Management by Motivation

MANAGEMENT
BY
MOTIVATION

Saul W. Gellerman

American Management Association, Inc.

For
F.E.T-C.G.

Preface

After the publication of *Motivation and Productivity*, a number of managers said that while it had clarified motivational theory for them, it had not made clear just how these theories might be applied in practical ways to specific problems. Of course, *Motivation and Productivity* was not intended to serve as a how-to-do-it book and, for that matter, neither is this one. Still, I was troubled by the realization that ideas which my colleagues and I had found to be of great value in our own practical work were not as readily useful to at least some of the people who were—potentially, at least —in a position to apply them on a much wider scale.

The motivation for writing this book originated in that troubled feeling. I felt that the task which I had originally set for myself was still incomplete. So I began to consider ways of closing the gap between intention and accomplishment, between explaining theories and applying them. This led me to several conclusions.

If *Motivation and Productivity* were to have a sequel at all, it should not be a how-to-do-it book, since that would almost necessarily have to oversimplify what the behavioral scientists have learned that is relevant to management. Neither should it simply compile more theory, although there may eventually be a need for that as new research compels revision of existing theories. Instead, the most practical sequel to a theoretical book would be a problem-oriented book—one that focused on the major managerial problems to which

7

the behavioral sciences and motivation theory address themselves, and then restated those problems from the perspective of what the behavioral sciences have learned about them. The objective of such a book should *not* be to make an amateur behavioral scientist of the reader—no single book could do that. Rather, its objective should be to teach him to look at problems the way the behavioral scientist does. To paraphrase an eminent Dutch psychologist, G. H. Hofstede, the best practical application of the behavioral sciences is to learn to look at organizations through research eyes.

I began by examining my own assumptions, the working hypotheses which form the basis for my approach to organizational problems. I think these are essentially the same as those of most behavioral scientists who are concerned with practical applications. They form the underlying argument of this book:

1. The behavioral sciences have a uniquely important contribution to make to the solution of modern managerial problems.
2. There are not and never will be enough qualified behavioral scientists to meet the needs of industry, government, and other organizations.
3. This shortage can be alleviated by enhancing the effectiveness of the behavioral scientist. This happens when management understands his basic strategies and how and why he arrived at them.
4. Such an understanding requires no special academic training. It does require a thoughtful confrontation with information that is usually inaccessible to managers, because it appears in scattered sources and is usually written for other behavioral scientists rather than for laymen.

But the effective use of behavioral science knowledge also requires a strategy. That is, both the manager and the consultant need to use this knowledge selectively. They need to distinguish between motivational influences on which, as a practical matter, they are able to exert some leverage and those which, regardless of their potency, are not really subject to much control by managers or consultants. A good deal of the prevalent confusion about motivation arises right here: Too much emphasis is given to motivators which could, *under conditions that no longer exist,* exert a powerful influence on behavior. But in fact these motivators have relatively little influence, precisely because those conditions no longer exist.

The behavioral scientist has no quarrel with conventional ideas about motivation *in the abstract*. For example, he would not dispute the notion that rewards (employment, money, recognition) and punishments (dismissal, threats, criticism) have a motivating effect. What he does quarrel with is the beliefs that rewards and punishments are management's *best* motivational tools and that their motivational effects represent an efficient use of human resources. Instead, the behavioral scientist holds that the desirable effects of conventional rewards and punishments tend to be short-lived and that the undesirable effects not only tend to be more lasting, but often actually outweigh the benefits. His position, in brief, is that conventional rewards and punishments do not offer a *practical* motivational strategy. To achieve such a strategy, we must identify motivational levers which management is not only in a position to operate, but whose effects produce a favorable long-term balance of advantages over drawbacks.

The plan of this book is to deal with both kinds of levers: to explain the degree of control we really have over them, to consider their effects, and to outline what appears, on the basis of available behavioral science knowledge, to be a sensible strategy for using them. The book begins with an examination of how this knowledge can be applied to organizational problems, of why it is usually not applied, and of what might be done about this. It then proceeds to a brief review of motivational theory, with emphasis on a few recent contributions from behavioral research. There follows a consideration of one of the most powerful and yet most misunderstood sources of leverage upon the motivation that actually becomes available to an organization: the selection of the people who will belong to it and of those who will manage it.

Following that, the book turns to an examination of the process of individual growth and development and of the factors which influence it. In this connection, it reviews some of the more sophisticated programs for identifying people whose potential for development is greater than that of their peers. We then consider the opposite side of the developmental coin: the processes which tend to make people *less* motivated to develop their abilities or to adapt themselves to changed circumstances. Next comes an analysis of the effects of money upon motivation: what these effects evidently are under ordinary circumstances and what would have to be done to those circumstances to produce different effects. The book then closes with an examination of organizational climates and the process of organizational development.

Throughout, I have tried to stress the options management already has for affecting motivation through administrative action and to give only secondary emphasis to techniques which, because they demand a detailed understanding of social and psychological processes, are probably best left to the professional behavioral scientist. Indeed, it is one of the principal arguments of this book that the application of behavioral science knowledge to organizations can usually be accomplished best through wiser and more imaginative administration, and only secondarily through using the sophisticated techniques of behavioral research and development. If this book succeeds in showing opportunities for affecting motivation administratively and for working knowledgeably with the professional practitioners of behavioral science, it will have amply fulfilled its purpose.

                                                                        S.W.G.

Contents

Contents

Chapter 1

Diagnosis and Prescription

IN TOMORROW'S WORLD A PROGRESSIVELY SMALLER FRACTION of the population will be available to do producing, while the demand for things to consume and services to use will probably be higher than ever. Education will claim a larger share of most people's earlier years, and retirement will begin earlier and last longer than it does now. Despite the proportionally smaller workforce, the economy itself must grow if it is to provide increasingly higher living standards for generations that have never known anything else. All this clearly means that the foreseeable future will undoubtedly bring an ever increasing emphasis on productivity.

Financing this kind of economic growth will call for investment on a huge scale. Although technological improvements may ultimately lead to savings, they are very costly in themselves. The money that pays for these improvements will come largely out of profits, and anticipated profitability will be the main determinant of where the investments go. Even publicly financed enterprises will tend to compete for tax funds on the basis of how efficiently and usefully those funds are expended.

There are many sources of profit and efficiency, and personal productivity in such forms as ingenuity, sustained effort, and teamwork is only one of them. But it is an important source, and often an indispensable one. It can hardly be doubted, then, that tomorrow's managers will face a permanent need for fostering personal productivity among the people whose work they direct.

To a greater degree than ever before, the way to personal productivity will mean adapting to change. This means adjustments of all kinds: not only to new machines and methods but also to new organizational arrangements, new superiors, new locations, new jobs, even new careers and, quite possibly, new ways of being rewarded for one's efforts. Despite the well-known human propensity for getting into comfortable ruts, ways will have to be found to help more people than ever before to welcome change—or even to seek it. But change always brings risk with it, which is basically why it is resisted in the first place. Most people prefer the devil they know to the devil they don't know.

The most obvious and talked-about risk incurred through change is to job security. It is probably neither the most common nor the most serious problem that change creates. Nevertheless, a great deal of collective bargaining and some strikes are centered on the question of whether change should deprive people of employment. This is at the bottom of such diverse controversies as "full crew" laws affecting railroads in some states, litigation regarding plant shutdown and removal, and reduction in the number of "full time" working hours in a normal week.

Whether technological change can create (or indirectly induce) as many jobs as it eliminates is perhaps a moot point, but there is no doubt that it benefits the well-educated part of the labor force and threatens the less-educated part. This leads to a paradox: The lifetime educational demand (in the sense of having to be retrained for new occupations) will probably be greater upon the high school graduate than upon the college graduate, and greater still on the high school dropout. Management will be faced with a twofold challenge: to maintain the productivity of the labor force through retraining and to keep business strong enough to employ as many otherwise marginal workers as possible.

Indeed, the most serious and commonplace way in which change will complicate the task of management may be through its impact on education. Many organizations have recognized that, merely in order to continue functioning, they must invest in the maintenance of human productivity through training. In fact, the training budgets of some large enterprises already exceed those of a good-size university. But, as they have discovered, it is one thing to provide adults with a classroom, textbooks, and a teacher and quite another to make them learn. Obviously, they must also *want* to learn. But love of learning for its own sake is, to say the least, a rare virtue. It is going to be necessary to present the learning process to adults as the indispensable means to security, prestige, and self-fulfillment. It already *is* all of that, of course, but adults too often look upon the prospect of additional learning as a threat of boredom or mortification. A successful transition to an economy with a constant high rate of internal change will demand some way of overcoming this attitude.

The training process itself must be fashioned differently for adults and for youngsters, partly because adults and children can learn differently and partly because the typical methods of instructing children can be potentially humiliating to adults. But more than just a pedagogical problem is involved. Organizations must foster an internal climate in which periodic retraining is expected and even welcomed. Education must, in other words, become a "way of life" for the employees of many organizations. Until recently, it was possible for most people to acquire all the formal learning they would ever need *before* commencing their careers, but the accelerating pace of change means that education can no longer be confined to a preparatory phase. Careers will have to be interspersed with periodic training and retraining, and this may lead to the discovery that learning is more efficient when distributed over a lifetime than when it is basically confined to one big initial dose.

There are also other, subtler dangers involved in change. Since the ways in which people earn their living affect their social status, any change in their work can affect what their colleagues, family, and neighbors think of them. To be an expert in an obsolete craft usually means a loss of prestige. But it is a remarkable fact that many people are reluctant to give up a favored social position, however illusory it may be, even for the sake of preserving their employability. Once a person has run the race and perhaps even won it, it is not easy for him to have to go back to the starting line for a new race. However, the introduction of frequent and ceaseless change means that most people will not be able just to prove themselves once and then rest on their laurels; they will have to prove themselves several times.

Resistance to loss of prestige is not new; what *is* new is the scale on which it is likely to be encountered. It is probably at the root of most discriminatory hiring practices, most restrictions on admission to union membership, and the tendency to keep some managers in office long after they have lost contact with the work they are managing. The problem goes deeper than one might think, for it cannot be solved merely by exhorting people to develop several competences in a lifetime. The organization itself must change by developing new roles and new ways of allocating status. Prestige is about as intangible as any problem management has ever had to deal with, but it exerts too powerful a pull on human behavior to be ignored.

It will also be necessary for managers to go beyond the problems of prestige allocation to the broader problem of motivation itself. Management has traditionally been content to deal with this passively through compensation, fringe benefits, and various tangible rewards given in exchange for time spent at work. But we already know that more active forms of motivation, which are not a matter so much of rewards as of experiences, can be extremely important. In many kinds of jobs they make for greater productivity, greater adaptability to change, and smoother relationships between management and labor. Further, both the structure of jobs in the economy and the character of individuals in the labor force will increasingly accentuate this trend.

All this means that management must find ways to make work itself a more rewarding experience. There does not seem to be any simple "cookbook" way to do this, if only because jobs vary tremendously and people vary even more. *What management needs, therefore, is not so much a method for motivating as a way of thinking about it.* Most of what we know about motivation has been learned in retrospect; that is, we have analyzed situations that have already occurred in order to discover what was and what was not motivating the people involved in them. To apply this knowledge, we have to anticipate the factors that are most likely to have a motivational effect on the work of the people involved in some future situation. (In a very general way, that is what the opening paragraphs of this chapter have been all about.)

This is where behavioral research can be of inestimable value to the manager. But while it is important to know about some of the results this research has yielded and about how to interpret them, it is even more important to know something of its method. Without having to become a behavioral scientist himself, the manager should learn to look at the world the way the researcher does. This is not easy, but it really requires no special knowledge or expertise. It does require some detachment and persistence and, at times, a willingness to abandon those favorite ideas that have not stood the test of experience.

The behavioral researcher starts with a premise that is easy enough to test: that everyone's behavior is reasonably logical and justifiable *to himself*. To understand another man's actions, you must see his situation the way he sees it. This does not necessarily mean agreeing with him; it means trying to discover his basic premises. Whether he or anyone else is "right" or "wrong" in the way he views his world is quite irrelevant. What matters is what *he* believes, because that determines how he behaves.

Going one step further, the behavioral scientist wants to know what cues in a man's situation have contributed to his view of it. Most people are neither introspective nor articulate enough to tell you this even if they wanted to. So the behavioral scientist has to infer—but being a scientist, he looks for practical ways to put his inferences to a test. If they stand up repeatedly under such testing, the chances are that he has guessed right.

The researcher's way of thinking is, in other words, a combination of intuition, rigor, and detachment. He searches far and wide for "causes" and then demands that these causes be related to events in some sensible, predictable way. He cannot afford to be sentimental about ideas that are appealing but do not stand up under analysis. He dares to dream, and he also dares to measure every dream against reality. It is this way of thinking—this mixture of a wide-open willingness to speculate and a cold-eyed insistence on analysis—that the manager must adopt if he is to practice effective management by motivation. With it he can anticipate, with some reliability, how the various actions he might take would affect the people whose work he directs. It is this habit of mind, more than "leadership," "human relations," and even a knowledge of motivational theory itself, that is the key to a better utilization of human resources.

Behavioral research has given us a more realistic way of analyzing what happens inside organizations than we have ever had before. In fact, we now understand the process of managing people much better than we practice it. In part, this is because behavioral research is an analytic tool and nothing more. It is not a list of specific things to do and not to do.

Motivational theory, which is the product of this research, is in some ways a product for which there is no ready market. Most managers are aware—sometimes acutely aware—of the need for more effective ways to cope with the human problems of running a business. But they are quite properly looking for ways to simplify their work, not to complicate it. Therefore, motivational theory, which offers no simple solutions at all and demands instead that a far-reaching analysis be made of every aspect of management, is a disappointment to many managers. It is just not what they want. Although the theory has its share of enthusiasts, many others find it "too theoretical" or "not practical enough."

Yet motivational theory may very well be about as practical as any other really useful tool we are likely to get. Research results show that managing by means of simple rules and simple assumptions has already caused many more problems than it has solved. The job of management itself, in other words, seems to demand more analysis and less "action," at least of the thoughtless variety, than many managers have supposed. A simple list of do's and don'ts, however fondly we may wish for it, is not going to get much accomplished. Consequently, the market is going to have to adjust itself to the product—which is never easy.

The gap between theory and practice is only partly the result of a desire for simpler answers. The theory also has defects of its own. One kind of defect, with which we shall not be concerned here, is that the evidence on which it is based is not yet extensive or conclusive enough to satisfy the more demanding behavioral scientists. Their job, after all, is to find answers rather than to apply them; therefore they have every right to worry more about the quality of those answers than about their usefulness.

For those of us who have to concern ourselves with getting things done, the main defect of the theory is that it isn't ambitious enough. That is, it still doesn't teach the manager who would practice it to look far enough afield for the causes of the behavior he is trying to manage. But if the art of managing people is going to be advanced very much, it must first be viewed from a larger-than-ordinary perspective.

We are accustomed to thinking about the behavior of people at work as if it were only the result of circumstances on the scene (such as the leadership style of the man in charge) or of circumstances that are closely related (such as wages and benefits). To this list of "causes" we could add job security, grievance channels, communications, and other factors that are in or associated with the job itself. Even behavioral research has made its main contributions so far by digging into the everyday transactions between managers and employees or between employees and their jobs.

We focus too narrowly on the job and its immediate environment to understand or manage it well. Work is not an isolated event that can be analyzed or controlled by itself. It occurs in a larger context that includes a great deal of current economics and politics and usually at least a generation of history as well. Therefore, the effective management of work requires a broad view of the forces affecting it, including the extracurricular ones. It also requires an understanding of how to work selectively with those forces, sometimes at very long range, to increase the probability that events on the job will turn out as constructively as possible. In brief, the effective management of work calls for a sophisticated point of view.

Motivational theory can help in developing such a point of view. It provides a strategy for thinking through the problems of effective leadership. It enables the manager who grasps it to identify the causes of behavior, and to anticipate the effects of policies, with greater realism than a more traditional approach would ordinarily permit. It is not—repeat, not—a set of tactics. For the manager who can learn to think about his job diagnostically and can follow the thread of his own reasoning into action, motivational theory is a tool. But it is a tool that demands an *intelligent* manager. Let there be no mistake about this: Management by motivation calls for a subtle mind. The art of stirring up enthusiasm, or of setting an inspiring example, or of imbuing a job with a glamorous "image" is not particularly relevant to management by motivation.

Many of the human problems of business are the unforeseen side effects of solutions to other problems. When we deal with problems that are not as simple as they look, we are prone to "oversolve" them. That is, not only do our plans change what we wanted them to change, but they produce a number of unplanned changes as well. These other effects can lead to a new set of problems for which our original solution may be altogether inappropriate. Most of the problems of running a business are, in fact, related to each other; it is when we overlook this interrelatedness and define problems too narrowly that our solutions are most likely to undo themselves.

In dealing with motivational matters, an indirect approach may be preferable to a perfectly straightforward one. The object, after all, is not merely to achieve a certain result but also to limit the result to what is desired. Consequently, the manager who would manage motivation must do so with a certain finesse. Like a good chess player, he must play with every piece on the board and not just the ones that can be most readily positioned for action.

Most failures by capable managers to manage people effectively are not due to using the "wrong" tactics or to subscribing to the "wrong" human relations theory. They are due to a failure to think diagnostically about the forces that shaped the situation they are trying to manage. We too frequently assume that the dimensions of the problem we are dealing with are limited to those aspects of immediate interest to us and that any other ramifications or side effects can be safely ignored.

To illustrate the problem, let us examine (with all of the advantages of hindsight) some unwise decisions which sensible men considered sound enough when they were made.

During the late 1950's a manufacturer of metering equipment expanded its sales, and consequently its sales force, very rapidly. This growth was due chiefly to some technical innovations in the product line which made possible important economies for the firm's customers. For several years the demand for these products ran well ahead of industry capacity. It was a lush period of high sales, high profits, and high commissions.

Eventually both this company and its competitors brought additional plant facilities into being. This stabilized the market and put the salesmen back on their mettle—which eventuality, of course, had been foreseen. But before it actually happened, the company had to pass through a curious and wholly unforeseen crisis. At the height of the boom period, several of its ablest salesmen resigned and a number of others made it clear that they were contemplating similar moves. Some of the men who left went to work for competitors.

The most astonishing thing about this episode was that the sales force in general, and a number of resigned men in particular, had enjoyed exceptionally high earnings. The majority were still young, having been hired after college graduation six or seven years earlier. In comparison with their classmates who were employed by other firms, these men had incomes that were very high indeed.

Even though this firm had raised an unusually high financial barrier to protect its men from the blandishments of other firms, it was clear that a way had been found to penetrate it. The main reason given by the departing salesmen was not higher incomes (some actually accepted reductions of 15 to 20 percent) but, rather, the opportunity to move into management or staff positions.

A review of the problem traced its origins to marketing and recruiting policies. The company was convinced that its most effective sales strategy was to stress the economies which its products would eventually make possible for its customers, rather than their engineering features. This meant selling at a fairly high level in the customer's organization, and this in turn seemed to require salesmen who were considerably more articulate and urbane than the type traditional to the industry. In other words, college graduates.

But college men were difficult to hire, since the selling of metering equipment was neither a traditional nor a glamorous occupation for them. This problem was finally overcome by a very liberal compensation plan that rewarded the successful young salesman with a remarkably fast climb to the upper income brackets. The plan worked so well that after a few years the company's recruiters were besieged by a more than ample supply of eager applicants.

In time, however, this solution undid itself. What had actually happened was that the graduates regarded the company primarily as a fast growth vehicle for themselves. That is, they interpreted the company's booming sales as a forerunner of corporate growth which would "inevitably" be accompanied by rapid access to the ranks of management. If that didn't materialize soon enough, they would at any rate have accumulated enough money to venture out on their own or enough experience to attract the interest of other, more growth-minded employers. The important point about their high earnings is that they were regarded, seldom as an end in themselves, but rather as a means to another end (independence) and as a promising sign of yet another end (managerial status).

The company's compensation policies had solved its immediate recruiting problem; but they had not solved, and indeed may have aggravated, its longer-range problem of retaining experienced sales talent.

This weakness in the sales force was inherent from the beginning, but it became apparent only when two new factors began to coincide in the experience of several salesmen. One was the attainment of certain earnings levels and the accumulation of personal financial resources high enough to make the continuance of high earnings a matter of secondary importance. The second factor was the development in the same men of the feeling that to continue selling (or "peddling," as they termed it) would somehow be demeaning to men of their capabilities and tastes. They were able to afford a standard of living which was ordinarily associated with high prestige, and they meant to have both. When a few competitors were clever enough to recognize this need and offer managerial jobs to a few of these men, a wave of discontent swept over the remainder.

Fortunately, the management of this firm was able to recognize the real source of its problem and could therefore react appropriately. It did not take the "obvious" step of raising commission rates. That would only have postponed this crisis and worsened the next one; it would hardly have represented a satisfactory return on the investment. Management realized that a high monetary income was not, at least for this group, a permanent motivator. In fact, it had changed the eager, ambitious young men originally hired into a group of affluent, overconfident, and not easily challenged salesmen.

As so often happens in business, the solution to this problem was a series of small practical adjustments rather than any one sweeping move. A reorganization provided a few staff and supervisory opportunities for some of the more promising men. Earnings growth was scaled down for the younger men, not without some vocal protests and a few more resignations, but with the salutary result that the majority remained responsive to monetary rewards for a longer period.

Perhaps the most far-reaching change resulted from a re-examination of the assumption that impressive young men with college backgrounds were essential to the effective marketing of the company's products. Experiments with able men who had less than superlative backgrounds, and with sales efforts aimed at operating management rather than at executive levels in the customers' organizations, soon showed that there was more than one way to sell metering equipment. Or perhaps the market itself had evolved. In any case, the company reached a more viable balance between its marketing requirements and the motivational requirements of its sales force.

It requires no great wisdom to solve problems in retrospect, and the exercise is useful only if we learn thereby to solve them in advance. Undoubtedly the most elegant solutions in the field of human relations are those given to problems that never occur because they were foreseen and prevented. This is the kind of wisdom that must be developed if effective management through motivation is to be achieved. When the aims of men and the aims of their organization are opposed, it is usually difficult and sometimes impossible to rescue the situation. Therefore real management, in the sense of arranging events so as to produce a desired result, demands the ability to think diagnostically about the probable effects of those experiences which managerial action creates.

It would be a fine thing if most managers, or even a substantial minority of them, were to develop the kind of subtle and far-reaching habits of thought that management by motivation demands. But experience and common sense both indicate that they probably won't. This is not because of any defects in their characters but because of their jobs. The problem is organizational, not personal.

The simple fact is that most managerial jobs are already more than full-time jobs. The typical manager has more than enough to worry about. His typical solution is to arrange his problems in order of priority, deal with the ones he has time for, and just ignore the rest. In other words, that which is urgent gets done and that which is merely important frequently doesn't.

Most managers, even though they may know perfectly well that a crisis is brewing which may someday break about their heads, will let it brew. Should it ever occur, it will move to the top of the priority list until it has abated, when it will be relegated again to oblivion. Motivation, like any cause whose effects occur only slowly over the long term, and accumulate in a gradual, unspectacular way, is not going to be high on many practical priority lists. In fact, it shouldn't be.

There is a very good reason why motivation is of intense concern mainly in seminars and on other occasions when executives pause to consider where they are going—and why it usually gets little more than lip service on a day-to-day basis. For most managers it *deserves* no more than lip service on a day-to-day basis. They simply do not have the time to give the problems of motivation the kind of analysis these require. This is not to excuse the superficial and sometimes foolish programs that are developed for the sake of "motivation"; it is only to note that the ordinary manager is not in a position to take advantage of motivation theory.

For this reason, whatever concern an organization may have about motivation is usually relegated to a staff function, typically to the personnel department. This is usually a mistake. The personnel department tends to be regarded, too often with good reason, as a housekeeping rather than a creative function. Even where it has managed to rise above routine administration and has learned to speak with some authority on the more profound problems of motivation, it seldom gets more than a polite hearing and pious agreement to its preachments. The reason, which affects most other staff departments also, is simply that personnel does not participate in the key decisions that affect motivation. It isn't invited, because the motivational impacts of these decisions are seldom recognized for what they are.

There is a potential motivational impact in decisions on budgets, production and delivery schedules, hiring programs, marketing targets, organizational changes, and indeed nearly every area in which an organization makes major decisions in the normal course of doing business. This does not mean that considerations of profit and efficiency must defer to considerations of keeping people well motivated. But when a business decision runs counter to the interests of effective motivation, that loss of motivation is a cost which must be charged against the benefits of the decision in any realistic accounting. Management has the duty to weigh the cost in advance rather than after the fact. Sometimes the cost is tolerable and sometimes it isn't; unfortunately, the latter case is usually discovered only after it is too late to rescue the situation.

Another reason why the motivational "cost" of a decision deserves to be assayed in advance is that frequently there are alternatives available which achieve the business goal just as well without jeopardizing motivation. Finally, and contrary to much popular belief, effective motivation is not always a costly purchase. While it must be sustained on a suitable financial base, it is usually lifted to its heights by intangible gestures rather than by needlessly opening the corporate treasury.

But if the personnel department, and indeed most staff departments, are not privy to all the key decisions that eventually impact motivation, and if the managers who make these decisions are as a rule too burdened to make the subtle analyses required, what practical way is left to introduce an attempt to use motivation as a positive management tool? In the traditional organizational structure, *no way is left;* it is precisely for this reason that motivation gets top billing at seminars and short shrift in actual practice. We can hold more seminars, of course, and we can exhort more vigorously that motivation deserves more attention than it gets, but these courses of action are likely to lead to little else besides agreement.

What is needed is a change in the organization structure. We need to create a role for a full-time analyst of, worrier about, and gadfly for motivation. He should be a member of every planning committee and every major decision-making conference. He should know as much as it is possible for one man to know about what is going on in the organization. But his only responsibility, or at least his chief responsibility, should be to assure that the motivational impact of all management decisions is weighed before those actions are decided upon.

To be effective, he would have to be a nuisance. He would have to press points that might seem irrelevant, unimportant, or esoteric. He would have to scent smoke and give the alarm before anyone else saw the fire. He would have to learn to think negatively and to expose the flaws in faulty reasoning. He would have to insist that managers look beyond their own immediate bailiwicks to the remote consequences of what they are doing. He would have to argue in terms of large-scale, long-term events before men who are measured in terms of specific, short-term results.

In a word, he would have to intrude. He would be, at least at first, a disruptive force in an otherwise smooth-running organization. And that is precisely why such a role is needed: An organization that is left to its own devices will seek to run smoothly, and this is all too easily accomplished by stressing what is superficial, by ignoring what is difficult, and by discouraging dissent. The organization whose members accept its ways passively is likely to congratulate itself and conclude that its ways are right. But organizations do not exist primarily to create harmony; their main purpose is to achieve results. The intrusive, wide-ranging "angels' advocate" might not contribute much to harmony, but he should make quite a contribution to results.

A man in such a position would not necessarily know more about motivation theory or behavioral research than anyone else in the organization. In fact, the job would have much merit as a training position for bright young managers who were moving rapidly upward, and that reason alone is sufficient to reserve it for employees rather than outside professionals. The job, after all, is not to keep the "client" happy but to keep him from becoming complacent. For that reason, the most essential characteristic this man needs—indeed, *must* have—could be conferred on him: He must understand that he will be measured by his ability to keep management aware of the motivational consequences of its decisions. He need not be gifted with unusual insight or foresight as long as he can get most other managers to use *their* insights to the utmost. It is only in this one crucial respect that he would need to differ from anyone else in management.

The experience of serving in such a role for a few years would equip the young manager to handle executive responsibilities with a maturity that would ordinarily take him much longer to attain. And marking the job as a proving ground for men with a future would be a powerful motivational tool in itself. As for titles, it probably would be best to dub the incumbent an innocuous "assistant to" some top executive rather than attempt to describe the job and its responsibilities too precisely. It lends itself too readily to whimsical nicknames anyway.

All this is not to suggest that putting one man in charge of analyzing the company's impact on motivation, and of pleading the case for it, is the only way in which the insights of behavioral research can be applied to running a business. It is not necessarily the best way, and it is certainly one with few precedents. But it would have the virtue of breaking motivation out of the departmental mold in which it too often becomes nothing more than a password that is repeated meaninglessly. It would also put several principles of motivational theory to work in their own behalf. Like any experiment that looks good in theory, it might work out only modestly, if at all, in practice. It might, however, work very well, and in any case it is an experiment that is eminently worth trying.

The man who found himself appointed to such a role would clearly need guidance. Much of it can be found in the literature of behavioral research. And the remainder of this book is, in a way, intended as a guide to the manager in this or any other role who would seek to manage through motivation.

Chapter 2

Motivation Theory

Behavioral research is not easy to define. The term came into vogue a few years ago as a sort of catch-all for studies which were not clearly identified with any of the traditional "applied" disciplines, such as industrial engineering or industrial psychology, but which were broadly concerned with human factors that affected productivity.

The kind of behavioral research that has affected management practices, and will continue to affect them, has two distinguishing characteristics. First, it is real research and not just a collection of anecdotes that happen to support somebody's pet theory. It is based on the systematic gathering of pertinent facts and measurements of pertinent relationships; it is as objective and logical as the sometimes illogical nature of its subject lets it be. Second, it is concerned with the ways in which people's habits, attitudes, and reactions to each other—in other words, their most characteristically *human* attributes—affect what they can accomplish in their work.

As for motivation theories, there are of course many of them, some with claims to scientific respectability and some without. It is precisely for this reason that we must specify which theory we are referring to. The behavioral research of the past two decades has had some fairly consistent implications about the ways in which people encounter their work, what factors influence that encounter, and how the encounter affects their accomplishments. These implications—or, if you will, these attempts to explain research results and to predict what further research may reveal—are what we will mean when we refer to motivation theory.

The results of behavioral research studies already fill volumes, and it is not our purpose here to speak of very many of them or even to cite many by name. With the exception of two recent and significant studies, which will be treated in some detail, this chapter will consist of broad summations and generalizations. The reader who would pursue the subject in more depth can refer to any of several books that have been written for this purpose.[1]*

Behavorial research first began to attract attention, and notoriety, by smashing a few idols. These were some very old assumptions about the nature of people and work that were seldom questioned (or even expressed) because their truth seemed self-evident. One such assumption was that mankind, being inherently lazy, despises work. Another was that mankind, being also inherently avaricious and fearful, would work only in the hope of making a lot of money or in the fear of losing the chance to make any at all. From this it followed that effective management consisted in paying people enough to arouse their greed but not so much as to "spoil" them—and in keeping them forever insecure as to the continuity of their employment. This is essentially the philosophy of the "carrot and the stick," which in one guise or another is the oldest management theory in existence.

Research has even illuminated the reasons for this theory's durability. First of all, the rationale of the carrot and stick is not altogether unrealistic, and in the not too distant past it was probably a great deal more applicable than it is today. Second, people tend to accept as self-evident anything their own experience has never contradicted, no matter how narrow, superficial, or one-sided that experience may have been. Given the facts that the psychology of the employed human has been changing under the impacts of technology and education and that the vantage point of the entrepreneur has not been particularly well situated for detecting these changes, it is

---

* All references are listed in "Notes to the Text," which appears at the end of the book.

not really surprising that some obsolete notions of how people should be managed continue to be popular.

As for the degree of truth in the carrot-and-stick theory, one could easily paraphrase Lincoln. Some people are motivated by the lure of wealth or the fear of being fired all of the time, and all people probably are so motivated at least some of the time. The only argument between the traditionalists in management and the modern student of motivation is over the relative proportion of the two. Whatever that proportion may be, the motivation theorist would argue that it is constantly changing anyway. Moreover, he would hold that this change is in the direction of a stronger response to the inherent interest and challenge of a particular job and toward a lessening dependence on what the employer himself can give or take away.

This means that the educated and mobile employee, whose security is created not by his docility but by the demand of the market for his services, is an altogether new problem for management. He cannot be dealt with in the same way as the man with little to sell besides a willingness to fit into the system. Therefore—to mix a couple of metaphors—the theory of the carrot and the stick is clearly not going to be the wave of the future.

The research assault upon traditional management thinking has come from several directions. One of the earliest was upon what one might suppose would be a citadel of traditional management theories: the factory shop floor and its population of blue collar workers. The application of the carrot-and-stick philosophy to factories has been quite straightforward. To encourage higher production, monetary incentives were offered to those individuals who turned out work in excess of a certain standard. To discourage slackers, failure to maintain that standard was punished by reproach, warnings, or even (before the advent of labor unions greatly diminished the power of management to wield the stick) dismissal. The "certain standard" itself was usually an attempt to estimate the level of productivity that could reasonably be expected; it was based on past performance or on the measurements of efficiency engineers. On the whole, the prevailing systems were objective, understandable, and fair.

Nevertheless, the results were often disappointing. In various ingenious ways, ranging from conspiracies to deceive the work-mea-

surement specialists to tacit agreements not to exceed certain production levels, the workers to whom the incentives were applied responded to them perversely. There were exceptions, of course, but by
and large the reaction of factory employees to financial incentives
was suspicious and obstructive. Although it was obvious that the
workers were deliberately restricting their output, the reasons for
this supposedly illogical behavior were not clear until research findings became available.

These were obtained by sending trained observers (frequently
graduate students) to work for extended periods on the shop floor.
With but one exception, they shared the ordinary working lives of
the regular employees. The exception was that these worker-research-
ers were systematically recording and analyzing their experiences, as
well as their observations of what their fellow workers said and did.
When all the notes were pulled together and tabulated, some extraordinary insights were provided into what management policy
looks like from the receiving end; that is, from the viewpoint of the
people who were presumably being motivated or controlled by these
policies.

The findings showed that most factory workers had a rather different attitude toward the prospect of earnings increases than most
managers might have had. While the factory employee was not indifferent to money, he was certainly not preoccupied with it, either.
Instead, he looked upon money as only one of many potential rewards he expected from his job, and by no means as a potential cure
for all his problems. Money was looked upon in a functional way, as
the stuff with which one pays the landlord and the grocer; it was not
seen symbolically, as the stuff which in sufficient quantities could
make any dream come true. In other words, the carrot of incentive
payments was a marginal carrot which very quickly encountered its
point of diminishing (psychological) returns.

Further, the price demanded by management for this additional
income frequently seemed too high to the workers. It was not so
much the additional effort they begrudged as the threat posed by
higher productivity to their relationships with each other and even
to their job security. As they saw it, unrestricted output by each individual would inevitably lead to enmity and dissension among them,
and the resultant ill-feeling would in the long run be intolerable, re-

gardless of how much they were paid to endure it. There was also a fear (even before the advent of automation on a large scale) that increased productivity would lead to a reduction in the number of jobs. From their perspective, therefore, the workers saw productivity incentives as a bad bargain, and they behaved accordingly.

Insights of this kind have focused attention on the need to understand the *subjective* point of view of the people whose productivity one would like to influence. Of course this is difficult, and many managers still shy away from the attempt. It is always somewhat troublesome to have to deal with problems whose very definition cannot be agreed upon. Rather than venture into such uncertainties, some managers prefer to scoff at the possibility of accomplishing anything concrete through "vague," "soft," or "unscientific" approaches to management. Perhaps the modern approach to human relations has been all of that at times, but it also works—which is the best possible reason for setting trepidations aside and trying to understand it.

A second and more serious assault upon the carrot-and-stick theory has come from research on positive forms of motivation. It is easier to understand these findings if we make a distinction between what might be called the external rewards that a person *receives in exchange for his work* and the internal rewards that he *experiences during his work*. External rewards would include salary and other forms of compensation, job security, and whatever prestige is associated with one's occupation, industry, or employer. Internal rewards would include learning new techniques or information, perfecting skills, solving problems, achieving certain standards of quantity or quality, and so on.

Traditionally, the types of experiences we have classified as internal rewards have not been thought of as rewards at all; rather, they have been viewed as requirements which the job imposed on the individual and which did not, in themselves, provide him with much satisfaction. In fact, the notion that work *should* be inherently satisfying and not just an unpleasant necessity is a more or less recent addition to managerial thinking. So is the modern concept that satisfaction on the job consists of more than working in comfortable or attractive surroundings, that it also includes subjective experiences of enlarging one's competence and of job mastery. One of the major discoveries of behavioral research has been that such experiences can be quite important, not only for a man's ego but also for his productivity.

The influence of internal and external rewards on job behavior is too easily oversimplified. There are enthusiasts of carrot-and-stick management who would say that external rewards (the carrot) are the most potent positive motivators available and that the so-called internal rewards are of little practical consequence. There are behavioral science enthusiasts who would hold that almost the opposite is true. Actually, the two forms of reward seem to work best in tandem with each other; for all practical purposes they are never entirely separated anyway.

It is usually the external forms of reward that attract a man to a particular employer and keep him there. It is usually a deficiency of external rewards that causes him to think seriously about looking for a new employer. On the other hand, it is usually the internal forms of reward that attract a man to a particular vocation and create a sustained desire to do excellent work within that vocation. A deficiency of internal rewards will not ordinarily motivate a man to quit his job, but neither will it motivate him to produce in a more than ordinary way. Clearly, to emphasize one form of reward at the expense of another is self-defeating. This is most clearly and sadly seen in organizations that are long on security and pension benefits but short on challenging assignments. All too often, the result of this combination is that the company has its strongest hold on its least productive people and either loses or fails to attract the more productive type of person.

Motivation within a given organization can, in other words, get out of balance, and when this happens it is usually to the detriment of the organization. But there is an important lesson to be learned from these imbalances: The reward system of a company is always motivating its employees in *some* direction, and this is not always consistent with the direction in which the organization itself is trying to move.

The combination of high security and low challenge, for example, tends to screen out the more enterprising and vigorous sort of person and to attract and hold the steady, methodical types. This is fine for a company that is not faced with technological or economic changes, but it could be fatal for a company that must face them. The combination of low security and high challenge usually leads to continuous turnover, with some employees (not all) achieving very high rates of productivity and earnings, only to leave when a less hectic opportunity presents itself. Some sizable operations have been built in this way (especially for making sales that tend to be nonrepetitive, as of magazine subscriptions and mutual funds) , and some industries have had to operate in this way because of the inherent instability of their markets (for example, the defense and fashion industries) . But such companies pay a high, continuous recruiting and training cost, and often premium wages as well, in order to offset the lack of security; and they very often face particularly militant labor union tactics for the same reasons.

The optimum reward system for a given organization would depend on the various markets (including the labor market) in which it deals. In general, it is probably wise to see to it that people are provided with as much security as they need and as much challenge as they can handle. Defining these "as much" points precisely is, of course, something that each organization can only do for itself.

External rewards are largely the handiwork of a company's salary administrators and benefits analysts or of its bargaining committees; in any case, these rewards are largely the construction of experts who do not actually dispense them. The technicians construct only a framework within which these rewards are given, and the role of the first-line supervisor in administering such rewards is greatly simplified by the existence of the framework. However, the impact of the first-line supervisor upon the motivation, and ultimately upon the performance, of the employees assigned to him is by no means negligible. Neither is it simple. The supervisor is, after all, especially well situated to influence whatever internal rewards are available to his subordinates. However, his actual effect on internal rewards seems to vary considerably from job to job and from person to person.

The motivational impact of a supervisor, like so many other aspects of motivation, is terribly easy to oversimplify. Nowhere is this so clearly indicated as in a question which (in dozens of similar variations) is probably posed by supervisors themselves more often than any other, at least when they meet an alleged expert on motivation. That question is, "What do I have to do to *motivate* people?" and it is usually asked with more than a touch of desperation. Unfortunately, it is nearly impossible to give a simple answer to this question, because it is based on a false premise. Motivation, in brief, is not the simple result of anything that a supervisor (or anyone else) *does to* other people.

To be motivated is to steer one's actions toward certain goals and to commit a certain part of one's energies to reaching them. Each person's pattern of steering and committing is usually learned over a lifetime; it represents his way of trying to come to satisfactory terms with his environment—or, rather, with what *he thinks* his environment is like. That is in fact a highly condensed, and in some ways simplified, statement of what motivation is really all about, but it serves to make a very important point: that the word "motivation" is a deceptively brief way of expressing a complex reaction to a complex of influences.

The signals which mold the individual's notions about his environment come in constantly from many sources; collectively they form a mosaic which changes (if at all) very slowly, because so many components are woven into it. To motivate people, you have to alter so many of the signals they receive from their environment that the world starts to look different to them. Hardly anyone is that omnipotent. Most supervisors simply do not loom nearly as large in their subordinates' world as they would have to in order to alter their motivational patterns by personal communication alone. This is why real motivational changes occur only when the individual learns either that his environment has changed or that his earlier ideas of what it was like were not completely accurate. Motivation is therefore affected to a much greater extent by the slow and sometimes completely arrested processes of growing up emotionally than it is by relatively transitory and superficial relationships with superiors.

A realistic view of the role of the supervisor in motivation begins, then, with a realization that his influence is necessarily rather indirect. That influence is strengthened to the extent that his actions are consistent with what the employee already believes about supervisors in general, about the company he works for, and about himself. To the extent that the supervisor's actions are inconsistent with any of these notions (regardless of whether or not he conveys such an impression deliberately), the supervisor's influence is diluted. His "message" is received as discordant noise that is hard to integrate with most other messages and therefore easier to suspect or dismiss than to listen to. All this simply means that the supervisor who has to get his subordinates to "unlearn" some of their biases before they can be positively motivated has a very tough row to hoe. Ask any supervisor who has tried it.

That word "bias" has come into disrepute in recent years, since it is usually used to denote some form of unjustified antipathy toward a particular social group. But in its larger sense, bias denotes a mind made up on the basis of too little evidence; and by that definition nearly everyone has biases about himself which, unless they are unlearned, can be detrimental to his accomplishments. The most common bias is an underestimate of what the individual himself is capable of achieving. As a result, relatively few people make a serious or sustained effort to reach the limit of their potentialities. To assume that a group of people is inherently incapable of exceeding a certain level of attainment is the easy, and regrettably common, consolation of a small mind; to assume that one's own potentialities are restricted to what one has already achieved is the equally regrettable rationalization of an unchallenged mind. Modesty is unbecoming when it makes a man comfortable with less than he could achieve.

There are other biases which can be equally serious impediments to achievement. Among "disadvantaged" groups, for example, it is not uncommon to find an underlying conviction that any success will be temporary and any reward will be counterfeit. Among groups that have a strong "proletarian" ideology, personal success is sometimes seen as a betrayal of the group's interests and unaccustomed rewards as an invitation to dishonor. Perhaps these observations also are biases in the worst sense, but there is a fair amount of published research that supports them.

Before proceeding to the question of what the supervisor can do to modify these perceptions of the self and the environment, it is pertinent to ask whether he should, as an ethical matter, do anything at all. By what right, after all, can a supervisor presume to understand another man's capabilities, and the environment that man lives and works in, better than he does? Even if the supervisor's understanding is better, is it right for him to tamper with that man's innermost self? Doesn't the whole notion of motivation by changing a person's perceptions smack of manipulation, of taking unfair advantage of people, of using them?

At first glance it does. Since it would be inexcusable to proceed with such a program if it did, indeed, violate the rights of the individual or society's sense of decency, it is necessary to examine this issue more closely.

First of all, it turns out that the human personality is, happily, exceedingly tough to manipulate. The foolish and the ignorant will probably always be the prey of the unscrupulous and the wicked, but that is the consequence of their foolishness and not the cause of it. Despite the publicity given to brainwashing, subliminal perception, hypnosis, and the like, it is *very* difficult under normal conditions to get a normal adult to do something he really doesn't want to do—much less to change his mind about it.

But that only means the danger is minimal; it does not touch on questions of right and wrong. Without attempting to turn this book into an ethical treatise that would be beyond the author's competence, let it be said that it would be wrong for a supervisor *not* to take whatever deliberate steps he could to help make the individual employee (and, by extension, the organization as a whole) more productive. It would be wrong for a supervisor not to help make that sizable fraction of an employee's life that is spent on the job more meaningful to him. After all, the supervisor plays more than just an organizational role; he also has responsibilities to society as a whole, if only because his decisions affect the ways in which resources of talent and energy are allocated. If the payoff in goods or services is less than it might have been, or if the cost of producing them included more frustration and less personal satisfaction than it should have, that is his fault.

What can the supervisor *do* to affect motivation? Broadly speaking, he has to convey to his men two ideas: that doing the job more effectively is inherently satisfying and that their own talents can be brought into such improvements to the fullest extent that they (the employees) want. In other words, effective motivation depends on effective communication. But this is another of those deceptively simple statements with which the psychology of motivation seems to abound. It is in fact extremely difficult to communicate either of these ideas effectively. It is not enough simply to *tell* them to people. What a supervisor says is after all only a small fraction, and seldom a very important fraction, of his total communication to his men. *In the last analysis, the most effective way to convince people that their environment is not what they may think it is, is to change that environment.* In the case of a supervisor, this means modifying that part of his subordinates' environment over which he has some control: his own supervisory style.

Supervisory style can be analyzed in various ways, but perhaps the most useful way is in terms of the degree to which the supervisor admits his men to the decision-making process. This process is most easily described by contrasting its two extreme forms. It should be understood, however, that rarely if ever does one encounter a supervisor whose natural supervisory style lies constantly at either extreme. The main reason for this is that to adhere to either extreme is usually a highly ineffective way to supervise.

Thus at one extreme we have what has been referred to variously as the "production-centered" or "old-fashioned straw boss" style of supervision. It goes without saying that this style is anathema to most human relations counselors; even behavioral researchers (who try to be objective) seldom have kind words for it. The premises underlying this approach to supervision are rather uncomplimentary toward the people being supervised. Its adherents declare that most people are not intelligent, willing, or interested enough in their work to perform it properly unless (*a*) they are told precisely what to do by someone who is wise enough to understand what work is needed; and (*b*) they are policed and, if necessary, disciplined by someone vigilant enough to detect slackening and tough enough to establish his authority over his men. In other words, the production-centered supervisory style is based on the assumption that the attributes of an adult are quite scarce among the people being supervised, and that the supervisor himself was appointed because he possessed considerably more of these rare qualities than any of the people whose work he directs.

It is easy to quibble with these premises, especially in the light of recent educational trends and the consequent wholesale upgrading of substantial parts of the labor force. But give the old-fashioned straw boss his due: Where workers *are* ignorant or uncooperative, it may take a disciplinarian to get things done. Unfortunately, this argument has been grossly overgeneralized. Because of an all too prevalent bias, workers who are at least potentially capable of self-discipline and effort are treated as if they were unreliable or witless. Perhaps it is just too tempting a boost to the supervisory ego to assume that the people one supervises *need* a presumably stronger, wiser man than they are in order to produce anything worthwhile.

Whatever the reason for it may be, the production-centered style of supervision continues to have many more adherents among supervisors than research indicates are needed. The decision-making process is, in other words, too often monopolized. This is usually because the supervisor is either too shortsighted to recognize the inadequacies of such a style or, more commonly, because he has never really examined the assumptions underlying his way of handling his job.

At the other extreme we have what has been referred to as the "employee-centered" or "human relations minded" style of supervision. Underlying this style is the belief that most people are reasonable and willing to cooperate if they are treated decently enough. In fact, supervisors of this type would hold that when workers do not cooperate with their supervisors, it is more likely to be due to resentment against callous or undignified treatment than to inherent unwillingness to work. The job of the supervisor is therefore a matter of organizing, informing, and supporting his men, not of threatening or policing them.

The employee-centered style is in so much better harmony with the mainstream of current educational and social thinking than the production-centered style that it is easy to assume it can be a panacea for all supervisors. It cannot. Research seems to indicate that while this approach to supervision is probably optimal for a very large part of the various working groups one encounters in industry, it can sometimes be inappropriate. Sometimes the personality characteristics of the workers are such as to make them more efficient and even more comfortable under a production-centered supervisor. This tends to be true, for example, with employees who dislike ambiguity and prefer a clear-cut set of do's and don'ts to general guidelines that leave too much room for their own judgment. Production-centered supervision also tends to have better results with employees who accomplish most of their work individually, rather than in teams, and who rely on their supervisors primarily for precise information as to what must be done rather than for support or expressions of appreciation.

In fact, the more thoughtful students of supervisory styles have concluded that the most effective approach to sustained productivity is neither the production-centered nor the employee-centered style in its "pure" form, but a mixed or flexible style that continually adapts itself to changing conditions. This would call for shifts in emphasis which could, unless they were handled sensitively, undermine the supervisor's claims to sincerity and reliability in the eyes of his subordinates.

The theoretically ideal approach to supervision demands, in other words, a virtuosity that few supervisors are likely to be capable of—at least not without considerable effort on their own part to develop it. It is not enough merely to know what must be done and tell people how to do it. The supervisor must somehow arrange things so that his men validate his decisions. They must agree, openly or tacitly, that his diagnosis is realistic and that his prescription makes sense. This can be achieved only by sharing the decision-making process with them or by winning their confidence sufficiently that they waive participation in it.

The most effective supervisor is a catalyst, not a drill sergeant. He creates a situation in which proud, intelligent men are willing to accept his leadership. He does not command; he convinces. He opens his work to review by his subordinates as well as his superiors. The only prerogative of office that matters to him is the silent respect of men who know as well as he does that their job assignment has been done well. The supervisor has a job to do rather than a role to play; he can elicit the teamwork he needs only by being a team player himself. The self-important, self-impressed supervisor with a passion for keeping his "prerogatives" to himself and his subordinates "in their place" may still be commonplace, but he is also obsolete. He is an inefficient mechanism for getting things done in today's industrial world.

Chapter 3

Some Recent Research

THE EFFECTIVE SUPERVISOR CONSIDERS HIS RAPPORT WITH HIS men the principal tool in his kit, and for that reason he takes care to keep it in good shape. The importance of rapport—that is, mutual understanding and exchange of information—has nothing to do with feelings, ethics, or vague notions about being nice to people for niceness' own sake. It has a great deal to do with the mechanisms through which groups actually get their work done. The process of communication—the flow of facts, ideas, and emotional reactions between people—is to a group what the flow of impulses through the nervous system is to a living body. Communication animates or paralyzes, excites or relaxes, coordinates or confuses a group. The process of supervision cannot really be understood without first understanding communication.

A great deal of twaddle has been written about communication. It is in reality subtle, complex, and hard to define or measure. Perhaps the most clear-eyed approach to the realities of communication that has been taken recently is contained in a series of studies that are well worth reviewing in detail, as much for their originality as for the light they shed on how communication actually occurs within organizations. They come from what may seem, to the American businessman, an unlikely source: the nursing departments of British hospitals. But defer judgment until the research has been described;

41

for what happens in hospitals is not, after all, so different from what happens inside other kinds of organizations.

These studies were conducted by Reginald W. Revans and a research team from the Manchester College of Science and Technology.[2] The occasion for them was the observation that in five otherwise comparable hospitals decidedly different records had been compiled in two key sets of statistics. One was the average length of patient stay; that is, the time it took each hospital to discharge, as cured, a patient who had been admitted for any of several more or less common surgical procedures.

Now, if one looks at a hospital dispassionately (which is not easy), it can be viewed from the economic standpoint as a sort of "factory" designed to produce a "product" in the form of patients who have recovered from their illnesses. In that sense the length of patient stay is an index of the hospital's efficiency. In this case, the Manchester researchers satisfied themselves that the differences between the hospitals were not merely the results of tradition or medical conservatism and that all five were endeavoring to send their patients home as soon as it was safe to do so. But the fact remained that people seemed to recover from equally serious appendectomies or gall bladder removals, for example, much faster in some of these hospitals than in others.

The other set of statistics that caught the attention of the Manchester research team was the rate of voluntary resignations by student nurses. About half of the girls in Britain who begin nurse's training programs fail to complete them, which constitutes a problem of no mean proportions. Again, the nursing schools, which are affiliated with the hospitals, can be looked upon as organizations whose function it is to produce trained nurses, and one measure of their efficiency is the percentage of girls who complete the three-year program. Of course, some girls leave to be married and others are unable to meet the training standards. The Manchester group, however, was concerned with those student nurses who left the program because they decided, for whatever reason, *not* to try to complete it.

Some of these hospitals seemed to lose considerably more of their student nurses than the others. These differences could not be explained by differing selection standards or differences in the training programs themselves. But the really interesting finding among all the statistics available was that the same hospitals that had managed to send their patients home more quickly were also able to keep the largest proportion of their student nurses. Conversely, the hospitals in which it took patients longer to get well were also the ones with the highest rates of turnover in their nursing staffs. It seemed, in other words, that some of these hospitals were definitely more efficient than the others, at least as far as these two measurements were concerned.

The Manchester group set out to determine what caused these differences, and it chose the internal communications systems of these hospitals as the focus of its research. What it found throws an unusually clear light on what the process of communication really is and how it affects the operating efficiency of an organization. The team members gathered their data by means of conventional interviews and questionnaires, supplemented by the infinitely tedious process of following nurses about during their duty hours for months on end to record what they did, how they did it, and how much time they devoted to each task. When the resulting mass of data was digested, it was shown that the patterns of communication within these hospitals were in fact quite different.

In the hospitals with high nursing-staff turnover and slower patient-recovery rates, information tended to flow mainly downward. The student nurses, for example, might simply be told what to do without being given an explanation of why it should be done. Or they might be discouraged from asking questions or, sometimes, be given no instructions at all. The problem was not so much that this sort of environment was unpleasant, although it was; what was much more serious was that it was *unintelligible*. That is, the senior staff made it very difficult for the junior staff to learn anything about nursing other than how to submit meekly and do as they were told.

In the hospitals with low nursing-staff turnover and faster patient-recovery rates, information tended to flow in a loop; that is, both downward and upward. The student nurses were encouraged to ask questions, and either these were answered on the spot or, if need be, an answer was found. The senior staff treated the junior staff more as partners—junior partners, to be sure—in a joint effort than as flunkeys who were there to do the dirty work. In other words, the senior staff created an environment in which it was possible to learn.

Given the life-and-death potentialities that are always present in hospital work, and given the youth and inexperience of the student nurses and their need to acquire some sense of competence in a hurry, the importance of being permitted to learn can be readily understood. It has nothing to do with the philosophical joys of learning for its own sake. Rather it is a matter of coming to grips with anxieties which, unless they are mastered quickly, can easily become overwhelming. The student nurse must learn a great deal more than just "what to do"; more important, she must learn that she can trust her own judgment as to what should be done and her ability to do it. Or as Revans put it:

> A girl in her first year may, in the sense of being able to answer questions formally put at a lesson in a classroom, know as perfectly as does the President of the Royal College of Physicians what should be done in such-and-such a bedside situation. But in the solitary darkness of her first night duty her approach to what needs to be done, what she knows about it, and how she does it may be very different from her confident exhibition under academic cross-examination. . . . At her first midnight it may be of major importance that the superintendent on duty promptly answers her call, if only to reassure her that she is doing the right thing.

It comes as no special surprise that the quality of communication affects the quality of learning. Neither is it unusual that to make learning inaccessible or difficult creates anxieties which may make a job too uncomfortable to be tolerated. It is not immediately clear why communication should affect patients' recovery rates, but one may speculate without becoming too implausible that hospital patients have their own needs for explanations and reassurance which, unless they are satisfied, could raise anxieties that may interfere with recovery. What *is* surprising in all this is that the effectiveness of communication should have so much to do with what is *unspoken:* with attitudes, with the openness or defensiveness of superiors, and with whether reassurance and support can be communicated right along with facts and instructions.

The student nurse who finds that too little reassurance is given her has a simple, but wasteful, solution available: she can cease to be a student nurse. The frustrated patient cannot solve his problems so easily; he has little choice but to endure his frustration, and this makes him a "less efficient" patient. (That is, he makes less effective use of the hospital than he otherwise might have, because his recovery occurs more slowly.) *Now, there is really very little difference between the situation of the student nurse and that of the employee in any organization who is free to leave it—or between the hospital patient and the employee who is not so free to seek new employment elsewhere.* And this is where the British hospital study begins to have very important implications for the management of any organization anywhere.

The more intelligent the members of an organization are, or think they are, the more vital it is to their morale that the organization be intelligible to them. They want to understand why decisions are made, what standards or values are likely to affect future decisions, and how their own roles fit into the overall organizational scheme of things. In a limited sense, they can do their own jobs well enough without having much of this kind of information; but they cannot do them comfortably, and that is extremely important. When they do not *know*, they speculate, suspect, and interpret in their own way every shred of information and misinformation that comes along. They become, in other words, rumormongers. Alternatively, they may become apathetic.

To dismiss either reaction as a moral failing of the excessively bright is to miss the main point altogether: that these are the natural results of a job environment that makes little sense to the people who work in it. And, either way, they are considerably less than fully committed to the organization they work for—which is very likely to reduce their tangible accomplishment on the job.

Effective communication is necessarily a dialogue. For all our preoccupation with *techniques* of transmitting information—with learning how to say things clearly, crisply, even beautifully—no message is as well understood as the one whose receiver can discuss it with its sender. No matter how precisely a message has been phrased, the person to whom it is directed still faces the problem of translating it into terms that fit his own experience, his own idiom, and his own ways of thinking. Until he is able to integrate the message into the patterns of understanding he has already developed, the message will be understood only dimly, if at all.

The problem of having to communicate with someone in a foreign language differs only in degree, not in essence, from the problem anyone faces in trying to interpret information that does not fit readily into his own ideas. This is why the enormous efforts that are put into communicating may be wasted if ample opportunity is not provided for the people on the receiving end to discuss what has been communicated with the communicators.

Effective communication—that is, transmitting information which influences its receivers to behave in a manner acceptable to its senders—is built on *feedback*. The receivers must be able not only to make sure that they understand what the senders mean, but also to *influence the senders*. Here is the nub of the entire communication problem: The sender, to be certain that his message will be accepted by the receiver, must be prepared to let the receiver influence him. He must even be prepared to let the receiver alter or modify the message in ways that make it more acceptable to the receiver. Otherwise it may not be understood, or it may not be accepted, or it may simply be given lip service and ignored.

In this sense there is a certain aspect of negotiation, or at least the possibility of negotiation, inherent in any effective communication. The message is communicated best in the context of communicating something else as well: the sender's willingness to consider the receiver's reaction to his message as relevant. The message is much less likely to get through if it comes in the context of another attitude: that the receiver should content himself with being a consumer, not a critic, of ideas.

It is essential to understand that any communication carries more than that which is deliberately conveyed; that every message is affected by the context and manner in which it is sent. No human confrontation is sterile; no exchange of ideas takes place in a vacuum. Consequently, effective communication depends more on the *attitude* of the sender toward the receiver than on the sender's gifts for speaking, writing, or standing up in front of an audience. The communicator who gets his message across is prepared to negotiate, not just to lecture. If he begins with the premise that he knows all the answers and that his audience can contribute nothing to his own knowledge, he is doomed to failure before he says a word.

Every communication communicates attitudes, either directly in what is said or indirectly in the context and the manner of saying it. The implications of a message can be much more influential than the message itself. Consider, for example, Revans' account of the interviews at one of the "less efficient" hospitals:

> According to the student nurses themselves, the nurses generally did not give them very much helpful instruction on the ward. Some nurses spent too much time drinking tea in the duty room, not infrequently waited upon by a student nurse. The majority of nurses in the hospital did not seem to be interested in teaching their juniors, and were said to discourage questions. One nurse re-

plied to the query of a student . . . , "Don't you dare ask me; you should have learned that in the [preliminary training school]."

> Some nurses thought that making casual remarks to student nurses and just ordering them to do things were adequate vehicles of clinical instruction. A few minutes before a student nurse [was interviewed], the nurse had said to her, "Don't let the patient sit up." But why the patient should not be allowed to sit up was not explained, and the student was quite unable to offer any satisfaction to the protesting patient.

The attitude that cannot help but be communicated in any encounter between a superior and a subordinate (or between a corporation and an employee) is the superior's estimate of the subordinate. It is communicated not so much because the superior wishes to send it as because the subordinate needs to know it. The employee, unless he is extraordinarily indifferent to the opinions of others, has needs of his own for feedback. The organization he works for is, typically, his main source of income, security, social status, and—not infrequently—self-respect. His relationship with the organization is usually too important for him to take it for granted.

This tendency for men to become dependent on their employers has caused a certain amount of intellectual hand wringing among those who profess to feel that rugged individualism is in danger of extinction; but whether we regard this as lamentable or inevitable, the fact remains that many employees—perhaps the majority—develop precisely this kind of relationship with the organizations for which they work. Therefore, since the supervisor largely shapes the organization's estimate of the employee, what the supervisor thinks or even seems to think about the subordinate is of vital concern to him.

This is why there is no hint too subtle, and no implication too remote or irrelevant, for the subordinate to notice and weigh along with the more obvious and deliberate things that his supervisor does. Given this continual alertness by the employee to potential signals that may reveal something of his boss's regard for him, *the superior is in effect communicating all of the time,* whether he intends to or not. Further, what he deliberately conveys to his men must be consistent with what he conveys when he has no intention of communicating; otherwise his "message" will be unbelievable. This inconsistency between what a supervisor says and what he conveys through gesture, intonation, expression, and even omission is what subordinates often have in mind when they complain that they don't really know where they stand.

Of course, there are exceptions; the relationship between a man and his superior is not always fraught with so much interest. Some employees become quite alienated from the companies that employ them, either because they can afford to be complacent or because they have only a temporary interest in their job of the moment. Also, some supervisors are regarded as mere messengers for the real decision makers in a company, in which case the opinions of the supervisor are of little consequence to the employees. But it is precisely where the potentialities for effective motivation are strong—that is, where the employee is eager to have the organization confirm his own estimate of his capabilities and where his supervisor can be regarded as a valid spokesman for the company—that the communication of attitudes is vitally important.

Every overt message we may wish to communicate, be it written, spoken, or merely hinted at, must carry its own "passport" of credibility. That passport has little if anything to do with the elegance, or lack of it, with which we manage to say what we have to say. It is instead the sum of *all* the evidence the receiver has about what kind of man we think he is. This is why a certain leavening of generosity, tolerance, and goodwill is indispensable in the make-up of any man or company that needs to communicate effectively with other men or companies. For *the real art of communication lies not in how things are said, but in getting people to listen.* Unless we are able to convey a certain amount of respect for our audience in the process of communicating with it, dialogues tend to become monologues and all the communicative artistry in the world deteriorates into just so much paper and talk.

The essence of communication lies in creating a receptive atmosphere. Almost any message, even a clumsy or garbled one, will get through to an audience that is eager to understand. But a hostile or suspicious audience can twist, or even wholly reject, the clearest and simplest of messages. This is the point at which our understanding of supervisory styles and our understanding of communication flow together. For the creation of a "receptive atmosphere" depends on whether a mutually satisfactory set of roles can be worked out for all the members of an organization, superiors and subordinates alike, so that each feels sufficiently comfortable in his role to accept all the others in their roles. This does not mean humoring every little egotistical whim of every employee, but it does mean a willingness to share some authority and to compromise on some of the more obvious forms of prestige.

At the bottom, whether effective communication can occur in an organization depends largely on whether it can dignify and support its members, at least to the limited extent necessary to make membership in the organization a positive, rather than just a necessary, experience. The difference between companies in which managers can make themselves understood with almost no explanations at all and companies in which management's aims are consistently misinterpreted or distorted is usually nothing more than this.

The importance of the emotional interactions within an organization—that is, the feelings its various members have toward each other and toward the organization itself—is becoming much clearer as a result of recent behavioral research. Whereas the Manchester group focused its attention on the ways in which these feelings can affect internal communications (and through it, the operating efficiency of the organization), another recent study has concentrated on the emotional interactions themselves. This study was conducted by Harry Levinson and a group of associates at the Menninger Foundation. It was based on extensive field observations and clinical interviews among the employees of a large, privately owned electric and gas power company in the Midwest.[3]

The Menninger research team was primarily interested in the effects of organizational life on the *mental health* of the company's employees. The members defined this term much more broadly than the layman does; that is, they were not so much concerned with questions of "sanity," or even with whether some employees were "neurotic," as with whether conditions on the job permitted them to deal with their jobs and with each other in a realistic and reasonably tolerant way.

Mental health, as the Menninger group (and most modern psychiatrists) defines it, means more than just the absence of disease: It means being able to live, as it were, at the top of one's form. The mentally

healthy person by this definition is not necessarily "happy" or overflow-
ing with zest, but he can face the ordinary nonsense and disappointments of life without yielding any of his basic honesty with himself. He
knows full well that life is not going to be unfailingly kind to him, and
he is prepared to accept his share of trouble without retreating into
peevishness or self-pity. We would call a person mentally healthy, then,
if adverse circumstances could not ordinarily frighten him into becoming less fully human than he otherwise might have been.

The Menninger group wanted to learn the ways in which the experience of working for a large company affected this quality: what kinds of
experience enlarged a man's ability to be his best self and what kinds
of experience diminished it. Thus their focus was chiefly in the area of
what might be called preventive psychiatry; and while that is a worthwhile subject for managers to know something about, we will not pursue
it here. However, it is obvious that a company which has managed to
enhance and preserve the mental health of its employees could expect
greater resistance to stress and adaptability to change, and possibly
greater productivity, than a company whose internal atmosphere is
somehow harmful to mental health.

The research team interviewed well over 800 employees at all levels,
and in most of the far-flung locations, of this utility company. Further,
the various members of the research team spent days in the field with
line crews and in offices with clerical groups, observing their daily routine and familiarizing themselves with the details of their working lives.
When all these interviews and observations had been culled and classified, several main themes emerged. These were the concerns which
seemed to be most important to most of the employees most of the time:
not the transient crises of the moment which flare up briefly but are seldom remembered for very long, but the lingering, quite ordinary stuff of
which most careers are actually made. For our purposes, the most interesting of these concerns was with what the Menninger group called *interdependence*.

This is a very useful concept which goes considerably deeper into the
psychology of superiors and subordinates than it might at first appear.
Basically, interdependence means that a company and the people it employs have certain expectations of each other which are seldom articulated but which nonetheless are the real cement that holds the organization together. Each party expects to receive certain benefits from the relationship which make the continuation of that relationship worthwhile;
or to be more precise, each side expects the other to do what it can to
make satisfaction possible. If either party should disappoint the other by

failing to live up to its side of the unspoken "bargain," a downward spiral of mistrust and mutual dissatisfaction can be the result.

For its part, the organization usually expects the employee to handle his current duties reasonably well and to get along, at least most of the time, with the other employees. It also expects him to adapt himself to whatever changes the future may bring and to await the satisfaction of his own desires with reasonable patience. (Many a sad story has resulted from differing interpretations of what constitutes "reasonable patience.") As for the employee, his expectations frequently go well beyond a steady pay check and decent working conditions. Since a good deal of any man's fate is influenced by the kind of bargain he is able to make with the economy, his relationship with his employer can easily become the focus of some of his most profound and personal expectations. For example, the kind of work a man does for a living, and the kind of company he works for, may significantly affect the answers he can give to such ultimate questions as who he is, what he is likely to become, and where he is likely to go.

A man who has had an opportunity to get to know his company and his own role in it can, unless he is an utter fool, estimate with some reliability the likelihood of his ever receiving any of the rewards he may be interested in; and on this basis he can set up some fairly realistic expectations for the future. Most men make their peace, as it were, with the realities of organizational life by staking out certain goals for themselves which they regard as both satisfactory and possible to attain. The expectation that these goals may eventually be achieved within the organization then becomes a person's principal motivation for continuing to do whatever he thinks the organization expects of him; in other words, he fulfills his part of the understanding in the expectation that the organization will keep his goals within reach. Thus an implicit bargain is struck which may never have been voiced at all, much less negotiated. However, this bargain has a very compelling power as far as most employees are concerned, because the *quid pro quo* includes their self-respect. The Menninger group refers to this tendency by an employee to assume that his organization has tacitly accepted the responsibility for enabling him to fulfill his unstated aspirations as the "psychological contract."

That such "contracts" exist was known prior to the power company study. The clinicians on the Menninger research team were interested primarily in learning how and why they developed. To understand their findings, it is necessary to know a few things about the character of the company they were studying.

Like many utility companies, this one was growing at a slow and steady rate, more or less in pace with the population of the extensive region it serves. Management put a great deal of stress on service, and employees understood that their basic missions were to keep power available to the company's customers, to answer their questions and process their payments, and so on. The company offered its employees steady work and considerable security, although some of the jobs could be unpleasant or hazardous and none was unusually well paid. The progress of any individual employee was likely to be slow but predictable. There was relatively little turnover, and a high proportion of each year's new hires eventually became long-service employees. Most of them entered the company in relatively unspecialized jobs and gradually became proficient in their various specialties through experience; relatively few employees came to the company with well-developed professional skills (such as electrical engineering or cost accounting).

Although this was a large company, in many of its locations it consisted of small- to moderate-size local operations. Therefore, the employees usually had plenty of time to get to know each other well and to work out comfortable ways of handling the necessary routines. It was on the whole a well-run and, from the employees' standpoint, a relatively placid company.

In reviewing the reasons why these people had chosen to join this company in the first place, the Menninger group found two main patterns. The majority came to the company in search of employment, rather than any specific type of job, and they came to this particular company either fortuitously or because it was readily accessible and therefore a logical employer to consider. A minority came to the company with definite roles in mind; they had selected this company either because they wished to specialize in work that was specific to the power industry or because they had highly transferable skills which could be utilized in any company of this size. The underlying expectations of each group were rather different, and so were the psychological contracts that tended to develop in them.

Suppose we refer to the first group as "employment seekers" and to the second group as "job seekers." As for the employment seekers, they were concerned with all the usual bread-and-butter motivators: steady work, job security, and fair pay. But as time went along and the likelihood of their ever opting to leave the company diminished, a new and subtler expectation emerged. This was the need for a defined vocational role—for a suitable "label," as it were, with which to tell the world (and indeed themselves) what they were. To have no skill, no calling, or no expertise is—at least in that part of society that works steadily and leads an orderly life—to be nobody. What happened was that the employment seekers came to expect the company to provide them with a suitable vocational role—one in which they were interested and could become qualified, but also one that conferred an acceptable degree of prestige upon them.

In effect, the company was expected to function as a sort of vast vocational guidance agency, discerning each man's interests and abilities and assigning him, through trial and error if necessary, to the kind of job in which he could happily make a career. Further, it became part of the psychological contract for the company to preserve that role or, if necessary, an equivalent one for the individual. But "equivalence" has as much to do with dignity and with a man's comfort in a job as it has with skills and salary level. Having once provided a sort of vocational identity, the company was expected not to tamper with it.

Such attitudes are quite common among the long-service employees of most organizations. In companies where changes occur gradually (as in the power company studied by the Menninger group), expectations of this kind do not necessarily present a serious problem. But they can and do create serious difficulties in companies which are required, because of rapidly changing technologies or markets, to "break" the psychological contract. This can be seen vividly in the reluctance of employees to leave obsoleted jobs, even at no economic loss, when the alternatives appear to require the loss of a favored role and adaptation to an uncertain one.

As for the "job seekers," their need was not to find a role but to be confirmed in one. They were qualified (or at least, felt themselves to be qualified) for a somewhat more prestigious role to begin with. What they wanted of the company was to be accepted as experts in their various professions or skills. The psychological contract in such cases usually calls for the company to preserve that expert role. This might involve, for example, not questioning the expert's professional judgment, not assigning him to work outside his chosen field, or not assigning a nonexpert to that field. In other words, there is a tendency for people who enter an organization with certain advantages to expect the organization to preserve those advantages for them. A similar privilege for nonprofessional but strategically placed workers is often the subject of written labor contracts. The only real difference is in the explicitness of the contract; the psychology is identical.

When this type of contract (between job seekers and their employer) is fulfilled, the two parties enter into a sort of partnership in which neither is truly dominant. The individual is secure in the knowledge that the company needs him, and he has the added assurance of knowing that there are markets for his skills elsewhere if the contract should ever be broken.

When the contract is not honored fully, the employee will not necessarily leave, but he does tend to retreat more and more into an identification with his profession rather than with his company. He thinks of himself almost as an itinerant professional who happens, at the moment, to be selling his services to a particular client; and even if that relationship should continue for quite some time, he will treat it as a momentary thing of little lasting importance. If carried too far, this attitude can turn him into the very opposite of a professional—someone who puts in time and attends to the obvious, with little regard for whether problems are discovered or resolved. The abrogation of a psychological contract can be that destructive.

Thus the so-called psychological contract, born of expectations and validated by simply never being questioned, has a powerful influence in determining how fully an employee can commit his abilities to the service of his company. But where does the contract get its power? Why do expectations of which people may be only dimly conscious, and which are not always very realistic, play such an important (if hidden) role in management-employee relations? The answer seems to have a great deal to do with mental health, which was of course the main focus of the Menninger study.

A man's occupational role forms a large part of his self-concept; or to put it another way, a man *defines* himself in large measure in terms of the way he earns his livelihood. His work constitutes the bulk of what he contributes to the world at large and provides most of the justification for whatever stature and dignity he assumes relative to the world at large. Therefore his job inevitably involves his self-respect, and a mentally healthy person values his self-respect and will go to considerable lengths to defend it. When his actual job role fails to satisfy his need to be the kind of person he pictures himself as being, he is compelled to take some kind of action to preserve his self-respect.

Some men do this harmlessly enough by inventing fancy job titles for themselves that rather overdignify their real jobs. Others learn to treat their jobs as secondary and rather unimportant parts of their lives and devote their main energies to hobbies or outside interests. Some cling stubbornly to their dreams of what they should be and grumble ceaselessly about the unfairness of an organization that denies them their due. Their choice of tactics has an obvious impact on the effectiveness with which they can be expected to perform their work. Yet in every case, the maneuver serves the vital function of preserving a man's self-respect from the abrasive effects of working for a company that seems to think less highly of him than he does of himself.

These various maneuvers must be understood for what they really are: not as mere escapism, but as natural and necessary attempts to fend off humiliation. These kinds of reactions to a broken psychological contract are the rule, not the exception; and in the context of mental health they are healthy, not unhealthy. In that same sense, the skeptical audience that does not interpret a message the way a sender wants it to be interpreted may be acting just as naturally to protect itself from what it perceives as a deception.

The company can only be the loser when a psychological contract is broken: Its options are limited; and with perhaps one exception, they are not very promising. It can opt to live with an undermotivated and possibly troublesome employee, which is probably the most common solution but hardly a productive one. It can threaten him with dismissal or some other sanction if he doesn't change his attitude, but this is unlikely to have a lasting effect since the causes of his attitudes will not have changed. Perhaps the company can actually discharge him, although that is not so easily done with a long-service employee and long-service employees are precisely the ones with whom one can expect to encounter the broken psychological contract. Lastly, and most difficult of all, the company can reassess the man. This may lead either to giving him a way to change his status or to helping him to gradually change his expectations.

Supervisory styles, monetary rewards, attempts to communicate, and job roles all enter an employee's experience, are filtered by certain notions he has acquired about himself, and are somehow combined through that complex interaction to form his attitudes toward his work. Motivation is the result of an encounter between the individual and his environment. It is not solely the result of the ways in

which that environment is managed, as some human relations enthusiasts seem to suggest. It is not determined entirely by the individual,
with his various interests, aptitudes, and personality traits, as some
enthusiasts of personnel selection seem to imply. It is determined by
both. Further, since the encounter is a continuing experience rather
than a static, unchanging circumstance, it can change. Motivation is
changing all the time: usually too slowly to be noticed, usually fortuitously, sometimes for the worse; but sometimes it is changed deliberately and sometimes for the better.

So, having completed this brief tour of behavioral research and
motivation theory, let us turn to more practical considerations of
how they can be applied.

Chapter 4

The Strategy of Selection

THE ASPECT OF MOTIVATION OVER WHICH MOST ORGANIZA-
tions can exercise the greatest control, yet which is typically left
largely to chance, is the selection of their people. That statement
stands despite the fact that selection is written about, talked about,
advertised, maligned, and generally worried over far more than any
other single aspect of personnel administration.

Most managers are more concerned than they need to be with
techniques of selecting people. It is more important to understand
the logic of the selection process, and the context within which selection occurs, than it is to know just how one ought to decide whom to
hire, promote, or reassign. Only when the logic and the context are
understood do the various techniques of selection make sufficient
sense to be used—and, for that matter, selected—intelligently. In this
chapter we are concerned with those all-important underlying realities.

First, a word about why selection can have such a pronounced
effect upon motivation. The extent to which a man commits his abilities to the accomplishment of his work—that is, his motivation—is
the end product of a process into which many influences can enter.
We have already discussed several of these inputs: supervisory styles,
compensation, communication, and the like. Each is too important
in its own right to be dismissed lightly. But even when each of these

is being managed reasonably well, another factor nearly always stands out as the main determinant of motivation, and that is simply whether a man likes his job.

If he finds his work interesting, reasonably dignifying, and capable of providing him with an occasional thrill of accomplishment, the experiences inherent in the job itself will draw his energies and talents to his work. If on the other hand he finds his work a bore, or degrading, or incapable of tossing an occasional bouquet to his ego, no amount of supervisory artistry or anything else can keep him devoted to his work. He may do it in the minimal sense of just doing what must be done, but he can hardly be expected to lavish any extra care or ingenuity or effort upon it. The crucial difference lies in how well the job is suited to the man.

This degree of "fit" (or, if you will, "misfit") between a man and the work he is assigned to do is the consequence of a chain of management decisions. That chain begins with the decision to hire him in the first place, and it usually leads to the most recent decision to place him in his current job. All these decisions were *selection decisions:* the man was assessed in comparison to other available men and in the light of the apparent probability that he could handle each assignment ably enough to satisfy management. All this is an extended way of saying that a great deal of every man's potential motivation is already inherent in him when he is hired, or even before that, and is certainly inherent in him at the time he is given a particular job to do.

In this sense, motivation can be hired; and indeed, the same can be said of the lack of it. The quality of motivation that appears in a man's work is not so much instilled *in* him by managerial practices as it is elicited *from* him by his job. The individual is his own reservoir of whatever motivation he is capable of; he may draw upon it extravagantly or sparingly, but in any case he derives it from within himself and not from the people who pay his wages. They can influence his willingness to draw from this reservoir, but they cannot, except at the time he is selected, influence how much or what kind of motivation will be available to their company through this man.

These potentialities for motivated action—that is, these "reservoirs"—vary enormously between people. Some people can, at the peak of their form, pour truly heroic efforts into their work. Others achieve much lesser heights, and even then more rarely. Some people can tolerate, with good humor and undiminished efficiency, stresses that would turn other men into grumbling ineffectuals. These differences are all present, at least latently, at the time a man is the object of some manager's selection decision. It is precisely for this reason that so much attention should be given to the selection of new personnel: It determines so much of the kind and caliber of motivation that will be available to the company in the future.

Just *how much* of all motivation is determined in this way is difficult to say. In general, the manager making a selection decision is in a position not unlike that of a tomato grower who has just selected the seeds he will sow: He has not solved all his problems by any means, but he has taken a very significant step toward determining the kind of crop he will ultimately harvest.

Now let us consider the logic of selection. Any selection decision is an attempt to predict something about events in the future on the basis of evidence that is available today. Typically, it is a matter of trying to predict somebody's job performance—or, rather, the way in which some future manager will evaluate his job performance—on the basis of such things as previous work history, test scores, interview impressions, or some other standard. Selection is therefore a problem of anticipating one person's (the manager's) impressions on the basis of a second person's (the selector's) analysis of whatever he has been able to learn about a third person (the candidate). Small wonder that the predictions are so often wide of the mark! The selector is often in the position of having to play a fool's game which he can lose through no fault of his own or of his methods, and which he can win (if at all) largely by chance. There is, in other words, a considerable amount of *illogic* in selection, at least in the way it is too frequently practiced.

There is a better way. But, before describing it, we would be wise to regard the entire process of selection soberly and without enthusiasm. There are no panaceas, and can be no panaceas, in the business of choosing people. Even when selection is practiced as rationally as possible, it is an inexact and somewhat frustrating art. The manager who expects too much from it will inevitably be disillusioned or defrauded, or both. The best that can be said for personnel selection is that, when it is handled intelligently, the results will probably be a significant improvement over the chaos and confusion which are the almost certain aftermath of unintelligent selection. (Lest that statement seem too carefully hedged, note that it is actually claiming quite a lot: "significant improvements" in selection can make a mighty difference in productivity.)

Yet it cannot be overemphasized that personnel selection, regardless of whether it is carried out by the wise or the unwise, is *always* a guessing game. It is always based on incomplete, and sometimes on unreliable, information. But the main problem in selection is not so much the inadequacy of the information on which it is based as the inability of *any* current information to control the events it is supposed to predict. A man's future job performance and the way his manager will rate it will be affected by many circumstances that cannot even be anticipated, let alone measured, at the time a decision must be made as to whether or not to hire him. The things we can learn about a man today, even if they are relevant to his future effectiveness in his work, are seldom more than a small fraction of *all* the circumstances that will ultimately be relevant to it. Our tomato grower may know all there is to know about his seeds; yet, on the day he decides to sow them, he cannot predict the weather during the growing season or the market for tomatoes at harvest time. The manager who is thoroughly familiar with the aptitudes and personality of a candidate is in roughly the same position.

But, as any good poker player knows, there are ways of playing a guessing game to good advantage. There *is* a basic logic that underlies the selection process; and, if this is understood and sensibly utilized, the guessing becomes more educated and the game becomes considerably more susceptible of being won. This logic is not complex and may be visualized in a series of simple diagrams.

To begin, we should note that selection is always a matter of trying to relate one set of variables (the various ways in which we are measuring the candidates) to another set of variables (the various ways in which their performance might be rated if they were put to work in a particular job). No matter how the measurements of the candidates are made, they lead eventually to some sort of estimate of how likely it is that each man could handle the job in an acceptable way. These estimates can range all the way from rating a man's chances as remarkably promising to rating them as utterly unpromising. At some point between these extremes, the selector will usually have in mind (at least implicitly) the minimum degree of "promise" he is prepared to risk having to work with. All this can be represented as follows:

Remarkably promising

Minimum acceptable risk

Utterly unpromising

We can also represent the possible *outcomes* of any selection decision in much the same way. This time, for the sake of being able to show both scales together conveniently, we will use a horizontal line; but the principle is exactly the same. After a man has been hired and put to work, his managers will eventually arrive at an assessment of his performance, and their judgments may range all the way from concluding that he is utterly incompetent to rating him as exceptionally effective; more likely, he will be found to be somewhere in between. Further, those managers will probably be thinking (again, at least implicitly) of some minimum level of effectiveness that can be tolerated in this type of work: a level below which they would have to conclude that it had been a mistake to place the individual in this particular job. All this may be shown in the same fashion:

Utterly incompetent	Minimum acceptable performance	Exceptionally effective

Putting both these scales together, we get a combination which makes it possible to show the relationship (if any) between the ratings that were made at the time of selection and subsequent ratings of job performance. This can be done for any individual by locating the coordinates for the rating he was given when hired or assigned, and the rating he was given on the job, and by placing a dot, an X, or some other mark where these lines intersect. By extending the coordinates of the two minimum acceptable points into the graph, we can then place any individual in one of the four possible outcomes of any selection decision.

Note this carefully: *There are only four possible results of a selection decision.* Thus:

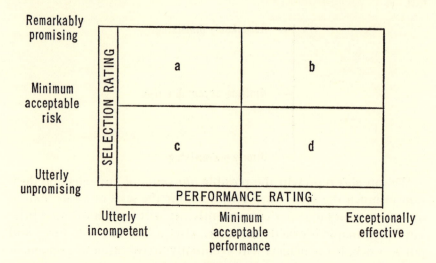

The section of the diagram marked "a" would include all candidates who, at the time they were chosen, were considered to have at least an acceptable chance of success, but who did not in fact manage to do well on the job. In all such cases the selection decision was an error. The section marked "b" would include all those people who not only looked good to the selectors but also performed well on the job. All such selection decisions were correct.

Ordinarily, our knowledge of the outcome of selection decisions is limited to the "a" and "b" varieties, since few companies would run the risk of placing a man in a job for which he seems to have little chance of success. To round out the full range of possibilities, however, it is useful to consider at least theoretically what might happen if candidates whose chances of success had been given a low rating were given a chance at the job anyway. Those who failed on the job, thereby fulfilling the gloomy prophecy that had been made for them, would be represented in the section marked "c." These selection decisions were correct in the sense that it would have been wiser for the company to heed its selectors. On the other hand, those candidates who managed to do much better on the job than the selectors thought they could would be represented in the section marked "d." All these decisions would be errors.

There are, then, two kinds of correct predictions (verified success and verified failure) and two kinds of errors (the promising failure and the unpromising success) that can follow any selection decision. Therefore the basic purpose of any selection procedure can be stated quite simply: to maximize the correct predictions and to minimize the errors. The only justification for adding or subtracting any particular procedure from a company's selection system is to improve its ability to accomplish either or both of these basic goals. Any technique for evaluating a candidate's chances, no matter how elegant or attractive it may be, has no place in a rational selection system if it cannot be shown to *better* the system's performance in reaching these goals. An appalling number of tests and other procedures, many of them time-honored and hoary with age, would fall into disuse if they were measured against this simple but exacting standard.

Although very few do it, any organization which took the trouble to plot the outcome of its selection decisions on such a chart as we have shown, and which found that most of these decisions turned out to be of the "b" or "c" variety, would have ample reason for congratulating its selectors. On the other hand, if "a" or "d" results predominated, the selection system would be properly suspected of doing more harm than good. If there were a roughly equal scattering of individuals in all four sections, the selection system would appear to have been largely ineffectual. (The latter, alas, is perhaps the most common result of engaging in this revealing little exercise.)

Although outcomes "a," "b," "c," and "d" seem abstract enough when displayed on a diagram, they are all familiar friends of any manager who has had to make many selection decisions. While the "a" type of error does not necessarily occur very often, it is rather unforgiving. To select a man who subsequently fails to vindicate the selector's judgment is a galling error, not only because of the loss of time and money that it causes, but also because the error occurs in public and becomes a matter of record. In this sense, outcome "a" is less merciful than outcome "d," even though they can be equally costly, since an error of the "d" type is almost never verified.

It is perhaps for precisely this reason that managers who are in a position to be choosy sometimes become very conservative about their selection decisions. That is, they may prefer the risk of wasting potentially useful men (the "d" error) to that of betting on a man who fails (the "a" error). This kind of reasoning is likely to be found in companies that have a choice between filling a position through internal transfer or promotion, on the one hand, or through outside hiring on the other. A few negative observations will almost inevitably be recorded on any employee who has been known for several years, especially when the company's appraisal system demands it; therefore the internal candidates will usually have some degree of "taint" to their qualifications which is apparently lacking among the better outside candidates. This is not because the outside candidates are better men, but because the qualifications of the inside candidates are better documented. Nevertheless, in order to be able to avoid the charge of having gambled imprudently on a "known" poor risk, some managers would prefer to take the outsider whose deficiencies are unknown or at least unrecorded. It goes without saying that this practice is wasteful of talent and destructive of morale and that it is also unworthy of a professional manager, but it is a prevalent practice for all that.

Outcome "d" therefore conceals a host of errors, and more often than not they are errors of managerial timidity. The known risk is not necessarily more dangerous than the unknown one unless the company takes a punitive attitude toward mistakes that were presumably "avoidable"—but that is a problem for another chapter.

The next diagram shows what actually happens in most selection systems: The operation of the system prevents its own evaluation. This is simply because the candidates who fall short of whatever standards the selection system imposes are almost never given a chance to prove the system wrong. The data available for checking the efficiency of the selection system usually consist almost entirely of the "a" and "b" kinds of outcomes. In other words:

a	b
c	d
??? ???	???

We would ordinarily hope to find that the number of individuals in "b" exceeded those in "a"; or, to put it more simply, that most of the people whose chances of success had been rated highly would actually succeed. But, even when they do, it is still possible that the selection methods are wasteful of available talent. That is, there may be too many rejections of potentially effective men represented by the "unknown quantities" in "d." Further, even if the number of individuals in "b" does not exceed the number in "a," the system is not necessarily faulty. It may be that the majority of rejected candidates would have failed; that is, the number in "c" would exceed the number in "d" if we had some way of knowing these quantities. In that case the selection system would be doing a useful screening job even if it was unable to identify all the potential failures. But the important point is that we almost never know for sure how well a selection system is working. Indeed, we cannot know unless we are willing to ignore the system long enough to accumulate a sizable sample of people whom the system would ordinarily reject, and hire the lot of them.

To find out whether a selection system is useful or fatuous can be a costly business. Not to find out can be even costlier. It is unfortunately true that the majority of selection systems are accepted on faith alone, and that the question of whether they deserve this sentiment is seldom raised. This is why few organizations are in a position to say for certain whether the processes by which they acquire, utilize, and to a large extent motivate their people are really systems or merely rituals.

What determines how well a selection system really works? Basically, there are two factors: One is the diversity of the available candidates, and the other is the extent to which the selection techniques measure something that is actually related to job performance. Regarding diversity, most selection systems have to operate within a relatively narrow range of ability. As a rule, the people among whom a company can actually make its choices are limited by job requirements or by the labor market itself to a comparatively small number. Only rarely are selectors confronted with a really wide range of talent within which to exercise their arts. (The Selective Service System probably comes closer to that condition than most employers ever do, especially in wartime when there are relatively few grounds for deferment.)

This restriction in the range of choice is important, because it makes it quite difficult to demonstrate the virtues (if any) of a selection system. If the system works at all, it usually works on a grand scale rather than a microscopic one. That is, it makes gross distinctions between groups of people but not fine distinctions between individuals. Selection systems work on the principle of comparing one individual to a large group of people having similar characteristics and stating the probability of his success in terms of the historic record achieved by that group. Thus we might conclude that the odds in favor of a particular individual were, say, 3 to 2 because 60 percent of the people to whom he seems similar have made the grade in the past. But until we actually put that individual into the job, we do not know whether he may become part of the 40 percent that do not make it. Consequently, if the available candidates are all relatively similar to each other (that is, if the range of the odds on the success of all candidates is narrow), the relationship between selection ratings and performance may be indistinct or even invisible.

The problem can be likened to what happens when a reproduction of a photograph in a newspaper is examined under a magnifying glass. The picture actually consists of a pattern of small dots which, when clustered closely together, produce a dark area. Looser clusters produce gray areas, and the omission of dots produces a white segment. If we examine only a narrow strip across any section of the picture, we see not a picture but only an apparently meaningless series of dots. It is only when that segment is viewed in the context of all the dots that the picture itself can be seen. Most of the evaluations that can be made of selection systems are not unlike the narrow row of dots in a newspaper photograph: they show only what the system can do with a small part of the available population.

The ordinary restrictions on the choices available to an employer place a heavy burden on the selection system. The narrower the range of available talent, the more sensitive the system has to be, and the more likely it is to make errors of either the "a" or the "d" variety. On the other hand, when the range of available talent is fairly broad, even a relatively crude selection system can sort them out with acceptable accuracy. This is why it is very much to any organization's advantage to maximize the range of available talent, at least for initial screening purposes. (More about that later.)

The "sensitivity" of the system might be defined in terms of how well it managed to sort candidates into the four possible outcomes. A sensitive system would be one which made relatively few errors. (Psychologists use the term "validity" when applying this concept to tests.) Here is how different degrees of sensitivity can affect the results of selection:

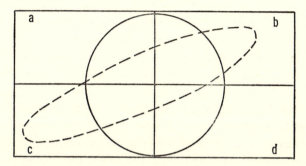

The diagram is not meant to represent Saturn, although perhaps it would be useful to conjure up a vision of that planet when assessing a selection system. What *is* represented is two very different degrees of sensitivity. Remember that any individual can be placed on our outcome chart by marking the point where the coordinates of his selection rating and his subsequent performance rating intersect. If we record the fates of a large enough group of individuals in this way, the chart eventually becomes filled with marks. Unless the selection system is entirely meaningless, these marks will not be scattered randomly all over the chart. Instead there will be a certain pattern to them. That pattern is the key to evaluating the selection system.

Ordinarily, one could draw some kind of loop that enclosed most of the marks. Such a loop would be a rough-and-ready way to visualize what a statistician does when he calculates what he calls a "correlation." Basically, a correlation expresses numerically what the loop expresses visually: the degree to which the marks in the chart adhere to a detectable pattern. Or to put it in terms of people instead of marks or numbers, correlations show how reliably the selection ratings have actually predicted job performance. If whatever the selectors were doing was really quite irrelevant to the way in which peo-

ple handled their jobs, this irrelevancy would show itself in a pat-
ternless scattering of marks in all four quadrants. In numerical
terms, this would show up as a correlation close to zero. In our example, this situation is represented by the solid circular line that en-
closes a roughly equal number of both kinds of errors and both kinds
of correct predictions. In actual practice, however, a zero correlation
is seldom enclosed so neatly. It usually looks more like an irregular
blob than a circle!

On the other hand, if the selectors knew their business and were
able to predict performance reasonably well, the marks would have
coalesced into a roughly elliptical pattern, somewhat like the dotted
loop shown. Numerically, this would result in a correlation between
zero and plus one. In terms of people, most of them would have been
correctly assessed by the selection system and would therefore appear
in the "b" or "c" quadrants of the chart. There would be a more or
less regular increase in the likelihood of successful performance as we
moved from the lower to the higher selection ratings. The ellipse, in
other words, would be tilted from the lower left to the upper right.

The shape and tilt of the ellipse that was drawn around the marks
representing the outcome of selection ratings have a great deal of significance for evaluating those ratings. But before elaborating on that
point, let us note in passing what a selector's nightmare would look
like on our outcome chart. It would be a narrow ellipse tilted in the
opposite direction; that is, from upper left to lower right. This
would represent a selection system so out of tune with reality that
one could do an effective job of selection by going exactly opposite to
its recommendations every time. Numerically, this would be a correlation close to minus one.

The ideal distribution of people on an outcome-of-selection chart
would not be an ellipse at all; it would be a straight line. That would
represent an infallible selection system in which every rating pointed
with absolute certainty to a particular level of performance. It need
hardly be said that this has never happened and probably never will
happen. The "next best" distribution would be a fairly tight ellipse
like the one we have illustrated: one in which the marks that represent people are mostly located at points that are fairly close to a theoretical "straight line." In other words, most of the selection ratings
would come quite close to predicting how well the individual actu-

ally handles his job. This also is relatively rare. The practical standard of a good selection system, then, would be an ellipse which is at least clearly discernible as an ellipse: not as tight as our dotted loop yet not shapeless or merely circular, either.

To achieve even a "fat ellipse" distribution on an outcome-of-selection chart is no easy task. The value of such a distribution should not be demeaned, since it can mean a substantial saving in time and money. Still, as more and more people deviate further and further from that theoretical straight line—that is, as the ellipse gets fatter—more and more people turn into predictive errors. This brings us to one of the hard, cold facts of the selection business: *Errors can not be eliminated.* They can only be minimized, which is difficult enough but very useful when done intelligently.

To do this, the selectors must appreciate a little-known and somewhat paradoxical fact about selection errors: that *while they can not be eliminated, they can be selected.* It is possible, in other words, to decide which types of errors would be least damaging to an organization and which types would be most damaging and then, deliberately, to increase the likelihood of the less damaging errors in order to minimize the chances that the more serious kind would occur. This is an expensive form of insurance, since it amounts to buying inefficiency to stave off calamity. But it is often necessary to make this unpleasant choice, simply because the ellipse is too fat—in short, because the selection system is relatively insensitive. The best reason for trying to increase the sensitivity of selection systems is to minimize the harshness of this choice.

Since the choice must be made, it is best to make it wisely; so let us review the problems that are involved in it. The two errors to which a selection system is exposed are the unforgiving "a" type of error, in which a highly rated individual turns in a disappointing job performance, and the hidden "d" type of error, in which people who could have succeeded on the job were underestimated by the selection system and therefore were not assigned to the job. Neither is desirable, yet there are times when, owing to the availability of qualified candidates or the importance of the job to be filled, or to both, the one is clearly preferable to the other.

Availability of candidates may refer to the external labor market or to the internal supply of employees who could be considered for an opening. When the labor market is tight, the selectors must become increasingly reluctant to turn away a potentially qualified candidate, simply because it may be difficult to find anyone more suitable and, meantime, there is pressure from line management to get those jobs filled. In these circumstances, the "d" error becomes the more intolerable of the two, and the selectors are increasingly willing to take chances on men about whom they have some doubts. Translating this willingness into the structure of our charts, they lower the minimum acceptable risk line from its *original* level (the solid line at "o" in the following diagram) to a *revised* level (the dotted line at "r") :

```
           ┌────────────────────────┬────────────────────────┐
           │                        │                        │
           │  a                     │  b                     │
           │                        │                        │
           │                        │                        │
        0  ├────────────────────────┼────────────────────────┤
           │        1               │            2           │
        r  ├─ ─ ─ ─ ─ ─ ─ ─ ─ ─ ─ ─ ┼ ─ ─ ─ ─ ─ ─ ─ ─ ─ ─ ─ ─┤
           │                        │                        │
           │  c                     │  d                     │
           │                        │                        │
           └────────────────────────┴────────────────────────┘
```

The sections marked "1" and "2" include people who would previously have been rejected but who would now be put to work. In the case of section "1," we see an increased exposure to potential failures. This represents the cost of employing this strategy. Surprisingly, executives who consent to (or even insist on) this strategy, for the sake of filling out crews which would otherwise remain undermanned, are sometimes bitterly disappointed when the new hires produce less than average results. This is tantamount to insisting on filet mignon and then expressing shock when the bill for it is considerably higher than for hamburger. Human ability is no exception to the laws of supply and demand.

The section of the chart marked "2" shows the payoff of employing this strategy: an increased flow of scarce and capable people into the company from among those who would ordinarily, and erroneously, have been turned down. It is not uncommon, by the way, for companies that turn to this strategy in times of labor shortage to discover that their standards have been too high all along. Minimum hiring standards (and minimum assignment standards, too) are often rather arbitrary, having been adopted for the sake of convenience rather than on the basis of evidence that they could effectively separate the hopeful from the hopeless. Thus, when candidates with high school diplomas are abundant, it is easy to adopt the diploma as a minimum standard even though many of the people who lack one can learn to do the job as well as graduates can. The same principle is, if anything, even more true of college degrees. Minimum standards have a way of creeping upward needlessly, thus harming the selection system (by forcing it to make its choices within an unnecessarily narrow range), the company (by forcing it to make inefficient use of the available labor supply), and the candidates themselves (by excluding and frequently demoralizing men whose abilities are not fairly represented by the standard). This is precisely what happened, by the way, in the case of the metering equipment company described in Chapter 1.

None of this should be construed as an argument in favor of encouraging students to become dropouts. The economy does not always have to contend with a labor shortage, and whenever it doesn't the inexorable upward creep of minimum standards will unquestionably be resumed. Nor can it be doubted that the lifetime earnings of an individual, as well as his satisfaction with his work, are directly related to the educational background he brings to it. There are, of course, exceptions to the rule, but they are all exactly that: exceptions. No sensible young person can afford to plan his career in the slender hope that he will somehow turn into an exception.

Whenever hiring standards are reduced as a means of contending with an inadequate supply of qualified candidates, a great hue and cry is likely to arise from some managers about diluting the quality of the workforce. This apprehension would be justified only if the selection system had been unusually precise and if the previous minimum standards had been set at a point which efficiently utilized the available talent. Since these two conditions are not really very common, the reduction of minimum hiring standards does not *necessarily* result in bringing in less capable people. That could happen, of course, especially if a fairly large number of new men were brought in as a result of the revised standards, but it is by no means an inevitable result of this strategy.

There are two main reasons why reducing hiring standards does not necessarily reduce worker productivity. The first, as we have already noted, is that the standards may have been set too high in the first place. The second reason concerns the limitations of the selection system: Unless it is unusually sensitive, it will not define all risks clearly. Instead, there will be a fairly extensive "gray area" of more or less intermediate risks—people whose chances would not appear to be either good or bad. Selection ratings of this indeterminate type are very often given to the majority of available candidates.

Since most managers prefer to deal, whenever they can, with something more hopeful than a 50:50 risk, this group of candidates is not extensively utilized. The minimum acceptable risk line, in other words, is often drawn so as to exclude them. But this is often due to a problem in semantics rather than a problem in assessing candidates. That is, the intermediate risk is *not* someone for whom "average" or mediocre performance is predicted; rather he is someone who appears to have about an average chance of turning into a good performer. Or, if you will, about half of the candidates so rated will (assuming the selection system is working well) turn out to be just as effective on the job as those men who were given higher ratings and went on to succeed. The rating is given to probability or to the "odds" of success, not to the quality of the man himself. More about this later when we discuss the "descriptive fallacy."

In passing, however, we might note a related semantic problem. Many managers have become allergic to that word "average." Somehow, the prospects of having to accept an average risk, or even of having to add an average performer to one's department, have become unattractive to the average manager. (The pun is intentional.) Although the term has a precise mathematical meaning, its connotation has slipped from the center of a distribution toward the lower end. In most jobs an average performance is quite sufficient, and in many labor markets an average risk is about as good as we are likely to find. Although to some managers this may seem to be a surrender to expediency, a closer look at the real requirements of their companies may reveal that they have unwittingly allowed the high standards they set for themselves to spill over into those they set for their departments—probably to the detriment of their companies. They may, in other words, have permitted their own pardonable pride in their own ambitions to contribute to that upward creep of standards: to insist on filet mignon when hamburger will do.

In any case, dipping into the pool of available average risks does not necessarily dilute the quality of manpower. The real problem is not with these men but rather with our own inability to define their potentialities more sharply. For this reason, the labor shortages that tend to show up at the peaks of economic cycles can have salutary effects. They can reveal the inefficiency with which companies have utilized available manpower, both in their employees and in the outside labor market. They can help to demonstrate that a selection system has pitched its standards too high, perhaps as an easy way to compensate for the imprecision of its measurements. Labor shortages can compel a company to take a harder look at the talent it may have been wasting: internally in the form of employees who have been underutilized and externally in the form of candidates who have been rejected unnecessarily. They can cause a company that has been actively—and perhaps at some cost—upgrading the abilities of its employees to thank its lucky stars. They can motivate a company that has been indulging in the luxury of not doing so to begin such a program without waiting for the next painful lesson in the unwisdom of not developing its human resources.

One final comment about the strategy of deliberately electing to increase the "a" type of error in order to minimize the "d" type. It is primarily useful when the kinds of ability we are seeking have become scarce, relative to our needs for them, and it is forced upon us by the relative insensitivity of most selection systems as well as by the inefficiency with which we tend to use them. But there is one other consideration that must be taken into account before resorting to this strategy, and that is the consequence of failure in the particular jobs we are seeking to fill. Obviously, there are some jobs in which failure is annoying but hardly catastrophic as far as the company's overall operations are concerned, and there are some in which failure would be catastrophic and therefore considerably more than just annoying.

In general, executive jobs, key professional and supervisory jobs, and certain highly skilled jobs are all in that second category in which failure is quite intolerable. In none of those cases would this strategy be wise. But for the vast bulk of the other jobs in most companies, it can be a very useful strategy indeed. Even where the success

of a particular individual can have a crucial effect on the fortunes of
the organization as a whole, it can be helpful to assess realistically the
question whether the traditional standards of selection have been set
beyond the limits that prudence alone would dictate. No manager in
his right mind wants to bet his company's future on an asset that is
both perishable and irreplaceable, yet that is precisely what happens
when access to key jobs is overly restricted.

A further diagram demonstrates the effect of employing the opposite strategy:

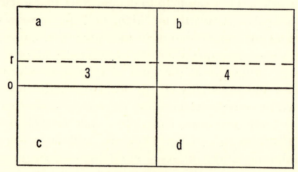

The section marked "4" indicates the increased exposure to the "d"
type of error that results from deliberately raising the minimum acceptable risk level. The cost of this strategy is additional wastage of
talent. This in turn could endanger internal morale by seeming to
close what some employees might regard as natural routes of advancement. Or it could gradually reduce the abundance of willing
outside applicants by giving the company a reputation for being arbitrary in its hiring standards—or, at any rate, too severe to make it
worth the candidates' trouble to apply. The potential payoff for accepting these added costs is represented in the section marked "3,"
which shows the decreased exposure to the "a" type of error. By applying a severe selection standard, the company gets additional insurance against assigning men to jobs in which they fail. This second
strategy makes sense, therefore, in very loose labor markets or in cases
where the position to be filled is so crucial to the organization that
the risk of failure must be minimized at any cost.

Because the cost of this second strategy is usually hidden and does
not become apparent for a long time, it is elected much more often
than the first. Yet its costs can be severe, and it is very much in the

organization's best long-range interests to hold them down. Once again, the real problem is, not the labor market or the importance of the job to be filled, but the relative insensitivity of most selection systems. However, the second strategy also helps to illustrate an important point about selection: When there are plenty of candidates available, even a relatively crude selection system can do an effective screening job as long as the minimum standard is raised to a high level. The obverse is even more important: If a company knows that its selection system is not very sensitive, it makes sense to maximize the number of candidates on whom it is exercised.

This long exposition of the logic underlying selection systems has been somewhat oversimplified from the very first diagram. For the sake of clarity, we have dealt first with underlying principles; for the sake of reality, it is now necessary to add the surface confusion and imprecision that typically help to obscure the problems that selectors have to face. These are shown in one final diagram, which illustrates the essentially illogical context in which most selection decisions must be made:

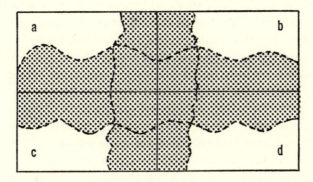

We have until now been resting our arguments on assumptions that are not, alas, very often justified. These are that the minimum standards of the selection ratings (the central horizontal line in all previous diagrams) and of the managers who rate job performance (the central vertical line) are consistent. They almost never are. The so-called minimum standards are seldom defined very precisely, and even when they are (as in the case of cutoff scores on tests) the precision tends to be illusory owing to random influences which can always account for a few points. The question of whether a given individual constitutes an acceptable or unacceptable risk for a given job can vary from day to day, or from selector to selector, especially if he is one of those average risks anyway. Therefore the line that separates the two kinds of risks on the outcome chart must be represented as rather fuzzy in order to correspond to reality. Selectors just aren't as precise as our arguments have implied they should be. This is not necessarily to detract from their efforts. After all, they are charged with measuring a very hard-to-measure animal and with making predictions about how he will fare under conditions which are themselves largely unpredictable.

The same argument is, if anything, even more true of performance ratings. The vertical line also is quite fuzzy. In part this is due to the well-known tendency of humans to react to each other's personalities in ways that are protective of their own. Consequently, so-called performance ratings are too often compounded of the "chemistry" of interpersonal reactions more than of dispassionate measurements of what a man has accomplished. Even when subjectivity is not an important factor, many managers are handicapped in making performance ratings by the lack of suitable standards with which to measure what they are supposed to rate. Most performance appraisal systems give the appraiser little guidance as to what, for example, would constitute average performance. Is it average for the department, for the company as a whole, or for this type of worker in general? Or is it just a euphemism for people whose work has caught no one's eye? Since performance-rating systems are likely to be ambiguous themselves, two perfectly honest and competent managers can arrive at two utterly different evaluations of the same man's work. This sort of thing can obviously play hob with determining whether a given individual turns up as an "a" or a "b" on the outcome chart.

One might be tempted to conclude from this that attempting to impose logic upon a selection system is itself illogical, and that selection itself must forever remain a black art whose few successful practitioners would seem to be guided by unfathomable instincts. Nothing would please the so-called intuitive experts more, and nothing could be further from the truth. Illogic may be endemic in selection, but it is not inherent in it. Selection systems are often freighted with bad habits, most of which are the result of never having had to think through the full implications of what was being done. It is this failure to think straight about selection, and not the use of a particular method or the retaining of a particular expert, that is at the root of the trouble with most selection systems. This is also why so many companies populate themselves with carefully chosen men who turn out, years later, to be incapable of sustaining the kinds of motivation the company needs in order to prosper.

Both selection itself and the thing it is supposed to predict—performance ratings—can be rationalized to a considerable extent. Further, this can be done without making superhuman demands on the ordinary mortals who have to operate these systems. Just as war is too important to be left to the generals, selection is too important to be left in the hands of the experts. Management can and should control its own selection system. But first it must get rid of some illusions.

Chapter 5

The Difficult Art
of Choosing People

A SENSIBLE SELECTION PROGRAM MUST BE BUILT ON SOME-thing firmer than fantasy, and fantasy is too often the chief under-pinning for expensive selection systems. What makes many selection systems expensive is not only their initial cost but also their failure to man the organization with enough people who can respond, over the course of their careers, with the kinds of vigor, flexibility, and initiative that most organizations will sooner or later require of their key members.

Most of the unreality and illogic in selection systems is caused by assumptions that turn out, on examination, to be fallacies. It will be useful to explode a few of the more common ones here. Any one of them is capable of wrecking an otherwise well-constructed system. Let us look briefly at the "hero" fallacy, the "descriptive" fallacy, the "permanence" fallacy, and the fallacy of "determinism."

Most of the world's work gets done, and done well enough, by rather ordinary people. All of it gets done by people who have some flaw or deficiency that is not altogether desirable in their work. *The hero fallacy* is the notion that there must be somebody somewhere who fits the specifications of a job, and the whims of its managers, perfectly. A corollary of the hero fallacy is the notion that no one but such a mythical hero can really handle the job satisfactorily. A company which accepts the hero fallacy has a fairly simple strategy to follow: All it has to do is find such a person, put him to work, and then forget about him while he proceeds to fulfill his destiny. When the strategy doesn't work, the hero fallacy also provides a convenient and comforting explanation: Yesterday's hero was obviously overrated—a mere error in selection. By choosing more carefully next time, all the company's problems with this particular job will vanish. But somehow they never do so, which is the reason for the principal complaint of managers who are addicted to the hero fallacy: There just aren't enough really capable and dedicated people in this world.

Managements that are afflicted by the hero fallacy are likely to try to solve too many of their problems through selection. Even the best selection program does no more than narrow the field of available candidates to those among whom management has the best chance, through intelligent leadership, of tapping inherent motivation. Selection is the indispensable beginning of effective management by motivation, but it is never more than a beginning. The insidious aspect of the hero fallacy is that, by providing such an attractive rationalization for its own failures, it closes management's eyes to the harm it is doing. It is easy, much too easy, to write off the results of inadequate managerial planning as just one more poor choice of talent.

The almost inevitable result of the hero fallacy is experimentation with one selection system after another, one recruiting source after another, and, of course, one key employee after another. This endless experimentation has secondary results: low morale, excessive turnover, and usually an unattractive reputation in the labor market. These problems serve to compound the underlying difficulty by making it that much tougher for even a well-qualified "hero" to resolve the dilemmas he is expected to resolve. So a vicious circle is set up, much to the profit of a succession of consultants, perhaps, but not to the company's. One of the more ironic results of the hero fallacy is that a company that tries to solve all its problems through "better" selection is destined to have no end of selection problems.

It is seldom realistic to try to staff an organization, especially at executive levels, with men who were "made" for their jobs. It makes far more sense to select the best men available, and then tailor the organization to benefit from their strengths and to offset, or at least minimize, the effects of their weaknesses. Or, to refer the problem back to our outcome-of-selection chart, there is little profit in raising the minimum acceptable risk line too high.

It is easy, by the way, to accept this argument without really abandoning the hero fallacy. One can agree with the notion that, after all, everyone has his faults (if only because it would be arrogant to deny it) and then proceed to inflate the requirements of the next job to be filled because it is "exceptional." One can agree that it is management's responsibility to support each of its key men in ways that compensate for their deficiencies and then load the full blame for the next organizational disappointment onto the shoulders of one hapless executive who "obviously" was unfit for his job. *Nobody is fit for his job in a company that is encumbered by the hero fallacy.* The idea is basically an absurd one that leads, tortuously and expensively, nowhere. For all that, it is perhaps the main reason for the excessive enthusiasm, and the excessive condemnation, in managerial attitudes toward personnel selection.

The descriptive fallacy is the notion that if a man's qualities can be described precisely enough and completely enough, he can then be matched against the requirements of a job in a way that permits a reliable decision as to whether he belongs in it or not. This is why some testing programs take days to complete, why there is such a persistent demand for "insights" into candidates' personalities, and why selection specialists are asked to couch their reports in graphic terms that evoke familiar images of behavior on the job. The logic of all this seems impeccable until one begins to insist on clear definitions.

The descriptive fallacy actually rests on some rather shaky assumptions. For one, it is questionable whether a person can be "described" at all in the sense of conveying an accurate portrait in words or numbers of how he can be expected to conduct himself in what would be, for him, an unfamiliar situation. Further, the language with which we ordinarily talk about someone's style of acting, thinking, and communicating—in a word, his "personality"—is itself quite imprecise and loaded with private meanings that are seldom easily conveyed. Consequently, when selection specialists attempt to describe a person whom they have been measuring with their various yardsticks, what they describe is not necessarily the person, and what their managements infer from their description is not necessarily what they have described. Or—in terms of our outcome-of-selection chart—attempts to establish the degree of risk in hiring a candidate by describing his personal qualities result in a very, very fuzzy notion of what his chances really are.

The descriptive fallacy also involves a sort of psychological version of the law of diminishing returns. There is a point beyond which further testing, interviewing, and probing add little to what can be usefully known about a candidate. That point is usually reached fairly early, especially when the probing is in the hands of sophisticated selectors who know what is essential and what is not. To continue the examination further does little but duplicate what is already known or, in some cases, confuse the issue by introducing meaningless or misleading information. But the descriptive fallacy seems to demand that the candidate be measured by every yardstick we can find; and a long list of tests, interviews, and background investigations creates a comforting, if illusory, feeling that everything that needs to be known about the man *is* known. The danger in this approach lies not so much in its unnecessary cost or its unnecessary imposition on the time of the candidate as in the spurious sense of certainty which the sheer weight of information gives to the people who use it. Where, as is generally the case, the candidate is a comparative stranger and the selectors must make up their minds about him within a reasonable period of time, it is questionable whether they will really know much more about him after four days than they did after four hours.

In the last analysis, every selection decision involves prediction, not description, and prediction is always an attempt to estimate probabilities. Whether the description of a man that emerges from his session with the selectors captures the essence of the man or misses it altogether is really an academic question. For practical purposes, all that matters is whether what the selectors have done can be translated into a reliable estimate of the candidate's likelihood of measuring up to the job. It is precisely because descriptive information is so difficult to translate into accurate estimates that its value is questionable, regardless of how "uncannily" it may agree with other people's preconceptions about what the candidate is like. The proper business of the selector is therefore to know how people who are comparable to the candidate have fared on the job and to be sure that he really is comparable to that group.

Regrettably, the descriptive fallacy leads many managements to turn to selection specialists for confirmation of what they think they already know, rather than for an estimate of probabilities. That is, they measure the usefulness of the selectors by the extent to which the selectors describe the candidate in essentially the same terms that they would use. Whether the opinions that are thus confirmed are relevant or irrelevant is seldom considered. This is not unlike trying to decide whether a horse is likely to win a race by consulting an expert as to the color, height, and general appearance of the horse, without timing him in a trial race or reviewing his record.

The permanence fallacy is the assumption that, once a man has been evaluated by selectors, everything that may need to be known about him in all future selection decisions is already known. This is why relatively few people are ever re-evaluated after having once been put through whatever procedures their companies used to select them in the first place. Yet people can and do change over the long course of a career, and it is a comparatively rare man who is not wiser and more competent today than he was, say, five years ago. This is especially true of the younger men and women who make up the bulk of the candidates who pass through a company's initial selection procedures. But many companies have an unfortunate tendency to "type-cast" their employees quite early in their careers, with the result that gradual maturation and learning eventually overqualify them for their assigned roles. This is a major cause of serious morale and turnover problems.

But a more serious result of the permanence fallacy is the tendency to assume that if a man is qualified for a particular job today, he always will be, and that therefore he can be safely left to handle it with a minimum of support. Almost inevitably, a man who is so regarded by his superiors will disappoint them in some way, either because of a normal human lapse or, more likely, because management will have taken him so much for granted that it fails to communicate its needs to him effectively. Either way, there is a real danger that management will overreact by concluding that the man has lost his touch or that the job has outgrown him. It could have happened, of course, but if management has been operating under the permanence fallacy it is just as likely that he has stayed too long in the job and lost interest in it.

Men who are capable of learning and personal growth on the job (and that includes most of them) are always in potential conflict with their organizations. It is precisely this capacity to grow that enables them to gravitate toward the key jobs in their companies: management, professional work, or various highly skilled occupations. Therefore, their companies rely on them, and this reliance increases as they become more and more proficient in their particular jobs. Theoretically, the ideal organization would have seasoned experts in all its key posts, each of them with many years of service ahead of him. In actual practice, such organizations are impossible, simply because people don't stop growing.

In time, a job that has been thoroughly mastered becomes routine and even boring. Consequently, just at the time when the company's investment in the man who holds it reaches the point of maximum payout, the man is likely to want to discontinue the arrangement and get into a new job in which he will necessarily be less proficient. Especially when there is a strong outside demand for the services of such specialists, there is a limit to how long a company can keep a man in a job for which he is maximally qualified without running a serious risk of losing him.

It is a paradox that many experts don't want to *be* experts; they would rather be continually in the process of *becoming* experts. The permanence fallacy fails to take account of this inconvenient but important aspect of human nature. As a consequence, people who may have been quite properly selected for their jobs several years ago may be unwilling to stay in them, or at least to devote their best efforts to them, today. This is not the result of faulty selection; it is the result of faulty career planning.

The importance of effective career planning in a program of management by motivation is impossible to overemphasize. The selection process must be a permanent feature of organizational life, not just an introductory ritual. It is probably impossible to plan full careers in any kind of detail, especially when they are subject to technological change, but it is usually possible to make fairly reliable forecasts of a person's potentialities over a limited (say, five-year) range. The job itself and the prospect of future assignments play such a vital role in motivation that the administration of job placement cannot be left to chance. In many companies it is. This is why there is a more or less constant "fallout" of potential executives and specialists from such firms.

It is of paramount importance to have an effective means for periodically taking stock of the directions in which people have been developing. It is equally important that they be aware of that system and have confidence in it. Otherwise the corrosive idea that "there is no future for me in this company" can take root, and nothing can be more damaging to the motivation of an ambitious person than that. (More about ways of preventing this in the chapter on employee development.)

The fallacy of determinism is the idea that a man's success or failure in a given job is determined entirely by his possession of certain qualities, and that the presence or absence of these qualities can be assessed at the time of his initial selection. It is probably true that short-run results on the job can be predicted fairly well by a good selection system, but the more time that elapses between the initial selection and the actual performance rating, the less reliable the prediction is likely to be. We have already noted one reason for this gradual loss of predictability: People change. There is another reason: Jobs change, too. Very often the content of the job, the skills required, or the concept of what the man in the job is supposed to accomplish changes in the course of several years. It should come as no surprise when men selected under one concept of how the job should be done do not work out as predicted when that concept changes. Even when the job itself remains relatively stable, management or supervisory changes can bring differing standards of evaluating performance or differing emphases as to what is important and what is not.

For all these reasons, it is well worth regarding every selection decision as a relatively short-range affair. When the selection job is done properly, it can steer men into jobs for which they are prepared now, or for which they can be prepared in a relatively short time, with considerable efficiency. It may even provide some useful clues as to what kinds of jobs they ought to be considered for next. But no selection decision should be regarded as the last word on any man's potentialities. Selection isn't that accurate, and it isn't ever likely to be that accurate. Besides, no organization can afford either the misclassification of manpower or the widespread feeling of being "trapped" on a particular vocational track that unrepeated selection programs can cause.

So much for fallacies.

We can now outline a general strategy for a rational selection procedure. This can be summarized in five simple principles. The reason for this comparative brevity is contained in the first principle: *Every selection program should be tailored as specifically as possible to the requirements of the particular company and jobs for which it will be used.*

We cannot, in other words, go into much detail in describing a general program, because most of the details can be added only by the selecting organization itself. Only it can know the jobs well enough, and know the kinds of results that would constitute effective job performance well enough, to tailor a selection program to its own needs. Most firms fail to avail themselves of this privilege—some because they prefer not to take the trouble, and others because they do not appreciate its advantages. Either way the results are usually regrettable. In fact, the ready-made selection system, without local validation or local comparison with alternative techniques, is one of the main justifications for our strong initial statement about the chance nature of most selection systems. When ready-made selection procedures work at all, they do so largely as a result of undeserved luck; when tailor-made selection methods work, and they usually do, it is by design.

Yet it is legitimate to ask what is wrong with using a selection system that has been highly recommended by another firm or is offered by a reputable agency. Unless a company is in the selection business itself, must it not rely on recommendations and reputation in deciding which methods to use? What is wrong is simply that ready-made selection methods that are purchased from a catalogue or transported wholesale from somewhere else have to rely upon luck to produce, in their transplanted environment, results that are as good as those they produced elsewhere. Good luck is, by definition, a scarce commodity. Consequently, selection methods that are merely bought or adopted usually work about as well as an honest roulette wheel. They are tolerated mainly because of ignorance—sometimes blissful, sometimes uneasy, always handicapping.

Tailoring a selection system to the needs of a particular company involves each of the next four principles, but *always* with a specific focus on the company and jobs in question and always with a coldly skeptical eye toward claims that cannot be substantiated within the company. There is, unfortunately, a great deal of quackery, as well as honest incompetence, in the selection field. In the absence of suitable legislative protection, a firm has no better safeguard than its own insistence on having all claims proved in its own context and with its own people. Proof, by the way, should never consist of falling for the descriptive fallacy. A selection system that cannot predict performance with reasonable accuracy, regardless of whether or not it can "describe" the personality or behavior of the people on whom it is tried, is largely useless. A business stands or falls on what its people accomplish, not on the adjectives that may or may not describe them.

The second principle is extremely important as a means of insuring effective selection, yet paradoxically it has nothing whatever to do with selection itself: *Always maximize the number of available candidates.* Most selection programs are badly handicapped by failure to look far enough, or wide enough, for people on whom the arts of selection could be practiced.

There are two reasons why this principle is so very important. One is the relative insensitivity of most selection systems. The larger the number of available candidates, the more readily the selectors can compensate for the insensitivity of their system by simply raising the minimum standard. They can elect, in other words, to risk the "d" type of error because of the greater likelihood that the "a" type can thus be minimized. When the supply of candidates is restricted, *as it usually is,* the selectors have no choice but to keep the minimum standard fairly low so as to permit a sufficient number of candidates to pass. But this exposes the selectors increasingly to the merciless "a" type of errors—the disappointments who looked good when they were chosen. In fact, this is precisely why errors of the "a" type occur so often: The selections were made from too narrow a pool of candidates.

The second reason for maximizing the number of available candidates has to do with the laws of chance. Although we seldom pay our respects to those laws, they govern the processes of selecting people and many other aspects of managing an enterprise all the same. When the job to be filled demands some skill or ability that is not particularly abundant, the selectors really face two problems. That is, they must be able to recognize a promising candidate when they see one, and they must also make sure that enough of the candidates whom they get to see are promising. They must have some kind of control over the input of raw material flowing into their system, so that there will be promising people to be identified. It is very much the same sort of problem that a fisherman would face if he had to catch not just any fish but a particular fish. He would rather know a particular pond in which his fish could be found than have to seek it in a huge lake.

But the problem of knowing "where to fish" is subtler than it may at first appear. This is because the process of selection is in reality a two-way street. Especially when the talent being sought is relatively scarce, the candidates may do more selecting of employers than the employers do of candidates. Before the selectors can even begin their work, the candidates must first decide whether they want to become candidates for the firm that is doing the hiring. The effect of this "selection of employers" by job seekers is largely negative, and therefore its effects are largely hidden. When potential employees decide, for whatever reason, not to apply to a particular company for employment, that company's pool of candidates is that much more restricted and the task of its selectors is that much more difficult.

This happens all the time, much to the detriment of the firms it affects and sometimes to the detriment of the candidates themselves. It happens because of various myths, scraps of information, half-truths, and full truths which combine to form all that an outsider knows about a company and which indicate to him that he probably wouldn't like it there. In recent years it has become popular to refer to this collection of popular, if not entirely accurate, ideas about a company as its "image." An effective selection strategy necessarily starts here, in a consideration of how to maximize the attractiveness of a firm to the kinds of people it needs to hire. However, there is a good deal of fiction in most company images, and for this reason executives sometimes tend to dismiss them as untrue and therefore insignificant. This is a mistake. Like it or not, the flow of talent into or away from any organization is regulated by the opinions of people who are usually ill informed about what the organization is really like and quite indifferent to whether their impressions are reliable: the potential candidates themselves. If the best men available choose to make themselves unavailable to a particular company, that company is in trouble, and no amount of expertise in selection can save it.

Images probably affect whole industries and professions to a greater extent than they do individual companies. Thus people will tend to judge the First National Bank of North Southfield by *what they think they know* about banks in general, regardless of whether they think they know anything about the FNB of North Southfield in particular. Similarly, they will assume that the architectural firm of Rice & Raisins, Inc., has whatever characteristics they think *all* architectural firms have, regardless of how little they actually know about R&R or even about architecture itself. Of course, very large firms that are nationally known, and even smaller firms that are locally prominent, often acquire distinct though not necessarily accurate images of their own.

It is unfortunately true that most outsiders have only the dimmest ideas of what the inside of an organization is like, and these dim ideas may be largely erroneous anyway. But the outsiders are usually content with what they think they know; after all, what reason have they to question whether what they believe about a strange company is fact or poppycock? Only too rarely does this blissful outside ignorance cause any dismay among the insiders, either: only when they realize how dependent their organization is—ultimately—upon an adequate supply of sufficiently capable outsiders!

However, images can be managed, not in the sense of manufacturing a favorable reputation out of thin air or slick public relations, but in the sense of intelligently placing needed information where it will do the most good. As a rule, this has to be a continuing program rather than a project with a definable start and finish. Usually at least four considerations are involved. The first is to find out, to the extent that this is possible, what the organization's outside image as seen by prospective employees is really like. This is seldom an entirely flattering exercise, but it usually reveals both strengths to be built upon and weaknesses to be reduced or eliminated. Since the unpleasant aspects of an image not only act as a deterrent to potentially desirable employees but also tend to have at least a little bit of truth to them, the act of defining an image can be a useful way of focusing upon what has been wrong about an organization.

The second consideration in dealing with images is to improve the reliability of the information available to the group one wishes to attract. This group may consist of students, employed professionals who might become interested in changing jobs, or, in some cases, rank-and-file employees who might be interested in an internal transfer. The problem of improving the reliability of information is usually approached with what amounts to an advertising campaign; it may include brochures, posters, or even published advertisements, all of which attempt to state the company's case in an appealing manner. However, all advertising has a tendency to raise suspicions, if only because it is obviously intended to sell something, and in any case it cannot be cross-examined so as to clear up doubts or clarify ambiguities. Consequently, the advertising approach to image making is useful chiefly as a supplement to, and not as a substitute for, more persuasive forms of communication.

By far the most persuasive influence on images is face-to-face contact between the outside audience and representatives of the organization that wants to influence them. But that word "representatives" must be understood in a quite literal sense: The people who make the outside contacts must themselves be typical of what the outsiders could expect to become if they were to join the firm. The personality, habits, and "style" of a firm's employees rub off on the firm's image; and, willy-nilly, *everyone* connected with the firm who meets the public becomes its living trademark. Therefore, these contacts should not be left to chance, and neither should they be irrelevant to what the outsiders need to know. There should not be too great a discrepancy in years, education, or interests between the people whom the outsiders will learn to identify with the company and the outsiders themselves. The best image makers for a student group are recent graduates from the same or similar schools, and the best image makers for experienced professionals are the company's most distinguished professionals in the same or similar fields. There is plenty of time to slip the seasoned manager and the selection expert into the recruiting process after the work of attraction has been done. They definitely do not belong in the early stages of the campaign to upgrade the quality and quantity of applicants.

To be effective, contacts between selected employees and groups that include prospective applicants must occur fairly regularly. They should take place several times during the year or so prior to the time when applications would normally be expected, and somewhat less often before that. This means, among other things, that the job of maintaining contacts with potential employees will become a fairly significant part of the workload of those employees who are themselves relatively recent "graduates" of those groups.

These contacts should occur in a persuasive context. This usually means giving the "audience" something it can use, such as a lecture or a demonstration, instead of merely showing up to pay for a party and singing the company's praises. Prospective employees are usually more interested in the specific nature of the work a company is doing than in the conviviality of its representatives. This is especially true of young people, who frequently look upon their next job as a preparatory step toward something better, and who are therefore less interested in a career with their next employer than in whether they can grow on the job.

A company's reputation can be affected by any event the public associates with it. Consequently, the company's various deliberate attempts to influence its reputation will constitute only part, and not necessarily the most persuasive part, of the potentially influential information that reaches the public. Even when a public relations program is well administered, it can be drowned out by the sheer volume of "unadministered" information that reaches the outside world. Bad news travels fast; when there is dissension in the executive suite, discontent on the shop floor, or dissatisfaction among customers, not only does this reach the public quickly, but its effects tend to adhere to the company image long after the event that caused it has passed into oblivion.

Consequently, the third element of what might be called "image management" should be a policy of reviewing every company decision from the standpoint of its potential effect on the company's reputation. It cannot be overemphasized that most reputations are made or ruined by the unintended side-effects of actions having no obvious connection with images. It is, of course, impossible to control every last potential opinion-shaping influence, but we typically attempt to control very few of them. We make the mistake of assuming that our audience is not watching us when we are not playing to it.

The external image of a company is every bit as much an asset as its credit rating and deserves at least as much consideration when major decisions are made. The main reason it usually fails to receive such consideration is not that executives are oblivious to it, but that they are charged with other responsibilities and are therefore willing to accept greater image risks than perhaps they should for the sake of advancing the functions for which they are responsible. Consequently, the company's most logical choice for the role of image protector in the councils of its management would be the same man whose functions are outlined in Chapter 1: the full-time worrier about, and champion of, motivation.

The fourth consideration with regard to images is undoubtedly the most important. For all their flimsiness and occasional lack of logic, most images are simply imperfect reflections of reality. They are seldom very wide of the mark. Thus the best way to improve a company's image is to improve the company. For example, if a firm is unhappy about having a reputation for stodginess, it will accomplish more by eliminating its stodginess than by concentrating on its image. In due time, images catch up with reality, but they never lead it.

There are other reasons—probably more important ones—for paying attention to images than merely to enlarge the number of applicants. Images are probably the most powerful motivational screening tests in existence. (Note that we called them "powerful," not "accurate.") If, for example, a company has a reputation for giving capable young men heavier responsibilities as quickly as they become ready, that company will attract more than its fair share of achievement-motivated candidates. Even a relatively insensitive selection system will suffice, in those circumstances, to fill the company with men who are eager to get ahead. On the other hand, a company with a reputation for slow but certain advancement will be sought after by more than its fair share of men who are primarily motivated by the desire to make themselves as comfortable as possible. It would take an extremely sensitive selection system to detect the occasional high-potential candidate in such a group of applicants.

Now let us turn from images to the third basic principle of effective selection: *Validate the system*. This is simply another way of saying that no system should be used until it can be proved to work. This proof should be as rigorous as possible and should be repeated periodically. Failure to adhere to this principle is the logical equivalent of measuring with a rubber ruler, yet validation is unquestionably the least frequently observed of all the principles listed here.

Validating a selection system is neither difficult nor expensive. But it does involve a lot of administrative detail, and this is one reason why many companies decide, foolishly, not to bother. It may seem like a lot of trouble to go to simply for the purpose of confirming what is obvious, although what is obvious is not necessarily what is true about selection systems. Perhaps the main resistance to validation, however, is the naïve belief that a selection system must work simply because it is a system. This kind of opinion usually rests on a variety of isolated incidents or irrelevant observations, all of which are taken as proof of success. And, as the old fallacy goes, no one can argue with success. But selection has too profound an impact on a company's long-range character and potentialities to be left to be measured by anybody's opinion alone—especially not the opinions of those who are involved in the selection system. The only form of proof that really matters is the system's demonstrated ability to minimize selection errors in the company that uses it. "Minimizing" in this sense also implies that the system does a better job than alternative systems with which it can be compared.

It is usually desirable to repeat the process of validation periodically. This is for two reasons: First, jobs sometimes change in the sense that a previously unimportant aspect of performance may become paramount, or vice versa. For example, a company that sold electronic communication devices hired sales engineers whose job was primarily to provide technical support to the salesmen. This strategy was used because knowledge of the way the devices worked and the way they could be applied was relatively scarce. In time, however, the customers became more sophisticated, and the role of the sales engineers gradually shifted to that of straight selling. It should have come as no surprise that a previously validated test for the selection of sales engineers proved to be inadequate when it was re-evaluated. The test was as valid as ever for the selection of primarily technical men, but the job requirements had changed. Consequently, a new test battery had to be developed and validated.

The second reason for periodic revalidation is that considerably more reliable data become available for this purpose with the passage of time than are normally at hand when validation is performed originally. That is, most initial validations are accomplished by seeing whether the selection ratings of the most effective and least effective employees differ. This calculation is based, of course, on currently available performance data. If the evaluations are clearly different, there is some basis for assuming that the system is capable of selecting new employees who are more like the outstanding employees than they are like the mediocre or borderline employees. However, this is a rather severe test to put the selection system to, since truly inadequate performers will ordinarily have been separated and are therefore unavailable to be put through the selection procedures. The difference, in other words, between the top and bottom performance groups will ordinarily be rather narrow; therefore, the system has to be unusually sensitive to demonstrate its usefulness in this form of validation. This is why many selection systems are better than they can be proved to be. Unfortunately, when a system gives ambiguous results in this form of validation, it is not possible to say whether it is, in fact, inefficient or whether its value has been hidden by the relatively small difference between the tested groups.

A second validation, usually after two or three years, can therefore be very helpful. It can supply the definitive answer to the question posed by an ambiguous result on the first try at validation. (If the results are still ambiguous in the second attempt, the time has come to search for a better selection system.) However, if the selection ratings made at the time of the first validation prove to be more accurate during the revalidation, that can be interpreted very favorably. Obviously, the purpose of all selection ratings is to predict future, not current, performance; and in the case of revalidation that is exactly what will have been demonstrated. Further, the performance ratings with which selection ratings are compared will be more reliable when they are based on a more extended period of time.

The fourth principle of effective selection is to *use tests selectively—if at all*. So much has been written about testing, both pro and con, responsibly and irresponsibly, that anything more than a terse treatment of the subject could easily become a volume in itself. This is obviously not the place for such a major digression. The reader who is interested in pursuing the subject in some depth—and it should not be pursued in any other way—may refer to any of the sources listed at the end of this chapter. For our purposes, a few major points will suffice.

Testing of various kinds is now a widely used selection tool, and for better or worse it will probably be even more widely used in the future. There is a good reason for this. For all its faults, testing usually makes a more effective contribution to the process of screening job candidates than any available alternative. That is, a selection system that includes an intelligently designed testing program will usually result in fewer errors of both the "a" and the "d" type than a selection system that does not include tests.

If justice in the selection process consists in steering as many people as possible toward jobs in which they can succeed and away from jobs in which they cannot succeed, then testing is unquestionably the most "just" selection procedure that has yet been devised. That statement stands despite the fact that tests are sometimes oversold, overinterpreted, and overly relied upon. The problem is not that the present state of testing is so bad, but that the present state of every other method for evaluating human potentialities on a large scale is much worse. From this it follows that people who are uncomfortable about working with imperfect instruments, and who would be disturbed by knowing that their most sincere efforts will inevitably turn up a certain percentage of the time as mistakes, do not belong in the selection business.

Before we go any further into the subject of testing, we must face the obvious question of whether tests can be used to determine what kinds of motivation—and how much—an individual has. In most cases I think the answer has to be no. It is true that some tests purport to measure motivation, or something, such as personality traits, that is closely related to it. Whatever these tests measure has not, however, substantially increased the accuracy with which selection systems are able to predict job performance—at least, not in the majority of cases where their effect has been properly weighed. And added accuracy is, in the last analysis, the only valid reason for adding any procedure to a selection system. In most cases, personality tests appear to have added nothing to a selection system but a certain illusory assurance in the minds of the selectors that they are being more "scientific" than they really are.

Sometimes there are exceptions. There have been occasions when tests of occupational interests, so-called biographical inventories concerned with personal history and background, or behavior-sampling techniques such as business games or discussion groups have added significantly to the accuracy of prediction that was obtainable without them. And, because many of the attempts to use personality tests for selection purposes have been relatively crude—involving, for example, the use of clinical or unvalidated "tests" which have little to recommend them but the enthusiasm of the inventors and their converts—there is reason to hope that further research with sophisticated instruments may yet produce a breakthrough in the area of personality measurement.

Every now and then a burst of press-agentry and sales promotion announces that the millennium has arrived. So far, all of them have been false alarms. It is probably worthwhile to continue trying to build various personality measurements into selection batteries, especially where personality factors have had a demonstrable effect on the success or failure of previous job holders. But the attempt should be made with extra caution and extra skepticism, and failure to produce a significant increase in the accuracy of prediction should be met with extra patience. That, after all, is the probable outcome in the present state of the art.

The question of whether personality tests are ethical, moral, or even legal has been given a considerable airing in recent years. There is certainly no ethical justification for using a test or any other procedure that adds nothing to an employer's ability to make a realistic decision about a job candidate. In that sense, most personality testing has been neither ethical nor, for that matter, economical. A more difficult question arises, however, in the case of tests which actually do make selection more accurate, but which the candidate might construe as improper, as embarrassing, or simply as nobody else's business. If we mean what we say about valuing the individual's integrity, then no organization has a right to put such questions to a candidate who objects to them. In fact, the organization should not even put him in the position of having to decide whether to bravely refuse to answer or meekly submit to what he regards as humiliation.

The practical difficulty in all this, however, arises from the fact that what one man may regard as an intolerable invasion of privacy another man may cheerfully reveal without the smallest qualm. There is no absolute standard as to which aspects of an individual's personality may properly be inquired into by a prospective employer and which may not. The choice would appear to be either to steer entirely clear of techniques which anyone might consider improper (which would leave the evaluation of personality to the long-since-discredited "method" of personal impressions) or to proceed with as much discretion and common sense as we can muster, inquiring into personality in ways which we have reason to believe will yield useful information and still be considered inoffensive by most people. The important phrase here is "reason to believe": The "reasons" had obviously better be backed by firm evidence rather than anybody's mere hunch or even the "informed opinion" of experts.

Given the choice between making unnecessarily clumsy predictions while hurting nobody's sensibilities, on the one hand, or offending some people while minimizing the number of selection errors on the other, I would vote for the latter course. Being unnecessarily rejected for a job, or being hired for a job in which one cannot do well, is in the long run a far more insufferable insult for most people than being asked to disclose something of one's personality. Life constantly exposes personality anyway to anyone with eyes to see and the wisdom to make judgments. Not even a hermit succeeds in preserving his innermost self (whatever that is) in absolute secrecy.

I would conclude that testing of all kinds is clearly worthwhile in certain circumstances and probably valueless in others. The sophisticated selection system therefore uses tests even more selectively than it recommends people for jobs. When they have been carefully chosen and validated, tests can be a useful aid to the selector's judgment. But no test can be a substitute for judgment, and carelessly chosen tests can mislead even the most experienced selector. The moral is plain: Tests must be handled with care. I would rather see even a highly effective test battery abandoned than permit it to become an excuse for mindless, mechanical sorting of human beings on the basis of scores alone.

The fifth and, in many ways, the most important principle of effective selection is, *never stop selecting*. This is, of course, the antidote for the permanence fallacy. During the course of a man's career, he will normally be the subject of dozens—perhaps hundreds—of selection decisions. Each of these should be made with as much care as the first. However, many organizations really evaluate the potentialities of their employees only once: when they are hired. After that, evaluation too often consists of little more than the subjective opinion of each employee's immediate superior. Admittedly, a man's manager is in a better position to evaluate his *work* than anyone else. But in most cases that position is not good enough for evaluating the man's *potentialities*. Entirely apart from the manager's skill in judging what a man can do, most jobs are not designed to demand all that a man can accomplish. The supervisor simply doesn't get to see his subordinate in a situation that reveals very much about his potentialities. In any case, neither the evaluation made at the time of hiring nor the periodic performance appraisal reveals much that can be projected very far in advance.

Periodic re-evaluations are therefore desirable, although they are not common practice. This is one reason why there are so many companies in which, on the one hand, executives are constantly dismayed by an apparent lack of promotable talent (they usually put the blame on supposedly lax recruiting standards) while, on the other hand, the same companies are filled with frustrated men who feel, often with some justification, that they are underutilized by their jobs. It is unfortunately true that when a company assumes its men are incapable of growth, not much growth will occur. Thus the very fact that the company shows no interest in uncovering hidden talent will, in itself, reduce the likelihood that talent will spontaneously blossom forth. Yet the very act of seeking for talent helps to motivate men with untapped abilities to develop and display them.

When a periodic re-evaluation is held, it naturally raises the expectations of the people who are asked to participate that something new is in store for them. The letdown that follows a re-evaluation which does not bring a significant change can be serious. Consequently, there must be some kind of screening procedure to insure that employees will not be exposed to such a re-evaluation unless there is a reasonable likelihood that the results will be positive. Re-evaluations should not, in other words, be handled on a wholesale basis, and neither should they be administered with the same techniques or philosophy as evaluations of candidates at the entry level.

It is here that the supervisor's evaluation of current job performance can play a useful role, not in merely nominating the outstanding performers (since they may or may not have the capability for equally outstanding work at a higher level) but in eliminating from consideration the less-than-average performers. In the nomination stage, the strategy is much the same as in the recruiting stage: Maximize the number of available candidates, eliminating only those who are quite unlikely to merit consideration.

A corollary of the "never stop selecting" principle is that, as time passes, evaluation data become less and less reliable as guides to the kind of performance that can be expected of the individual. Beyond a certain point (say, five years at the outside), old evaluation data should not be used for decisions that can have an important effect on a man's career. What is likely to change in the interim is not his abilities—as a rule, these are fairly stable—so much as his knowledge and his motivation. His experience will have taught him more than just facts and techniques; it will also have taught him more about what he can expect from himself and what kinds of attractions and opposition to expect in his environment. He will be, for better or worse, a man with an altered inner compass.

It is motivational changes of this kind that must be weighed in order to arrive at a currently valid forecast of the kinds of performance a man can be expected to deliver. Old evaluation data, no matter how carefully formulated, are seldom a reliable index to the results of this maturational process. This is because we cannot predict the kinds of experiences a man will pass through, both on and off the job, or the ways in which these will slowly shape his perception of himself and of his world. This is why all selection decisions should be made for a particular job at a particular time, not for all time.

Recommended Readings:

For a good general introduction to the problems of testing, especially for personnel men and others who will be directly involved in a selection system, see Robert B. Miller, *Tests and the Selection Process,* Science Research Associates, Chicago, 1966.

For a review of the ethical problems in testing, see Saul W. Gellerman, "The Ethics of Personality Testing," *Personnel*, November–December 1958.

For a review of the conditions in which testing is worthwhile and those in which it is not, see Saul W. Gellerman, "Personnel Testing: What the Critics Overlook," *Personnel*, May–June 1963.

Chapter 6

The Enlargement of Competence

THERE ARE, TO OVERSIMPLIFY A BIT, THREE MAIN THEORIES or strategies for the development of managerial talent: the jungle theory, the education theory, and the agricultural theory. Of these, the most popular and most widely practiced strategy is undoubtedly the jungle theory. It is also the least effective, and as time goes on it is likely to become even less useful as a means of providing an organization with the managers it needs.

The essence of *the jungle theory* is that talent will naturally make itself apparent, simply by outdistancing the competition. Therefore, the best way to discover it is to sit back and wait, hopefully, for some of its more obvious signs to appear. This is why managers are occasionally asked to "identify" their bright young men, on the theory that whatever it is that gives a man the potentiality for managing must surely be obvious to the man who supervises his work.

Unfortunately, the only thing that is reliably obvious to the supervisor of a man's work is the man's work. This causes no problem when management is looking for men to take over jobs that are no more than extensions of their present work. But it can lead to serious blunders when people are to be selected for jobs that are substantially different from what they are now doing. Managerial jobs are almost always substantially different from nonmanagerial jobs, and higher management jobs in particular are often quite different from lower management jobs.

The jungle theory has outlived its usefulness. In the days when most organizations had only modest managerial requirements, and when the available supply of men who were trained to think for themselves was rather thin anyway, it probably sufficed. Enough capable men came bobbing to the top, and were discernible enough by their distinctive attributes, to provide a company with all the talent it needed. This was the origin of management's gross overuse of the rating term "outstanding." This term used to refer to men whose qualities were so distinct from those of their peers that they almost literally stood out in bold relief from everyone around them. Today it has become simply a tired way of heaping an extra measure of emphasis into the ears of an audience that is already jaded by too many superlatives.

At any rate, the jungle theory is no longer equal to the task of providing a company with managers. The economics of the situation have changed. The demand for talent is greater; and, while the supply is also greater, the problem of distinguishing the potentially wise from the merely smart is too complex for natural selection alone to handle. Further, the ability to manage is not necessarily a weed; it often needs careful cultivation if it is to survive and grow to maturity. To sit back and wait for the talent to emerge by itself is to waste a precious resource.

The education theory is based on a recognition of the inadequacies of the jungle theory; it is very much in vogue in most companies that have management development programs. The essence of the education theory is that management consists of skills that can be taught, or at least induced to emerge, through an educational program. The result is often like an exclusive corporate prep school in which managers who have succeeded in attracting the attention of higher management are exposed to various internal and external programs and then turned loose to practice what they have learned. In effect, "raw" managerial talent is passed through a management development mill in hopes of transforming it into a finished executive product.

The educational theory represented a significant breakthrough insofar as it made these points: that management skills could be deliberately developed, rather than merely harvested, and that this development was the responsibility of the employing organization rather

than the local educational system or society at large. If it had not occurred, the resulting shortage of competent managerial manpower
could by now have seriously curtailed industrial expansion. If this
seems to overstate the case for an abundant supply of managers, one
need only look at the economies of countries in which managerial
talent is in shortest supply to see the results of such deficiencies.

The education theory has undoubtedly served us well. But, like
most attempts to exploit a breakthrough, this one made the right
diagnosis yet failed, in its first efforts, to find the most effective pre-
scriptions. The problems have concerned what is to be taught, how,
to whom, and when. None of these problems has been solved altogether satisfactorily, but we have learned a great deal about all of
them.

In the early days of management development, it was assumed that
whatever managers needed to learn in order to become better managers must be somewhere in the university catalogues. The courses to
which aspiring managers were exposed were often lifted or adapted
from curricula designed for much younger and less experienced students. The results were sometimes intellectually stimulating, sometimes bewildering, and seldom very productive of visible managerial
improvement. In fact, the results were so disappointing that management development went into a temporary hiatus from which it did
not emerge until it became fashionable to teach methods rather than
content to managers.

This phase is still very much with us. We have attempted a more
scientific approach to management development by subdividing the
manager's job into its components and then teaching what are presumably the most productive approaches to those components. Thus
we have the case and incident methods, in which managers are taught
to trace the various causes of a problem and to compare the effects of
various "solutions"; and sensitivity training, in which the manager is
taught to improve his own ability to communicate, and to be communicated with, by learning about the ways in which other people
react to him personally. We are concerned largely, in other words,
with teaching managers how to use various techniques which are presumably useful, at least potentially, to all of them.

One of the main arguments advanced in defense of these programs
when their results have been disappointing is that instruction has

been wasted on the wrong students. It is not uncommon for line managers to meet their quotas for sending managers to training courses by providing those whose abilities are not too highly prized. They do this partly out of skepticism that management training courses can really add much to the abilities of managers who are already doing well, and partly out of a genuine reluctance to lose the services of such men while they are being "trained." The trainers regard these tactics as a not too subtle form of sabotage; it should hardly be surprising, they object, if when second-raters emerge from training programs they are still second-raters.

That argument has some validity, but not too much. On the basis of what we know today, it would be very difficult indeed to draw a sharp line between managers who stand to benefit from a management training course and those who are either too dull or too advanced to learn much from one. It would be equally difficult to draw such a line between training programs that should be helpful to most managers and those that will be helpful to only a few. Since neither line can be drawn with great accuracy at present, we are not likely to see the end of the assertion that the wrong people are being sent to management development programs, or of our inability to say for certain whether this is just a trainer's convenient rationalization or a valid complaint.

Actually, most training programs suffer not so much from the wrong trainees as from the wrong timing. As a rule, men are sent to these programs when they can be spared. This seldom occurs at points in their careers when the things they learn in training have much chance of becoming permanent additions to their repertories of managerial skills. They rarely get a prompt opportunity to practice what they have learned when they return to their jobs; hence the new ideas and techniques are usually forgotten rather quickly. Even if the manager does emerge from training a better man than when he entered it, the results are all too quickly dissipated. It is disturbing to speculate on how many second-raters have been prepared to become first-raters when they completed a management training course, only to lose whatever advantage they gained by the lack of an opportunity to put their new learning into practice.

The scheduling of management training has been treated as a mere administrative detail, but it appears to be every bit as important for the success of the program as course content and trainee se-lection. If management training cannot be scheduled at the right time in a manager's career, it probably should not be scheduled at all. The right time is when he is on the verge of a significant promo-tion—or immediately after such a promotion. That way he can apply whatever he has learned to the new job unencumbered by the dead weight of his old habits and preconceptions.

There should also be a motivational benefit from this kind of scheduling. If training is tied firmly to the promotional process, it will tend to become both a status symbol and a sought-after advan-tage. When training is applied to managers in general, as it usually is, it can hardly escape the connotations of a compulsory and profit-less rest cure. Obviously, the trainees will learn more if they are pleased to have been sent to a course than if they regard it as an en-forced preoccupation with irrelevancies. (As an additional side bene-fit, the selection problem would be solved automatically if admission to management training programs were restricted to the beneficiaries of recent or imminent promotions.)

One final point about teaching managers: The actual techniques of instruction—be they case histories, seminars, business games, or audiovisual methods—are perhaps less important in the long run than the frequency of instruction. We too often assume, wrongly, that learning takes place only when somebody is deliberately in-structing. Much more managerial learning undoubtedly takes place in offices than in classrooms. But what managers learn on the job is necessarily narrowed by the limited perspectives of the job itself. They are seldom exposed *on their jobs* to new ideas or to the rela-tionship of those jobs to other jobs. They seldom have eye-opening encounters with gifted teachers or thinkers to the extent that they can in a training course.

This is both the reason why training is given at all and the reason why its effects nearly always dissipate over time—even when the scheduling and selection are handled as they should be. If manage-ment training consists only of an isolated episode in a long career, it can scarcely be expected to have more than a minor and temporary influence on a man's competence to manage. This brings us to one of those uncomfortable realities which are too often ignored, simply be-cause they were not obvious from the outset: *Management training is an open-ended investment.* If it is worthwhile at all, it is worthwhile only if it is repeated periodically. The course content itself can and should change, but the basic strategy of training—an interlude away from the job, devoted exclusively to the enlargement of competence—must recur fairly often to maintain lasting benefits. Ten times in the course of a career would not be too frequent an exposure to management training, especially for those men who rise to positions of higher responsibility.

If training should be timed to coincide with promotions, if training should be repeated periodically, and if training necessarily interrupts a busy working routine, it follows that there must be a centralized, high-level coordination of the training function. Whoever passes on promotions should also control entry into management training programs. In large organizations, this means that there will probably be several control points for both promotion and training, depending on the level and perhaps also on the functional specialization of the managers concerned.

The educational approach to management development therefore requires an extensive apparatus if it is to function well. Most of the complaints and disappointments that have been voiced about the results of this approach are probably traceable to a failure to provide enough of that apparatus; to trying, as it were, to buy management development at bargain rates. In this sense, the full potential of the educational approach has not yet been tapped, nor has a really definitive test of its potentialities yet been made.

The agricultural approach to management development is based on the premises that effective managers are grown, not born; and that, since most of this growth takes place outside the context of formal training programs, it is important that managers work in a job environment that is as growth-conducive as possible. Managers' jobs should be structured, in other words, not only to get the work itself done well, but also to increase the likelihood that the incumbents will qualify for promotion—and therefore for entry into formal training programs.

Competence can be encouraged to grow in the same sense that a tree can be encouraged to grow. This is not done by leaving it to develop as best it can in competition with others (the jungle approach) , and not solely by giving it an occasional dose of fertilizer (which is the essence of the educational approach, and wags can do with that what they will) . Rather, competence grows when it is systematically nourished, pruned of its errors, and transplanted, as it grows larger, to new ground on which it has ample room to flourish.

To get away from metaphor, what is a growth-inducing environment? It probably includes at least four factors: stretching, feedback, coaching, and career management. *Stretching* means assigning a man to responsibilities that are always a bit beyond those the man himself or any of his superiors feel he is ready for. Because we so often underestimate what a man is capable of doing, especially with regard to problems with which he has had little experience, stretching is much more likely to result in pleasant surprises than in disappointments. If it is gradual enough, the damage done by occasional disappointments can be minimized and easily remedied. Meantime, stretching not only accelerates the growth of competence but also delivers more productivity than would ordinarily be expected.

But there is a much subtler and more important advantage to stretching. It is often assumed that, when people achieve something of substantial importance, it is because they were highly motivated to do what they did. As far as cause and effect are concerned, the sequence is usually the reverse. That is, people who have achieved something of consequence for *any* reason frequently develop a taste for achievement. The process of becoming motivated to high achievement is not unlike the process of becoming motivated to eat salted peanuts: The motivation for the experience is touched off by the original encounter and sustained by further encounters. True, some people respond more strongly than others to having had to achieve something. But most people's interest in achievement can probably be increased by exposing them to what is, for them, a significant accomplishment.

There is a sense, then, in which people have to be thrust into achievement in order to awaken their appetite for more achievement, and this is precisely what stretching accomplishes. It also offers yet another advantage which can be of enormous motivational consequence for any organization. If stretching is used as a conscious policy for a period of years, it can eventually teach managers to stop underestimating people. It is precisely this habit which causes people to shrink—in despair, boredom, or frustration—to fit the undersized roles their superiors have conceived for them.

Feedback for managers is much discussed but still not really understood. First of all, there seem to be at least two kinds of information about themselves which managers need in order to develop optimally. Further, it is evidently important that these two kinds of feedback be given separately. One is the classical form of performance feedback in which a man is told how his work has been rated by his superiors. The second is less frequently provided, but it is at least equally important: periodic, frank reappraisal of the manager's promotion prospects.

When management people complain that they "don't know where they stand," they usually want the second kind of feedback (information on career prospects) , but the nostrum that is usually prescribed is the first kind of feedback (performance appraisal) . Not surprisingly, the complaint continues, and orthodox performance appraisal programs are regarded uneasily both by those who administer them and by those who are the presumed beneficiaries. There is no millennium in sight in the area of performance appraisal, but there does seem to be some merit in giving it in separate and clearly labeled doses. At least the man on the receiving end will then know what to expect.

By now it has been pretty well established that performance appraisal should deal largely with results rather than with ratings of such hard-to-define-or-measure qualities as "imaginativeness" or "aggressiveness." It is also preferable to measure results in terms of the extent to which previously agreed-to performance targets have been reached. It is generally considered wise to avoid having to appraise a man's personality in the process of appraising his work, since few people are capable (or, for that matter, desirous) of changing their fundamental make-up in order to please their supervisor. There is almost always room for more than one style or approach to any management job, and the appraiser should not quibble with style as long as the results are within range of target.

The function of performance appraisal is to teach, not to exhort or admonish. The manager can learn if it can be shown that his actions have been on or off target, especially when the target has been objectively defined. He can see the extent to which his actions have been effective or ineffective and adjust them accordingly. But he can hardly learn if the target consists of some vague adjective that can mean almost anything to anybody—if, for instance, he is told to become more "interested" or less "reserved." All such words point to is an image, not action, and that image is almost impossible to change without having enough clues to which kinds of action have created it and which kinds can dispel it.

Performance appraisal is on much firmer ground when it deals primarily with objectively defined operational results and when it deals with style or performance characteristics only to the extent that they can be shown to have affected results. It is better off when it deals with personality not at all. An effective performance appraisal statement—effective in the sense of promoting learning and growth—is really little more than a summary of what both parties should already know, since performance can be readily measured against objective targets. This gives rise to one of the most frequent criticisms of performance appraisal: that it should be unnecessary to summarize the obvious formally. But the truth is not so simple as that. If both parties are not aware that a summary will have to be written and discussed, the targets are not likely to receive as much attention; and the results, consequently, may not be so "obvious." There is also the question of authenticity: While higher managers often expect their subordinates to draw the "obvious" conclusions from their many day-to-day reviews during the year, the subordinates are likely to be much less impressed by their own conclusions than by a summary from the lips of the men who will have the most to say about their future. Lastly, a formal review of performance against one set of targets forms a logical and necessary basis for establishing a new set—especially if the manager is to be stretched.

A performance appraisal program would, however, be of comparatively little value if it stopped there. No human relationship is really quite so sterile as the restriction on "keeping personalities out of it" would seem to imply. The plain fact is that personality does enter into many decisions about a manager, especially promotional decisions. Further, since so much of a manager's time is spent in giving and receiving information, his personal impact on people can have a decided effect on his own effectiveness in higher positions. Therefore, while personality has no legitimate place in a review of what a man has accomplished, it inevitably enters into a consideration of what he will be permitted to attempt to accomplish.

This is why career counseling can be so difficult to bring off successfully. Perhaps it is also why we so seldom attempt to counsel our subordinates. Yet the costs of not making the attempt are often very high. When men are growing—that is, increasing their competence—they are naturally more interested in the future than in the past. The effect on their morale of an uncertain future, or a future that is simply not certain enough, can be profound. Some may decide that the gamble of staying in the company is not worth the risk of getting nowhere or of advancing too slowly. This is probably the main reason for the departure of high-potential managers. Other promising men who are faced with the prospect of slow or uncertain advancement simply lose their momentum and cease to grow as quickly as before. While most high-potential managers can tolerate some degree of ambiguity, few can endure too much of it for too long about a subject as close to their hearts as their own careers.

Career counseling is probably the most effective form of insurance against these risks. Its costs (in terms of bruised egos or personal animosities) can be minimized if the program is carried out with intelligence and discretion. To do this properly requires that certain ground rules be clearly established. At the very least, these should include three concepts: that the counseling is only advisory, not binding; that it attempts to forecast only the immediate future (say, the next two or three years), not an entire career; and that it is necessarily limited to generalities and estimates. These restrictions do not vitiate the program, provided the counseling is timed properly and, most important of all, is reasonably frank.

The best time for career counseling is when a manager is about midway to two-thirds of the way through a "normal" period of assignment to a specific job. This will vary from company to company and even, to some extent, within a single company. The important thing is that the issue be faced at about the time it usually tends to become uppermost in the manager's mind: when he can foresee the end of his present assignment or when he begins to feel that he has developed about as much mastery of it as he is likely to, so that the inherent challenge of the job is fading. That is when he will naturally wonder what is in store for him next. It is at precisely this point—and a similar stage will occur in every one of his major assignments—that *the manager's motives and those of his superiors are likely to be in conflict.*

His superiors, for their part, can now see the advent of a period of maximum return on their "investment," which is represented by the period during which the manager was learning to handle his job and gradually building up to top efficiency. They will naturally tend to feel that it is in the company's best interests to keep him there as long as possible. But the manager may feel quite differently about the matter. Instead of regarding the first phase of his assignment as a training ground in which he was prepared for a long and profitable tenure in one position, he probably will regard it as a proving ground on which he demonstrated his fitness to be advanced to another position. In other words, he may not want to be an expert in his present job—indeed, if he is strongly motivated to enlarge his managerial competence, he will probably look upon any opportunity to become an expert as a trap. He will want to broaden, not deepen, his experience so as to maximize his opportunities for further growth and achievement. As this conflict comes to the fore, he is likely to be increasingly disturbed by the possibility that the more effectively he handles his job, the more likely it is to turn into a trap instead of a stepping stone.

Career counseling that is timed to coincide with these natural periods of strain can serve three useful purposes. First, it can clear the air by demonstrating that management is neither oblivious nor indifferent to the problem. Second, it should aim to give the manager as realistic a perspective as possible of his own future, so as to prevent both gross overoptimism (which inevitably leads to disappointment) and gross overpessimism (which leads to needless demoralization). The third advantage is the most important of all: Career counseling compels both management and the individual to begin thinking seriously about the kinds of assignments for which he should be considered next. Failure to begin this kind of planning early enough leads to hasty and often ill-considered decisions later on.

The keys to effective career counseling, however, are frankness and realism. These must begin with a clear understanding that performance in a job at one level does not necessarily qualify a man for a job at a higher level. Neither does a man "earn" the opportunity to try his hand at a higher-level job through his performance in a lower-level job. This distinction is seldom made very clear, perhaps because it seems to be in the short-range interests of both the manager and his company to leave it vague. Thus the manager may expect his present performance to weigh in his favor, even if he knows it does not necessarily give any clue to his capacity for handling a higher-level job. The company, for its part, is eager to preserve the manager's present performance by supporting his morale, even if that means letting him believe his promotability will be measured by a possibly irrelevant standard.

This mutual reluctance to dispense with a myth has prompted one seasoned observer of management, A. T. M. Wilson of Unilever, Ltd., to remark that

> It is difficult to avoid an impression that many systems of appraisal permit a collusive blurring, as between senior and subordinates, of the difference between, on the one hand, immediate level of performance and, on the other, potential for future performance in a different working milieu with different responsibilities which demand different skills.[4]

It is equally difficult to avoid the conclusion that the myth is unnecessary and even harmful. Illusions make poor motivators, if only because they inevitably turn a man away from his proper goal. The point must be made, and made clearly, that while current performance has a great deal to do with a man's pay and reputation, and even with his ability to attract the attention of executives who can influence his career, it does not *in itself* determine whether he should be considered for promotion. This is one of the reasons why performance appraisal and career counseling should occur separately: to emphasize that one does not necessarily determine the other. There are, of course, standards for judging promotability, and to some extent these may be observable in a man's current work. We will review some of these standards later in this book. The important point now is that believability is the essential element in career counseling, and in the long run believability rests on candor and on looking facts straight in the eye.

In any case, specific career plans will probably not have been made at this point, and no realistic manager would be impressed by such long-range prophecy. There are, however, three kinds of information which *can* be disclosed. Together they can achieve the motivational purpose of career counseling, which is to provide the growth-oriented individual with a yardstick against which to measure both his progress and his ambitions. The first kind of information concerns the relative speed of advancement which can be expected during the forecast period. This can be expressed in terms of being faster than, slower than, or equal to the "average" rate—provided the average has been calculated and is generally known. The second kind of information concerns the range of organizational levels within which the individual can expect to be working during this period, usually expressed in terms of "example" jobs with which he is likely to be familiar. The third kind of information concerns functional groups and, when appropriate, geographical locations to which the individual might be assigned.

All this does is to give the manager some realistic parameters within which to focus his immediate hopes and plans. He knows that he must continue to deliver on his present job before any of the generalities expressed in his career counseling can harden into certainty. But he also knows that the opportunity for further growth is being held out to him. He knows which specific factors in his job or in his company may stand in his way and which ones are working for him. He knows, in a word, where he stands relative to the goals that matter most to him. Despite the fact that it has to be presented in a general and noncommittal form, this is precisely the kind of feedback he needs in order to maintain his motivation at a high level.

The third component of a growth-inducing job environment for managers is *coaching*. An opportunity to analyze problems, review plans, and "post-mortem" his mistakes can be invaluable for a manager. It sharpens his understanding of the environment in which he is working and fixes the lessons of his experience more firmly in his mind than they otherwise could be. This kind of relationship between a manager and an interested, well-informed associate is often found to have existed during the early phases of highly successful executive careers. It ought to be found throughout the careers of all managers, or at least of those managers who would appear to have more potential than most others.

Coaching is a valid but too often overlooked teaching tool. However, it is important to note that the function of a coach is quite different from that of a teacher. A coach does not give the manager the "right" answer to his problems; in fact, he may not even pretend to know it himself. Rather, he serves as a sounding board for the manager's ideas, as a friendly critic (when necessary) of those ideas, as a source of facts and ideas from his own broader experience, and sometimes as a sort of devil's advocate to test the strength of the manager's plans before they are formally implemented. The tactics used by the coach are not so important, however, as his basic commitment. He should be wholly committed to helping the manager to be as successful as possible, and this commitment should come from company policy, not personal altruism.

This is probably the main reason why coaching is so rarely used in industry. Most people in management are rewarded for making themselves successful, not for making other managers successful. In most companies there is simply no traditional role for a managerial coach: no job description, no compensation plan, no box on the organization chart. When coaching occurs, it is due to the wisdom and consideration of a thoughtful executive or sometimes to the efforts of a consultant who, usually, was retained for other reasons. Coaching seldom occurs as the result of a deliberate corporate policy to encourage it. But it should.

A tour of duty as a coach (perhaps "counselor" would be a more suitable title) could be highly productive for both a seasoned executive and his company. To be most effective, coaching should be a full-time job, not a secondary responsibility. An assignment to coaching should last at least a year, preferably two, and men should be selected for coaching on the basis of proven performance and experience at the level of the men they will be assigned to assist. Each coach should be carefully briefed by all the relevant executives—that is, those in the direct management line above the managers to be coached—both prior to, and periodically during, their assignment. This should serve the purpose of maintaining the perspective of overall company strategy, not "reporting" on the progress of the managers or evaluating their work. For reasons to be elaborated later, the coach's mission should be entirely to help the managers assigned to him; he should not give them marks for their work. Depending on the level, function, and location of the managers being developed, a well-organized coach should be able to work effectively with upward of half a dozen men simultaneously.

Coaching can and should be done by a manager's immediate superior, as well as by a specially appointed staff adviser. But, in the last analysis, the superior's main responsibility is to get the job done, and this is not always compatible with the patient and frankly partisan (pro-manager) role that makes the coach effective as a developer of managers. Because of the superior's fundamental commitment to line responsibility, he must regard each of the managers reporting to him as basically a tool for getting the job done—a tool which, if need be, can be discarded and replaced. To the coach, however, the manager is not a means to an end but a resource to be enriched and strengthened. It is in the company's interests that both of these functions, line management and management development, be performed and that neither have to suffer because of the other. This cannot be achieved by limiting either function to the part-time responsibility of anyone. There is room for full-time managerial coaching in addition to the necessarily part-time efforts of a manager's superiors. Indeed, it is probably no exaggeration to say that the function probably cannot be handled properly without full-time coaching.

All these considerations have profound implications for the ways in which companies are organized and managers are deployed.

Any organizational change in the direction of fostering a growth-inducing environment faces two major problems. The first is the obvious one of setting up the apparatus which will develop and administer programs designed to encourage men, and especially managers, to continually expand the range and depth of their competence. The second is subtler but at least equally important; and unless it is successfully solved, the effort expended in solving the first problem will have been to little avail. This is to make the shift toward a growth-inducing environment convincing by overcoming the notion, so widespread in most organizations, that despite occasional flirtations with new managerial fads the men at the top will always revert to a basically cynical and unresponsive style of management. Most companies, whether they like it or not, have been tarred with the same brush, simply because of the long tradition which holds that places of employment are meant for working and not for learning. That there is an enormous historical inertia to be overcome is evidenced by the gulf that separates work from growth in a great many minds.

Therefore, any company decision to treat the competence of its managers as an income-producing asset to be enlarged instead of, implicitly, as a commodity to be purchased will naturally create skepticism in the men it is intended to benefit. Strong, lasting, and convincing proof of a genuine conversion by top management to the cultivation of personal growth as a corporate way of life must be given. Otherwise, too many managers will find ways to circumvent or undermine the new policies; they will not want to be overcommitted to them when the "inevitable" reversion to the old philosophy occurs. Consequently, nothing less than a permanent change in the company's organizational structure, to accommodate a "career management" function with the avowed purpose of remaking the internal environment of the company, is likely to be capable of doing the job.

It may seem paradoxical to suggest that a growth-inducing environment is best established by executive fiat. There is little doubt, however, that a convincing commitment to personal growth as a company goal has to come from the top of the organization. So must the apparatus that can get the processes of growth into motion. This apparatus is more than an organizational necessity; it is tangible proof of the size of the bet that top management is willing to make on the potentialities of its own people. A growth-inducing environment can be created only when top management is sold on both the necessity and the possibility of doing so—and sold beyond lip service to the point of committing enough men, money, and power to the career management function to enable it to do its job.

Effective career management needs all three. Someone must be charged with administering these programs. In large organizations it may require several people or several decentralized departments; the responsibility, in any case, should be undivided. If career management is not somebody's full-time job and the principal basis for somebody's performance appraisal, it will stand in too great danger of not getting all the attention it deserves. Further, in order to insure that these programs are properly coordinated, without the tendency of so many well-intentioned personnel programs to be honored in the breach, the career management function should report to a high managerial level. At the very least it should report to a company's chief personnel officer; and if that official has only the modest organizational stature that many personnel managers have, the career management function should report instead to the same corporate officer to whom personnel ultimately reports.

This is not suggested merely for the sake of glorifying the career management function. Rather it is a matter of facing organizational realities. There is no point in establishing this kind of function if it is not to be given all the necessary means to accomplish its mission. Precisely because career management *must* intrude into so many citadels of traditional managerial prerogative—checking the timing of management training, for example, or reviewing assignment plans to insure that stretching takes place—it needs a sufficient measure of power to get its job done. To some extent, this kind of leverage may be earned by an incumbent who wins the respect of his fellow managers for his ability and fairness. But this is usually too slender a reed on which to allow the fortunes of career management to lean.

In most companies, power is represented mainly by the level of the executive whose wrath is likely to be incurred when a policy is ignored or circumvented, and the same principle undoubtedly applies to career management. The manager of this function must therefore be clothed with the authority to require, if necessary, that the company's career management policies be adhered to and that any exceptions to these policies be cleared with him. To those who object that this would alter the balance of power between line and staff in the direction of the latter, I can only agree that it does—and argue that the results would justify it. When a company is managed by men who are primarily motivated to increase their competence, rather than to guard their spheres of influence, the line-staff distinction becomes less important than the advancement of the organization as a whole—and the fun of being part of it.

There are at least seven functions whose control should be centralized in the career management group. These are:

1. Assessing the potentialities of managers for acquiring the competence to handle heavier responsibilities.
2. Appraising performance. This function is obviously re-

lated to the assessment of potential, yet there are important differences between the two functions which justify
their being treated separately.

3. Reviewing individual development plans and promotion
plans to insure that the stretching concept is being implemented judiciously yet without excessive timidity.

4. Scheduling, and helping superiors to prepare for, career
counseling.

5. Determining the proper time for formal management
training for each manager, as well as the types of course
content most useful for him to study during each of his
exposures to formal instruction.

6. Selecting, training, assigning, and evaluating management
counselors (or coaches). Since the demand for coaches is
likely to be chronically in excess of the supply, the career
management group would also have to decide which managers would most benefit the company by being coached.

7. Maintaining an up-to-date, relevant, and reasonably complete "inventory" of managers.

Of these seven functions, undoubtedly the most important and
most difficult to administer are the assessment of executive potential
and the appraisal of executive performance. In the next chapter, we
will look at both functions in some of the depth and detail they deserve.

Chapter 7

Predicting and Measuring Managerial Performance

IT SHOULD NOT BE NECESSARY TO BELABOR THE POINT THAT the kinds of men who are chosen to manage an organization, and the kinds of systems that are chosen for measuring and rewarding them, have a profound and lasting impact on the motivational climate of the organization as a whole. Therefore, to the extent that the executive in charge of career management acts as a sort of gatekeeper, regulating the flow of employees into management and of managers into the higher executive ranks, he is in a sense controlling the destiny of the company. He is, to paraphrase our statement in Chapter 1, working selectively with forces that affect the organization profoundly, but at very long range.

In most companies, the selection of managers is at best a fallible art. In a few companies, it is beginning to be converted into a more systematic and, in some respects, more scientific process. The best of these efforts have been made by American Telephone and Telegraph Company and by Standard Oil Company (New Jersey). Both are, of course, very large companies, and for this reason it would be easy to dismiss research results emanating from them as meaningful only to other corporate giants. But that would be a fallacy in this case, so perhaps it is best to begin by puncturing it.

Large companies do not necessarily need better managers than

Special thanks are due to Dr. Paul C. Baker II of Standard Oil Company (New Jersey) and Dr. Douglas W. Bray of American Telephone and Telegraph Company for reading portions of this chapter in manuscript. The opinions expressed herein are those of the author and not necessarily those of Drs. Baker or Bray or their respective companies.

small companies need, but they do need more of them. The sheer scale on which they must search for and evaluate managerial talent requires that the process be systematized as much as possible. This means that the elements of effective managerial performance have to be identified and that efficient ways of measuring them have to be devised. In other words, the larger companies, in order to get adequate control of the management selection process, have been compelled to take the lead in researching problems of universal importance to *all* organizations.

It was more than just necessity, however, that motivated the move by these big companies into research on management selection. Research is costly, and companies of this size can obviously afford to finance the necessary research effort more easily than a smaller firm could. There is also a statistical advantage that works in favor of large organizations that attempt this kind of research: their ability to try out various selection systems on more people, so that the sensitivity (or lack of it) of each system can be measured. These measurements on relatively large groups make statistical analysis worthwhile, and without statistical analysis it is impossible to say whether a selection system really works or merely tickles a selector's fancy. Lastly, research of this kind reflects a rather high order of sophistication. Again, large companies are not necessarily more sophisticated than small ones, and indeed many large companies have not yet ventured into research and development for their management selection procedures at all. The fact that this research has been done is one more testimony, if any more is needed, to the wisdom and high managerial competence of the companies that have done it.

In 1956 the Bell System began a long-term "Management Progress Study" that is destined to continue for some time. More than 400 young men were assessed in depth quite early in their careers. The purpose of these assessments was to determine whether measurements made in the beginning phases of a man's career could be predictive of his subsequent accomplishments and whether further assessments at various later stages of his career could add to an understanding of the reasons why he had developed as he did.

The assessments themselves had several unique features. First, they were unusually comprehensive: They took about three and one-half days from start to finish for each individual. Second, a variety of methods were used, including some unconventional situational tests in which groups of men were observed as they attempted to deal with simulated real-life problems. Consequently, the assessment staff could combine the predictive power of techniques as varied as orthodox interviews and paper-and-pencil tests, on the one hand, and the various situational tests on the other hand. The results of this potpourri of assessments were considered by a board of judges who had observed the men throughout the various exercises and had developed overall evaluations of each man's strengths and weaknesses on the basis of the combined data available on him from all these sources. In effect, each man who went through the assessment center was probed and measured by just about every kind of useful psychological technique that could be utilized.

The judges' evaluations, along with the data on which they were based, were filed off company premises and maintained in strict confidentiality, so they could not affect any subsequent selection decisions regarding the men who had been assessed. This insured that the assessments would not become "self-fulfilling prophecies" by influencing the decisions they were ultimately designed to predict. However, as the careers of these men unfolded, the research team followed their progress and correlated it with the original assessments.

Of all the many techniques used, the *situational tests* are of most interest, not only because they are less well known than paper-and-pencil tests, but also because the AT&T data clearly indicate that they were the most effective predictors of all. That is, judgments made about the potentialities of the men on the basis of their performance in the situational tests usually came closer to predicting their actual rates of progress than did judgments that were based on the other techniques. However, the best overall predictions were based not on situational tests alone, but on combinations of situational and other tests. The essence of a situational test is that men are presented, singly or in groups, with a more or less real problem to solve, and they are observed as they try to organize themselves to grapple with it. They receive relatively little guidance or instruction on how to proceed, and therefore they tend to become preoccupied with the problem itself and to be much less conscious than they ordinarily would be of the fact that they are being observed. Specially trained teams of line managers act as observers, rating the men's performance but not aiding them or questioning them as the exercises progress.

Situational tests are admittedly only an approximation of real managerial behavior, but they are a much closer approximation than most tests, interviews, and other off-the-job procedures can provide. A more important advantage is that, by providing for multiple observers and a standard set of problems to be solved, situational tests offer much better conditions for observing and measuring a man's performance than most on-the-job contexts provide. In that sense, situational tests can be compared to a physical examination: A man's heart may not perform "typically" in his doctor's office, but it is better to evaluate it in the room where the electrocardiograph is situated than to restrict the doctor to feeling the man's pulse while he is on the job.

There are many variations in the way situational tests are presented, but they all have essentially the same inner logic. They all simulate reality, provide relatively little guidance on how to proceed, and leave it up to the individual or group to devise their own strategies for handling the problem as best they can. There are three main variations to this basic strategy: the leaderless group discussion, the business game, and the in-basket exercise. The *leaderless group discussion* (sometimes referred to as the "LGD") consists of presenting a small group of candidates with a problem to discuss. The problem itself is almost always a general one about which all the candidates are likely to be equally knowledgeable or equally ignorant, as the case may be. Other than the fact that they are usually given a time limit and told that the judges will observe but not participate in their discussions, no guidance is given. No chairman is appointed and no rules of procedure are laid down.

The group must, in other words, find a way to organize itself; and in the process of attempting to do this the men have to compete and cooperate simultaneously. Leadership, if it is to emerge at all, must be achieved by consent rather than by assertion. The participants' social skills, verbal skills, and capacity to function in the face of frustration are all put to a direct test. Some variations of the LGD involve mock elections, evaluations of competing business plans, and so on. In every LGD the essential point is that the group must find its own way to begin functioning as a group before it can really deal with the problem it has been given to solve. Because the men are reacting to one another rather than reacting to trying to influence an interviewer, the judges are exposed to a much wider range of their behavior styles than could be the case in an ordinary interview.

In *business games,* a group of men is given enough background information about a real or mythical business firm to take over its management in a mock decision-making exercise. Usually the group is confronted with some major problem affecting the fortunes of the firm, such as financial overextension or the need to enter a new market. In most cases the men are not assigned specific roles and therefore have to organize themselves into some semblance of a management team; however, in some variations the men are randomly assigned to different functional roles (for example, "treasurer," "plant manager") in order to be sure that several conflicting points of view are championed. Despite the obvious artificiality and pretense, a well-constructed business game quickly captures the imagination of mature participants, and they work at it with considerable vigor and determination. As in the leaderless group discussion, both problem-solving and negotiating skills are called into play, and the judges have an opportunity to observe a wider range of each individual's managerial repertory than would ordinarily be possible. Business games are often used for instruction as well as for assessment, and they have the added merit of lending themselves to critiques from which the men can learn something of value to themselves.

The *in-basket exercise* is usually administered to individuals, although there is no limit to the number of men who can take it simultaneously. Because it too is a simulation of reality and requires the individual to call upon both administrative and social skills to solve the problems with which he is presented, it is properly classified as a situational test. Unlike most LGD's and business games, however, the in-basket exercise lends itself to some degree of standardization. This, in turn, makes possible an objective scoring system through which the performance of any individual can be directly compared to that of many others who have taken the same exercise before him.

The exercise takes its name from the ubiquitous desk-top box in which managers usually receive their mail. Typically, the individual being assessed receives a background briefing on the fictitious company for which he is supposedly working during the exercise, and a situation is posed in which he must make a large number of decisions during a brief period without being able to consult other people or obtain additional information. This is usually done by asking him to pretend, for the purpose of the exercise, that he has been appointed rather suddenly to take over a key job, that his predecessor and his new staff are unavailable, and that he has come to the new office on a Saturday morning to familiarize himself with the job by going through the papers in his in-basket. These are a wide assortment of more or less typical letters and memoranda, some more urgent than others. Working within a relatively tight time limit, he must somehow dispose of everything in the in-basket by writing replies, assigning documents to subordinates for handling, or setting them aside for later action. A special questionnaire has been devised through which he can record and explain the various actions he took, and this in turn can be processed by computers to yield a set of overall scores.

The in-basket exercise can be made so realistic that participants and observers alike become enthusiastic about its potentialities for tapping real-life habits and characteristics. This apparent realness is both the main advantage and the main disadvantage of the in-basket technique. On the one hand, close approximation of a real managerial job makes the exercise attractive and acceptable to managers, who regard it as a fairer test of their skills than a more abstract exercise would be. On the other hand, there is as yet very little hard evidence that the results of the in-basket test predict anything at all about a manager's *future* performance or that such predictions can be made more reliably with this than with other, less expensive techniques. However, the ready acceptance of the in-basket exercise makes it difficult to conduct the kinds of studies that would be necessary to put it to this kind of crucial test, simply because it seems hardly necessary. There is enough fragmentary evidence available about the technique's usefulness to raise very high hopes for it. But there have been other instances of promising techniques catching on too quickly to be thoroughly tested, becoming fads, and eventually falling into disrepute. These should encourage a more restrained and orderly approach to the in-basket exercise—and, indeed, to the assessment center concept as a whole.

The Management Progress Study has aroused enough interest that the basic concepts of assessment are now being applied to management selection decisions in a number of companies. The approach is usually cautious and research-oriented. That is, there is enough confidence in the techniques to encourage their use in addition to—not as a substitute for—the admittedly sketchy data normally available about most managerial candidates. At the same time, by passing large numbers of managers and managerial candidates through the assessment procedures, data can be gathered for eventual comparison with each man's progress in sufficient quantity to permit a more definitive test of the various techniques.

The Bell System itself has been the largest factor in this movement. Because of the interest aroused by the Management Progress Study in the parent company, the Michigan Bell Telephone Company organized an assessment center in 1958 for the purpose of evaluating the potentialities of employees who had been recommended by their supervisors as candidates for first-line managerial positions. This was quickly followed by similar programs in the other companies in the system. By now, there are more than 40 centers within the AT&T complex which have assessed more than 10,000 men and women for supervisory positions.

Although the techniques used in these assessment centers are essentially the same as those used in the original Management Progress Study, the data are treated entirely differently. The MPS data will remain strictly off-limits to line management so that the men in the study will be neither helped nor hampered in their careers by the assessment results. The Management Progress Study remains, in other words, a scientific venture whose full implications will not be known for some time. The results of the various Bell System assessment centers, on the other hand, are provided to line management and undoubtedly have an important influence on promotion decisions.

Similar assessment center programs are now operating in The Standard Oil Company (Ohio), Lever Brothers Company, and International Business Machines Corporation, among others. Incidentally, the use of assessment procedures for management selection has an even longer history in Europe than in the United States. The German Army is usually credited with having originated them prior to World War II. The British War Office Selection Boards ("Wosbies," as the troops called them) used them to select officer candidates during the war, and this has led to the very widespread use of these techniques by the British Civil Service since the war. Assessment center techniques were also used by the U.S. Office of

Strategic Services during World War II. Although the OSS procedures aroused considerable interest among American psychologists, they were not used industrially on a large scale until the AT&T Management Progress Study began more than ten years after the war had ended.

The reason for this long hiatus in the development of assessment techniques in the United States was their high cost relative to that of more orthodox methods for evaluating human potentialities. Paper-and-pencil tests are relatively cheap, interviews are not a great deal more expensive, and professionally administered tests are not much more expensive than interviews. It was not clear from the OSS data that the use of assessment center techniques would add enough precision to the performance predictions that could be made with orthodox techniques to justify the added cost. The AT&T Management Progress Study is the first attempt to answer this question on a sufficiently large scale, and with sufficiently tight controls, to permit a definitive conclusion to be drawn from its results.

Although the Management Progress Study is not yet complete, enough interim measurements have been made of the careers of the men who were assessed to permit some tentative evaluations of assessment itself. So far the available data indicate that the decision of the Bell System companies to establish their own managerial assessment centers without waiting for the conclusion of the Management Progress Study was probably justified. About 79 percent of the men in the original sample who have progressed to middle management had been correctly assessed as having that potentiality by the centers. Further, about 94 percent of the men who have not yet been able to progress beyond the first level of management had been assessed by the centers as probably being limited to that relatively slow rate of advancement.

The assessment centers have, in other words, come remarkably close to predicting how most of the young men in the MPS sample would fare in the Bell System companies five to eight years *after* they were assessed. Whether that rate of accuracy will change when the study has run its full ten-year course remains to be seen; for the moment it appears that the predictions made by the assessment center staff were very accurate indeed. A conclusive answer to the basic question of the cost-effectiveness of assessment techniques as against that of less expensive techniques cannot be given until the study is completed. However, the current opinion of the AT&T psychologists directing the Management Progress Study is that the extra costs of assessment are fully justified by the accuracy they are apparently able to add to the difficult and crucial art of managerial selection.[5]

The EIMP project (Early Identification of Management Potential) of Jersey Standard was actually begun prior to the AT&T Management Progress Study. However, there is a logic in presenting it after the MPS: AT&T assessed young employees at the beginning of their careers in hopes of gauging managerial potential; the EIMP project focused on managers at all levels who were already well launched on their careers. The two studies are similar in that somewhat more than 400 men were assessed in each and in that the resulting measurements were not permitted to affect the subsequent careers of those who had participated. They also have an essentially similar purpose: to determine whether long-range executive and managerial success can be attributed, at least in part, to characteristics that could be reliably measured years in advance.

The main differences between EIMP and MPS are in the maturity of the men who were assessed and in the techniques used. The Jersey Standard study included men from the entire spectrum of management, ranging from the chairman of the board and the president of the parent company to the lowest supervisory level in some affiliated companies in the New York area. Unlike the AT&T research, the Jersey Standard study included no situational tests or combined judgments. It was based entirely on paper-and-pencil tests, some of them standardized and some developed especially for this project. The only exception was a personal interview. A projective test was eliminated from the study at a fairly early stage when it was demonstrated that it could not discriminate between managers who had been advancing fairly rapidly and those whose careers had developed more slowly.

All other tests chosen for use in this study proved to have some predictive power. The standardized tests included a modified version of the Miller Analogies Test (a high-level verbal reasoning test, used chiefly to screen candidates for admission to graduate and professional schools) ; a nonverbal reasoning test; and the Guilford-Zimmerman Temperament Survey (a well-known test designed to measure a number of personality characteristics, some of which were presumed to be important in determining managerial success) . The experimental tests which were devised especially for this study included an "individual background survey," which was essentially a biographical questionnaire dealing with the circumstances and history of an individual's youth and early manhood; a "management judgment test," which presented various real managerial problems and alternative solutions; and a "self-performance report," in which the individual was asked to evaluate his own managerial performance.

The data provided by these devices were evaluated in two ways. First, the Jersey Standard research team worked out an index of "overall managerial success to date." This was calculated by combining position level, rate of salary progress during the previous five years (compared to the average progression for managers at comparable levels), and rankings of managerial effectiveness (prepared by current and former superiors of the men being ranked). Because the first two elements in the index—position level and salary progress—could be influenced by the age of the individual, a statistical correction was applied which had the effect of eliminating the influence of age on these measures. The three elements were then combined to yield a rating which reflected several relevant aspects of managerial success, instead of only one. This index made it possible to compare the relative success of each of the participating managers up to the time of the study, independently of the advantages which age alone gave to the more senior men. A second and more stringent way of evaluating the test data had to await the passage of time; that is, determining whether the test results were predictive of subsequent managerial success.

The results of the first (or current) analysis of the EIMP data were exceptionally promising and more than justified the burdens of continuing the study over a period of years to determine whether the second analysis would be as successful. The results were expressed in "expectancy charts," one of which is reproduced in the accompanying exhibit. An expectancy chart shows what can be expected to happen, on the basis of experience, if certain information is available which has a known relationship to subsequent events. The chart summarizes the *past* relationships between "certain available information," on the one hand, and "subsequent events," on the other hand. Expectancy tables can therefore be used for prediction only on the assumption that an individual will turn out more or less the same as the "average" individual having more or less similar characteristics has turned out in the past. Whether there is wisdom or the lack of it in making such an assumption depends largely on whether the relationship between available information and subsequent events is stable or transitory.

This is precisely why a second analysis, showing whether a relationship detected at one point in time still exists after a considerable period has elapsed, is necessary whenever a relationship is detected in the first analysis. It is worth noting that it is difficult enough to devise measures of human attributes that are related to *current* performance; when such a measure is devised successfully there is an understandable—but dangerous—tendency to assume that a stable predictor of *future* performance has finally been found. Psychologists have learned the hard way to treat their few successes with current data cautiously. Too often they do turn out to be peculiar to a particular set of individuals or measurements.

An important reason for this instability is that psychologists, in an attempt to rid their predictors of irrelevancies and to make them as precise as possible, deliberately weight the various test scores in such a way as to produce the maximum correlation with current performance. The logic in this is not unlike the logic in focusing a camera: The lens is moved forward or backward until the image of the subject is etched on the focal plane as sharply as the lens itself will allow. Whether the lens must be refocused to take an equally sharp picture on another occasion depends on whether the subject has moved.

Weighting test scores is both necessary and dangerous. It is necessary in that the predictors must be "focused" to operate efficiently; but it is dangerous in that their precision may be illusory and largely due to the particular way in which "current" data were gathered. Weighted current test scores must therefore be treated with caution until a second (future) analysis of their ability to predict behavior can be made.

The data in our exhibit are based on weighted scores, deliberately introduced by the Jersey Standard researchers to maximize (or, if you will, to focus) the relationship of the test scores obtained by the managers in their sample to their current managerial success at the time they were tested.

The exhibit shows the odds, as it were, that could have been quoted on the likelihood that a manager would be found in the top 33.3 percent of the Jersey Standard "overall success" rankings, judging only by his weighted test scores. If the scores had been entirely unrelated to the success measurement, the managers would have been distributed about equally across both the test and the success measurements. For example, the managers whose test scores were in the top 20 percent would have had about a 33.3 percent chance of placing in the top third—or anywhere else—in the success criterion; and the same would be true of any other 20 percent of the test score groups. Instead there is a regular, sharply defined tendency for the probability of being in the top success group to *increase* as the scores themselves increased. A manager whose test scores were in the top 20 percent was about *19 times more likely* to be in the top success group than one whose scores were in the lowest 20 percent. There can be little doubt that the Jersey Standard research team had focused very sharply indeed on psychological differences between managers that were related to their comparative success levels at the time they were tested.

Expectancy Chart

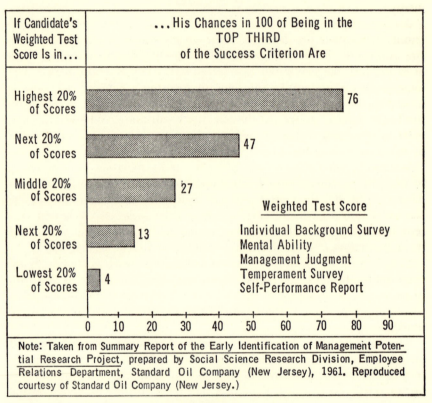

Note: Taken from Summary Report of the Early Identification of Management Potential Research Project, prepared by Social Science Research Division, Employee Relations Department, Standard Oil Company (New Jersey), 1961. Reproduced courtesy of Standard Oil Company (New Jersey.)

However, the proof of a psychologist's pudding is never in the eating but in whether it causes heartburn or happiness for years afterward. The EIMP project is still continuing, and the research team continues to follow up the careers of the managers who were tested as much as ten years previously. Although the results of this continuing follow-up have not yet been published, it appears that the system of weighted test scores worked out in the original EIMP study have withstood the test of time.

Whatever it was that the tests measured was stable characteristics that not only differentiated the more successful from the less successful at the time of the original study, but also have continued to influence the varying degrees of success ever since. If anything, the years have tended to heighten the differences detected by the tests. This means that the relationships between weighted test scores and later managerial success will probably be more sharply etched than the ones shown in the exhibit.

What was it, then, that the EIMP tests measured? Actually, a number of factors were involved. The most powerful single predictor in the test battery turned out to be the individual background survey, which was basically a means of recording data about the individual's early life and family background. It appears that biographical instruments of this type are really a sort of indirect personality test, in the sense that adult personality differences can often be traced to trends that had their beginning much earlier in life. However, a biographical survey is more objective than a typical personality test, since most of its questions deal with verifiable matters of record rather than with matters of opinion. This relative objectivity leads, in turn, to a more stable score (and therefore to more accurate prediction) than most personality tests can be expected to achieve.

Basically, the biographical instrument in the EIMP project was measuring the rates at which the managers in the study had become emotionally independent and mature during their youth and early manhood and their ability to set themselves on a well-defined, productive course at an early age. The men who moved farthest and fastest in the Jersey Standard hierarchy had been masters of their own fate from a relatively early age—bad luck and difficult times notwithstanding. They were, in other words, no strangers to success; and for the most part they achieved success by pursuing it, having made such pursuit a habit for most of their lives.

Similar findings have occurred in many other contexts, and their implications are rather profound. To suggest that most careers are, in effect, determined before they begin would be going beyond the facts. On the other hand, there is little reason to doubt that a head start in early life can be turned into a potent advantage by an adult. It is also clear that people who arrive at a full command of their potentialities more slowly, or less completely, than others carry a handicap with them into their adult years—at least as far as success in management is concerned. Neither the advantage nor the handicap is absolute: Both can be overcome. Yet it would appear that neither can be overcome easily. For all practical purposes, the vast majority of humans (managerial humans included) enter adulthood without a distinct advantage or disadvantage carrying over from their youth. Consequently, what they achieve as adults is a matter of effort, ability, and luck—not necessarily in that order.

Mental ability was the second most effective predictor in the EIMP battery. This is hardly surprising, since the higher a man rises in executive ranks, the more time he must spend in learning. Executive learning is not the same as children's learning, which is often a matter of memorizing details; nor is it the same as craftsmen's learning, which consists in becoming profoundly familiar with all aspects of a particular, usually rather narrow, set of problems. Rather, executive learning consists of the quick determination of what is essential in a mass of information which the executive is usually unable to comprehend in any depth. It also consists of determining how those essentials relate to other essentials gleaned from other technologies which he is equally handicapped in understanding. In effect, an executive is in the business of navigating through what are, for him, uncharted waters. Since he cannot know all these waters well, he had better know his navigation well. This is really just another way of saying that he had better be possessed of a fairly high order of intelligence. It makes sense, then, that the more mentally agile managers in the EIMP study had an advantage with respect to rising to higher executive levels.

There is also a sense in which the relationship of mental ability test scores to executive success flies in the face of managerial folklore; and indeed it is necessary to qualify any statement of that relationship rather carefully. Only a few executives are geniuses, and very few geniuses are executives. What is required of an executive is the ability to select, from among other men's insights, those which can be put to practical use—but not necessarily the ability to generate those insights. Consequently, while a highly intelligent man is better equipped for executive responsibility than a man of more ordinary intellect, a brilliant man does not necessarily have an advantage over a highly intelligent man in this respect.

Neither the AT&T nor the Jersey Standard research project has as yet been completed. Indeed, both are continuing programs rather than projects with a deadline. Yet it is already possible to draw some preliminary conclusions from them. Some of the characteristics that enable a man to handle an executive job effectively can be measured when he is still relatively young; these measurements can be made with a combination of situational, biographical, and mental ability tests; and, while he is still young, the individual with the best chance of rising to the top as a mature man is already brighter, more self-possessed, and more able to lead than his peers. The major implication of these results for management is that management development can be focused on men with the greatest probability of benefitting from it. Therefore, it is not necessary to rely on good fortune alone to bring enough well-rounded managers to the forefront when they are needed, because management development is itself a manageable process.

The discovery that the potentiality for high-level managerial work is identifiable at relatively early career stages can help to solve one of management's oldest problems. That is, what is the best way to allocate the necessarily scarce opportunities for optimal career development through rapid promotion and deliberate exposure to varied functional experience? Not even a large company can afford to offer such opportunities to its younger managers indiscriminately. Early identification techniques offer a rational solution to the problem. At the same time, they could create new problems, chief among which is overreliance on the techniques themselves. No matter how much they are refined, and no matter what new techniques are added to the assessment arsenal, all attempts at early identification will be vulnerable to both the "a" and the "d" types of selection errors.

Another potential problem which could be created by the use of early identification techniques is the development of a "crown prince" atmosphere in the organizations that use them. That is, when some young men are thought to be destined for top-level positions while others are seemingly out of the running almost from the start of the race, the effects on morale and indirectly on productivity are almost certain to be harmful. The solution to both the overreliance problem and the crown-prince problem is to use early identification techniques with restraint and common sense. This means that although the men who appear to have the greatest potentialities might at first be promoted more rapidly than the others, for all subsequent promotions they would have to compete on equal terms with all other managers at the same levels. Preference should be limited, in other words, to giving the selected men an opportunity to begin developing their managerial skills at a faster rate than their peers. Whether this preferential treatment is continued in further rapid promotions should depend entirely on whether it is justified by superior performance. In other words, if any man is to be given an advantage over his peers it must be clearly due to his accomplishments and not to his sponsors. Of course, the main implication of the studies completed thus far is that properly chosen men *will* tend to justify preferential treatment by performing more capably at every level than managers who have arrived there more slowly than they did.

There is a danger that a rapidly developing manager could be rushed ahead too fast. In that case, not only his career but management's confidence in the early identification system could be damaged unnecessarily. It is worth stressing that the one thing early identification techniques can be expected to do is to show which men are more likely than the rest to develop the capabilities for high-level management. Actual promotions to high-level jobs should be restricted, as they usually are now, to men who have *already developed* these capacities, regardless of whether their long-range potentialities were evident when they were younger.

Meantime, it can be stated with some assurance that further advances in the art of identifying people with high-level potentialities are likely to wait upon developments in other areas. There is no shortage of ways to assess men's potentialities; what is needed now is a much clearer notion of exactly which of their potentialities ought to be assessed. Surprisingly, we still know relatively little about the specific kinds of behavior that managerial assessment techniques should be designed to predict. There is, of course, a great deal of folklore about what constitutes effective management and what constitutes ineffective management; and much of this has the ring of wisdom to it. But it also has the ring of imprecision and inconclusiveness. In the scientific sense of precise measurement and unambiguous definitions, we really do not know just what kinds of behavior potentials to look for in prospective managers. This is not because any impenetrable mysteries surround the nature of managerial excellence. It is simply, and embarrassingly, because the necessary techniques for analyzing it have not been applied. This oversight, in turn, is due to a general failure to recognize the inadequacies of most current definitions.

It is at this point that the two subjects of this chapter merge: the *prediction of future performance,* which is the essence of selection, and the *evaluation of current performance,* which is the essence of appraisal. We usually consider the way a man handles his job in both contexts, but too often without a clear distinction between the two. As a result, attempts to forecast what a man *could* do get weighted down with a great deal of irrelevant detail, while attempts to improve his current performance and to maintain his motivation are blunted by other irrelevancies. We will consider the application of performance appraisal to both future and current performance—but separately. It is logical to continue our discussion on predicting managerial performance by considering the predictive aspects of performance appraisal first.

There are four good reasons why we need to define effective managerial performance more precisely, before we can expect to make much more progress with performance prediction. First of all, the principal ingredient of most management selection programs is and will undoubtedly continue to be nomination. Managers are asked to nominate candidates for other managerial positions from among their subordinates, on the basis of qualities that are presumably revealed in their job performance. The entire ethic of the merit system, promotion from within, and rising through the ranks is tied to the nomination process; it will therefore endure if only because it must endure. Few claims are made for its efficacy as a selection method. But this is precisely why nomination needs to be improved. The manager who is asked to name employees who have managerial potential usually gets little useful guidance on what to look for and what to ignore or discount. He is hardly to be blamed if he falls back upon a combination of current job performance—which often has dubious relevance to a higher job—and whatever favorite notions he happens to entertain about the qualities that make for good managers.

The typical request to nominate management candidates is in fact quite unfair to the manager who receives it and to everyone else involved. It is founded on the absurd premise that managers, *because* they are managers, somehow know how to identify potential managers. They very often don't. The fact that in some companies there are certain visible similarities among the men who are chosen for management posts only proves that their managers share certain preconceptions. It does not necessarily mean that the qualities of an *effective* manager have been successfully identified. If only to improve the nomination process, and thereby to provide a richer input to more precise methods of assessment, the *behavioral* qualities of effective management should be carefully pinned down. (The reason for laying stress on behavioral qualities in the preceding sentence will become apparent presently.)

Second, most attempts to measure the effectiveness of selection systems have run into a sort of semantic sound barrier—an upper limit beyond which measurement itself becomes balky—owing to the elusive nature of the things that selection systems are supposed to predict. For example, it is easy enough to *talk* about "success" or "effectiveness," or to find some other glib way of expressing something we want the selection system to help us to get; but it is not so easy to measure it. Sooner or later we have to face the practical problem of what to use for a yardstick. When we do that it turns out that "success" and other words like it express very dim concepts indeed. They are not adequately represented by any of the easily obtainable measurements of what people have actually done. The Jersey Standard study, for example, used salary changes as one of its several criteria of managerial success. But the research team used it more because of its convenience and objectivity than because they believed salary to be invariably a close relative of success. On this point, most managers would agree: "It ain't necessarily so."

Because success is such a loose concept, it is hardly surprising that managers who are asked to rate people according to their success are in fact rating many different things. There is *no* generally acceptable yardstick, and therefore they use whatever yardstick is at hand. The result is a hash. But when you try to correlate something that is reasonably well defined with something that is not, the correlation you obtain can be no more accurate than consistency of the ill-defined something lets it be. This is inherent in the nature of correlation, and correlation is by far the most convincing way we have of testing the usefulness of a selection system. One result of this dilemma is that psychologists have wondered for years whether their prediction techniques might not be considerably more accurate than they could prove to their own or anyone else's satisfaction.

This is, in fact, the main barrier to further advances in the state of the art of performance prediction. It is not that the search for newer, more sophisticated predictors needs to be pressed much further at this time. The problem is rather that we are not really sure which of our available predictors are worth the investment of time, money, and talent to develop them further. We won't know until much better performance criteria are developed to replace the ones we have today—better in the sense of being reasonably precise and independent of anyone's personal judgment. This can come only from a reasonably objective definition of the kind of performance that should be expected of managers.

A third reason for attempting to arrive at such a definition has to do with morale. The higher one goes in management, the more ambiguous the requirements of the job become, with the result that performance is not really measured so much as it is reviewed—in the same sense that a critic reviews a play. It is not uncommon for an executive to learn long after he has made a decision that his superiors considered it unwise, because he is in effect playing a game in which the rules are spelled out *ex post facto*. To some extent this is unavoidable, since the full consequences of high-level decisions are difficult to anticipate. But this uncertainty exacts a price from both the executive and the company he works for. It can hardly fail to make the executive uncomfortable. At times it may also make him defensive and unwilling to think or act independently. When men in high positions choose to play it safe when their business judgment indicates a need for action, it is easy to dismiss the problem as a simple defect in their characters—a selection error. But that would be to fall for the hero fallacy. There is something to be said, therefore, for removing at least some of the ambiguity that surrounds most higher-level jobs; and the way to do that is to define both the unpardonable sins and the unimpeachable virtues as precisely as possible.

The fourth reason for spelling out what we mean by effective managerial performance follows directly from the third. If the rules of the management game are stated unambiguously, it becomes incumbent not only upon the managers, but on *their* managers as well, to abide by those rules. The very act of stating the limits of acceptable and unacceptable behavior imposes a sort of discipline on top management to stay within them. With their own judges more predictable, managers are less likely to be defensive. As a result, the business of the organization can proceed in a more straightforward manner, with more emphasis upon results and less upon safety, popularity, and second-guessing the men at the top.

None of these reasons is new, and one may legitimately ask why they have not long ago impelled a large-scale effort to arrive at an improved definition of managerial effectiveness. The answer is that they have, and that so far none of these efforts has been very successful. The keenest analysis of what's wrong with current systems of managerial performance evaluation has been made by Marvin D. Dunnette of the University of Minnesota.[6] The analysis that follows draws heavily upon his work.

To begin with, many companies still have a predilection for rating their managers in terms of a list of adjectives that are somebody's idea of what a manager ought to be like. These usually sound like a sort of grown-up version of the Boy Scout Oath: Instead of being brave, clean, and reverent, the manager is typically expected to be decisive, articulate, and aggressive—or some other combination of qualities that one can hardly quarrel with. Aside from the unlikelihood that any mortal manager will ever be found who can look good if measured honestly against such sterling criteria, there are serious weaknesses in the adjective approach. For one thing, the words mean different things to different people and so lead inevitably to a hash. Further, the adjectives are usually rather obviously loaded in a positive or negative direction, so that merely checking them becomes a sweeping judgment of the individual rather than a sharply etched portrait of one aspect of a man. This leads managers to avoid "indictments" by giving nearly everyone a strongly positive rating. While this is understandable, it makes the ratings nearly useless. Finally, the adjective approach often fails to meet the test of relevance. That is, the qualities described are not always crucial to assessing the value of a man's services, and the adjectives nearly always omit qualities that are more important than those they include.

Another approach is to avoid trying to assess separate components of performance and to concentrate instead on global or overall judgments of what a man has contributed to his organization. One of the merits of the global approach is that it is easier to get judges to agree on generalized ratings than on ratings of separate parts of a man's performance. But balanced against this advantage are several weighty disadvantages. Assessments that attempt to rate everything about a man at once are so inherently vague that it is impossible to say for certain what goes into them. In effect there is no quality control, and under the circumstances it is fairly likely that irrelevant factors can sway the rating in one direction or another. Global ratings also tend to underestimate what a man could do at his best and overestimate what he could do at his worst, without indicating which circumstances would enable him to do his best and which would handicap him.

One of the more popular trends in performance rating has been to evaluate the results that men achieve, rather than rating the men themselves by their qualities or traits. This represents a laudable attempt to minimize the subjective side of performance rating, and it takes on added respectability from its apparent closeness to Peter Drucker's famous concept of management by objectives. Yet measuring by results and managing by objectives are not quite the same thing. To begin with, there is the inescapable and not-so-easily-solved problem of exactly which results to measure. In many jobs—and especially in managerial jobs—results are compounded of circumstances, luck, and many people's efforts; and the contribution of any particular person (including a manager) to those results could be anything from minuscule to decisive.

The man whose performance is measured by results may be credited with other people's successes or stigmatized for their failures, unless it can be shown that the results were his and his alone. But that happens only rarely in managerial jobs. Another problem is that the particular results selected for measurement may represent only a part of the job, and not necessarily a large or vital part. Lastly, it is difficult to apply standards to results, so one is often left with the dilemma that measurement by results was intended to avoid: Shall subjective judgment be used to decide which results are "better" than others? While setting objectives is a good way to focus a man's activities and to motivate him in a short-term sense, it is not necessarily an effective way to measure either his contribution or his potentialities.

Perhaps the most important observation to be made about performance rating systems is that they are seldom used with the punctuality or thoroughness that is prescribed for them. Performance rating scales are not, in other words, considered very important by the people for whom they were designed; and this in turn is usually due to the *way* in which they were designed. They are typically composed of loosely defined or even undefined terms which represent the opinion of someone—seldom the manager himself—as to what should be rated in a manager's performance. These forms are resisted by managers because they seem, and very often are, irrelevant and unnecessary. The importance of performance rating itself is seldom quarreled with; rather, it is the forms themselves, with their sweeping generalities and their lack of clear-cut standards, that receive the brunt of the criticism.

To be effective, a system of performance evaluation would need to have at least three characteristics: First, the ratings would have to be based on specific, verifiable *events,* not on traits that allegedly encompass a man's personality and not on results in the broad and essentially unaccountable sense. Second, these events would have to be demonstrably significant. It is not enough that anybody's opinion or even so-called common sense indicates that the events are significant; hard evidence should show that they are crucial to effective performance. Third, the scale used for rating each of these events should be firmly anchored in specific, easily recognizable behavior description, not in ambiguous terms like "average" which mean different things to different people. Attempts to build systems of this kind are currently being made in a number of companies.

Our insistence on basing ratings on events rather than on judgments springs from the need for a stable yardstick. We can usually assume that whenever a yardstick has to be interpreted, even competent interpreters will disagree on the measurements they obtain from it. Thus we are never sure whether such a yardstick has been read accurately or inaccurately, even when we use consensus or some other way of reducing its stretchability. Admittedly, not all the ambiguity is eliminated when we switch from judging traits to asking whether an event has occurred. After all, one can always quibble with the definition of the event. Still, a carefully defined question that seeks a yes-or-no answer is much more likely to lead to agreement between observers than any other kind of question.

There is, of course, a danger in relying on specific events instead of on generalized traits. The events chosen for the rating system may be either irrelevant or insufficient; that is, they may cast no light at all on what kind of performance to expect in the future, or they may reveal only a fraction of what the man has done. Fortunately, both of these dangers can be greatly reduced when the rating system is designed by means of the "critical incident" technique. This is a method originated by John C. Flanagan of the University of Pittsburgh. It requires the recollection, by persons who were in a position to witness and judge them, of many specific events in which a job was handled exceptionally well or exceptionally poorly. What results from collating and analyzing hundreds of such events is, in effect, the pooled wisdom and experience of the executives who made the judgments. This information can usually be reduced to a manageable number of make-or-break factors. These are, for all practical purposes, the anatomy of the job—its unimpeachable virtues and its unpardonable sins—expressed in terms of specific things that were done rather than in adjectives, adverbs, or other qualifiers. The pertinence of the factors can be guaranteed by selecting only those kinds of incidents that show up repeatedly in many separate recountings; their completeness is assured by thoroughly mining the memories of enough managers.

So much for predicting future performance on the basis of current performance. There remains the thorny problem of current performance itself—whether its measurement contributes to its improvement and, if so, in what way. During the past dozen years or so, this issue has probably generated more heat and less light than anything else in personnel administration. It will probably continue to do so, chiefly because the supporters of performance appraisal claim too much for it, while its opponents, by demanding too much, inevitably acquire a long and impressive list of disappointments with which to damn it.

The rationale underlying performance appraisal is quite simple, and this is indeed the main thing wrong with it. The premise is that if men are told in what ways their performance is deficient, they will naturally want to correct it. This is at best a gross oversimplification of human nature. It would be more accurate to say that most men would want to correct the deficiencies in their performance if they *agreed* that they were deficient and if there appeared to be enough *advantage* in correcting them to justify the effort. But these conditions are extremely difficult—sometimes, perhaps, impossible—to satisfy. This is the main reason why performance appraisal, when it is practiced at all, so easily leads to resentment and estrangement between supervisor and subordinate, on the one hand, or to a mere ritualistic pretense on the other.

Despite the difficulties in making so "straightforward" a program work, attempts to set matters aright continue. These are of two sorts: administrative and psychological. The administrative attempts consist of various control systems through which personnel departments try, usually with indifferent success, to persuade or coerce managers to confront their subordinates with a frank evaluation of their work. The reason given most often for the relative ineffectiveness of such systems is that top management ignores them and that the rest of management infers that performance appraisal is really only a pious hoax. The psychological attempts are aimed toward the heart of the matter. They try to remove the underlying resistance to performance appraisal by teaching managers to handle it more adroitly or by restructuring appraisal so that performance is measured against objective standards which the subordinate has helped to select. There can be no serious argument with the value of training and restructuring; but they are not, in themselves, sufficient to make performance appraisal the potent tool for betterment it was intended to be.

Whether an effective system of performance appraisal would actually improve performance is likely to remain an academic question—at least until a way is found, not only to make such a system effective, but to keep it that way. Some experiments suggest that systems based on joint goal setting by supervisors and subordinates can, at least during the life of the experiment, produce increases in productivity. But the real test of any experimental system is what happens when the experimenters, with their vested interest in the system, leave it to be operated by managers whose interest in it depends on how well it has been sold to them. Even effective systems will, in the long run, probably have to rely on the policing abilities of the personnel administrator to see to it that they are used consistently.

There is, however, a subtler advantage to performance appraisal which justifies its use, entirely apart from whether such appraisals improve performance. One of the most common complaints that employees of all kinds, including managers, are likely to express is that they don't know what kind of future they can anticipate for themselves in their companies—or, to use an overused phrase, they don't know where they stand. Traced to its roots, this is usually a way of expressing the discomfort of not controlling one's own destiny.

Assignments, promotions, salary increases—events that help to determine the quality of life in an organization—too often seem to be decided remotely, in ways that the individual can influence only indirectly if at all. The usual assurances about the merit system are not sufficient to set these anxieties aside, although they can help if they are demonstrably supported by fact. But what is really at stake in each case is a man's future. If he is young enough, he will face the problem of whether to commit himself to his present organization or seek a better future elsewhere. If he already feels committed, he must make the best of a situation from which he cannot escape. Either way, having one's future largely in the hands of someone else—even a benevolent someone else—is a rather insecure state of affairs. It is also endemic in organizations of all kinds and, in a sense, the price one pays for being part of an organization in the first place. In the long run, whether this insecurity is assuaged or aggravated can have a significant effect on the quality of a man's motivation.

Performance appraisal is not a complete answer to this problem, but it does give the individual some measure of control over his future in two ways. First, there is at least an implied commitment on the part of the organization to stand behind whatever appraisal the supervisor gives. However vague and inexact it may be, the appraisal is a sort of tacit guarantee, at least for the near term, of the kind of treatment the individual can expect to receive from the organization. Second, having to reveal the appraisal to the employee imposes a severe discipline upon the supervisor, so much so that many balk at it. Some overreact to the discipline by becoming excessively lenient, letting the employee believe that his work is better than it really is. But under such a system, supervisors are constrained from making the kinds of negative judgments that are too harsh or simply unjustifiable. And it is this constrained, distilled appraisal that becomes a sort of implied contract, at least in the employee's mind, between his organization and himself.

In limited and subtle ways, then, a performance appraisal system can let people know where they stand. Is that enough of an advantage to justify the system? It may not seem so, since employees who are appraised and told about it are not necessarily happy, and their work is not necessarily more efficient. But their complaints, if there are any, are likely to center on less corrosive anxieties, and that is a considerably greater advantage than it may at first appear.

Management too often expects that the elimination of a problem will lead to its obverse; that is, if the cause of unhappiness is removed, people will automatically swing to the other extreme and become happy. It is not difficult to understand why this does not happen. Morale is something like a spring: It can be depressed by a negative pressure or elevated by a positive lift. Releasing either of these influences does not send the spring hurtling in the opposite direction; it merely returns it to a neutral position. This *is* the normal condition of morale: neutral, indifferent, motionless. That is all you can expect from relieving a negative pressure upon morale. To move from there to the kind of zest and commitment associated with high morale would require further efforts—in other words, a positive lift. Performance appraisal, when sensitively used, relieves one of the more damaging pressures upon morale and permits it to rise, as it were, from a compressed state to a neutral condition. A potential danger is thus removed and the possibility of introducing a lifting force is at least opened. That is not at all a bad bargain.

Chapter 8

Competence Loss

THUS FAR WE HAVE CONCENTRATED ON WAYS OF HONING the capabilities of more or less gifted men in order to enable them to reach higher levels of competence. That is an essential but in itself insufficient strategy for organizational survival. It is also necessary to deal with the erosion of competence, which is perhaps more of a problem for ordinary men than it is for the unusually capable.

The man of promising potentialities is often provided with what amounts to an insurance policy against a decline in his abilities, simply because he is more likely to repay an investment in developing those potentialities than is someone of more ordinary talents. But in terms of overall productivity, small ways of preserving the value of the ordinary man's contributions can be at least as important as dramatic ways of enhancing the contributions of exceptional men. The point could probably be argued endlessly, but it can hardly be doubted that the *cost* of inefficiency among the rank and file becomes inflated, in most companies, by a much larger multiplier than can be applied to the activities of so-called key men. Hence it seldom makes good financial sense to base an organizational development plan solely on the flowering of the ablest people available. Neither does it make good psychological sense to plan solely for increasing competence. Unhappily, competence can also decline. We therefore have to find ways of preserving it, along with ways of enlarging it.

The problem of decline in competence is older than it may seem. During the past several years both management and labor have become concerned with the tendency for certain skills to become unnecessary, owing to the displacement of one product or process by another. But this so-called skill obsolescence is only part of a larger, less obvious problem that has been with us for a long time—the tendency for some people to become *less competent,* under certain circumstances, than they have been. True, the productivity of the average worker has been increasing for years, owing mainly to rising educational standards and to improvements in tooling. What is not so widely recognized is how often declines or standstills in individual productivity have acted as a brake upon the rising averages.

Competence is, after all, a relative rather than an absolute quality. It is a matter of being able to do what is expected of one. But these expectations change, and sometimes the things one is able to do change too—in either direction. So competence itself is essentially changeable, not fixed, and we can reasonably expect it to fluctuate to some extent during the course of any man's career. Nevertheless, we have traditionally regarded competence as being rather like a beard; that is, something not acquired until adulthood and never really lost thereafter. Regrettably, it is becoming increasingly clear that competence is more like the hair on top of a man's head, in the sense that it is not necessarily there to stay.

The changeability of competence has been obscured for several reasons. One is that the acceleration of technological change has only recently approached the point at which a man can no longer take it for granted that he will spend his entire working lifetime in one career. Another reason is that in an era when change came more slowly, losses in speed, strength, and adaptability could usually be offset by increases in wisdom. Still another reason is that motivation used to be considerably more stable over a lifetime than it has since become. That is, until fairly recently most men were never really free of the fundamental pressures of job security and income, and accordingly they were unlikely to knowingly permit their income-producing skills to wane. Today income per se is a less crucial problem, and men tend to become concerned with such esoteric motivators as dignity, recognition, and a sense of fulfillment in their work. Like it or not, the tendency is to demand more of one's job and less of one's self; and the result is sometimes a gradual decline in output. We will have more to say about this later, but for the moment it is important to clarify one point: When productivity declines because men are less motivated to produce, the fault is seldom with their moral fiber or with the climate of ideas around them. Rather, the fault is usually with a management that is unable to harness the reservoir of latent motivation that such men represent.

What we will refer to here as "competence loss" has a variety of causes and therefore calls for a variety of remedies. It is a class of problems rather than a single problem for which a single solution can be sought. For convenience' sake, we can refer to a variety of related problems under this single label, but it is neither convenient nor possible to handle them all in the same way. Perhaps it would be best to begin by reviewing what competence loss is *not;* since, despite its relatively recent discovery, it has already begun to be obscured by a mythology of its own.

First and most important, competence loss is not a well-studied, well-understood phenomenon. Despite the tendency of some writers to prescribe for it confidently, it is still very much in the discovery and definition stage. Useful research is only beginning to be reported, and we therefore have to rely heavily on both common sense and a cautious interpretation of common experience.

Second, it is already clear that competence loss is not the inevitable fate of anyone. In many cases it is preventable. To let it occur by default, which is why it usually occurs, is a gross squandering of human talent. Further, the shadow of competence loss can be just as devastating as its substance. This is because managers tend to overreact to it, relegating men who appear to have suffered some degree of loss to positions that are often of considerably less consequence than they are still prepared to handle. This practice is, if anything, more wasteful of talent than competence loss itself.

In particular, competence loss is *not* the lot of older workers in general. To be sure, age is no longer the advantage it once was, since education increasingly offsets experience (rather than vice versa), and wisdom is often no match for being technically up to date. But while older people may, as a group, be more susceptible to competence loss than other age groups, the majority of them compensate quite well for whatever handicaps age itself carries with it.

Therefore the apprehension that is often felt for the older worker in an increasingly sophisticated economy is seldom justified by the available facts. To write off a man's ability to rise to a significant new challenge merely because he has passed a particular birthday is one of the most profitless ways to create a self-fulfilling prophecy.

A third fallacy about competence loss is that it is both epidemic and incurable. Managers tend to diagnose it rather casually—and probably too frequently. We have no satisfactory way of measuring competence loss, and for that reason it often appears to be a much more formidable problem than it really is. To say that it often exists chiefly in the eye of the beholder is not to minimize it, but to place it in a more realistic perspective. The problem is bad enough without making a nightmare out of it.

It is useful to remember that there has been what amounts to an educational revolution in the United States during the lifetime of many men who are still working. Only two generations ago, a high school graduate was considered an educated man. Today college degrees are commonplace and graduate degrees are by no means uncommon. The education that was considered ample to equip an entrant into the labor force in the 1920's and 1930's is, in other words, considered minimal today. And thereby may hang a good deal of what appears, at first blush, to be competence loss. The jobs that are being created in today's economy often presuppose a more extensive exposure to formal education than the jobs that are being eliminated. Consequently, many of the men who are considered incapable of being retrained to handle the newly established jobs may, in reality, never have been educated to the point of readiness to learn them. Their deficiencies are, in short, remediable.

That deficiencies in education are remediable was illustrated in a careful study at International Business Machines Corporation conducted by Walter J. McNamara.[7] The company had embarked on a program of upgrading factory employees from various electromechanical tasks to inspection jobs on computer systems. This program involved 12 weeks of formal training in such subjects as computer organization, transistors, and printed circuits. As might be expected, the trainees selected for this rather costly training were among the best-qualified employees in the plant, from the standpoint of both ability and performance. McNamara's interest, however, was in whether employees who would ordinarily be considered poor risks for such programs—the less well educated and even the less able—could be trained successfully. He therefore deliberately chose a class of trainees from among the *least* promising employees available. They were well below the plant average in tested aptitudes and knowledge. However, since they had all volunteered for a course in which they knew they would be severely challenged, it is reasonable to consider them more strongly motivated than the average employee in similar circumstances.

In addition to the built-in motivational advantages that this class had, McNamara provided two additional educational advantages. One was to lengthen the total classroom time by about 25 percent over the regular courses. This was partially in recognition of the fact that the regular program had been paced for faster learners. However, the main reason for the added time was to permit a special precourse training program in arithmetic fundamentals and basic electricity. These were the subjects on which the training course itself was to be built and in which the trainees' own formal schooling had not given them an adequate background. In effect, the pretraining course brought this class up to the same educational starting line that the regular classes had been able to begin from, simply because they had had the benefit of better schooling.

Not surprisingly, the special class did not do quite as well in the main part of the training program as the regular, better qualified trainees. But they did considerably better, as a class, than would ordinarily be expected of a group that had begun with such handicaps. About two-thirds of them completed the program successfully, which is a very respectable result indeed in view of the problems they faced. Those failures that did occur were due to loss of determination nearly as much as to inability to handle the subjects that were taught.

There is nothing really new in the demonstration that presumably unpromising workers can, given a somewhat greater-than-usual investment and some extra motivation, be upgraded to handle relatively complex work. But McNamara's experiment demonstrated a great deal more than its most obvious finding. What is new and important in this study is its implication about the nature of the handicap that so-called unpromising workers carry. In many cases, this may be, not so much a matter of adaptability that time has taken away from them, as a matter of never having been given certain essential adaptive tools in the first place. The defect may, in other words, have dated from the time they discontinued their schooling and went to work, rather than from a slow erosion of learning ability as they grew older. There is reason to believe that many an old-timer could acquit himself reasonably well in advanced training if he were given some of the basic schooling that he either never got or has forgotten—schooling which the modern youngster with whom he must compete is given more or less routinely. In this sense, a good deal of what seems like irreparable competence loss may be largely a matter of a few missing but easily supplied prerequisites.

If a man cannot be built up to a skill level within reach of the job, sometimes the job can be brought within reach of the man. This was shown in another study at IBM, this one by Ernest F. Bairdain.[8] Once again, the problem was to upgrade the skill level of a group of workers who had been hired and trained for simpler tasks so that they could work on a considerably more sophisticated product line. Most of the workers in this plant were able to make the adjustment to their new jobs without much difficulty. However, Bairdain was concerned about the workers whose abilities did not seem to present a suitable match to the apparent requirements of the new jobs. He approached the problem from the job side by challenging the assumptions that had been made about the skill and ability levels they required.

Detailed analyses were made of the actual demands which various tasks made upon the abilities of the men who performed them. In many cases it was found that the requirements which had usually been assumed were, in fact, unnecessarily high. For example, in one process involving microminiaturized parts, it had usually been considered necessary to perform about 80 percent of the work under microscopes. This meant that most of the employees working in these departments had to have nearly perfect vision. But the new analysis revealed that only about 20 percent of the work really needed to be done with the aid of microscopes and that this portion could be consolidated into a limited number of the jobs. In this way, more jobs could be opened to workers whose vision would have disqualified them under the original distribution of work. Findings such as this in many kinds of jobs enabled the company to take great strides toward overcoming the problems attendant upon the apparent mismatch between people and jobs.

The tendency to overestimate the skill and ability requirements of a job is especially common in new jobs which, because there is little precedent for them, often appear to be more demanding than they really are. Sometimes exaggerated skill requirements persist for years simply because it has never been necessary to challenge them. For example, Bethlehem Steel Company completed a new mill in the Chicago area at about the time that a shortage of skilled labor became acute. The company was therefore obliged to begin operations with many inexperienced and supposedly marginal workers. The mill achieved efficient production much more quickly than had been expected, simply because many of the new workers were able to master their jobs faster than had been anticipated. The point is, of course, that many of them weren't really marginal at all; the requirements of their jobs had been overrated.

So it is clear that men can be underrated or that jobs can be overrated, or both; and for any of these reasons men may seem to be obsolete or incapable when in fact they are not. Even granting the possibility of these errors, there are of course many situations in which the gap between what the individual can really do and what the job really requires is too great to be bridged. In plenty of situations this dilemma is not at all illusory. Bairdain faced the dilemma by trying to change the only element in the picture he could change: the job itself. Those jobs that seemed to be beyond the capabilities of available workers were analyzed, broken down into their components, then restructured in new combinations so that the same manufacturing process was accomplished by a combination of redesigned jobs. Some of these jobs were within the skill limits of workers who might otherwise have been excluded by the original job designs. There is, of course, nothing sacred about *any* job designs; yet somehow they rapidly acquire a thick coating of tradition, and we tend to forget that alternative ways of getting the work done may be just as effective. By assuming, in effect, that jobs *have* to be done in the way they would be done by highly qualified or experienced workers, we relegate many potentially effective workers to an undeserved and at least partially fraudulent category of "incompetence."

The two IBM studies show that the real dimensions of obsolescence and competence loss may be considerably less than they might at first appear, even in processes involving highly sophisticated technologies. It is therefore vitally important to keep the problem in perspective and to avoid leaping either to excessively pessimistic conclusions about human capabilities or to excessively awed conclusions about jobs. Having issued this necessarily lengthy *caveat,* we can proceed to consider forms of competence loss that are neither illusory nor easily corrected.

It is useful to distinguish between three kinds of competence loss. They are all serious, but we will deal with them in descending order of the difficulty of doing anything about them. First, we will consider the person who is no less capable than he ever was, but who works in a field where the standards of productivity have been rising, so that they now exceed his abilities; second, the person whose ability to handle his work has actually decreased; third, motivational problems which, while they last, have the effect of reducing productivity. One seldom encounters a pure case of any one of these problems. They are likely to occur together; like locusts, they bring their relatives with them and thus worsen an already bad situation. But, even though any given individual could suffer simultaneously from more than one of these forms of competence loss, we will consider them separately for the sake of clarity.

Rising productivity standards that eventually have the effect of making a man's output marginal, thereby pricing him out of the market, are usually the result of technological changes of one kind or another. Work may arrive at his bench faster than it did before, or it may require more precise handling than it did before, or the workers to whom his finished work is sent may now be able to handle a larger volume of input than before. For these or similar reasons, an individual whose output has not changed may gradually become less competent, in the sense that he is no longer able to do what is expected of him. When this happens, he is likely to be regarded as an unfortunate but unavoidable victim of progress—rather like the dinosaur that, although just as big and powerful as its earth-ruling ancestors, perished anyway because it could not adapt to climatic changes. The worker in this situation is, in other words, regarded as one of a species headed for extinction, with little if anything that can be done about it.

This rather common point of view has led to much hand wringing over the plight of the ordinary man who either is no match for today's technology or will be no match for tomorrow's. But that whole line of reasoning is very loose. It is by no means a foregone conclusion that the average worker or even the marginal worker must be caught, sooner or later, in the rising waters of technology. Whether this happens may depend as much on management policy as on the limitations of the individuals involved.

When a job demands more in an intellectual or physical sense than an individual is able to contribute to it, his continued employability depends on how readily he can apply his abilities to other jobs. Thus the switching or transfer process, in which capabilities that have been invested through training and experience in one set of skills are reinvested in another set, becomes crucial. This switching process was seldom necessary in the days when a single set of skills sufficed for a lifetime. Consequently, management has had to learn relatively little about them. But it is now clear that a man's ability to transfer to another job what his hands or his eyes or his brains have learned in one job is nearly as important as his ability to learn those same skills in the first place. It is in preparing for one's second job, and for all subsequent jobs, that the ability to capitalize upon prior learning becomes crucial.

If learning transfer is new to industry, it is not new to the psychological laboratory, where it has been studied for years. It has laws of its own, and these laws have two fairly clear-cut implications for management that could minimize this particular form of competence loss. One is rather obvious: The more there are of common elements, or at least similar elements, between the old job and the new, the more easily the transfer occurs. The second is less obvious: The more experience one has had with learning transfers, the more readily they occur.

It would be difficult to overstate the importance of this second point. The ability to learn is not unlike the tone of a muscle, in the sense that if it is not exercised it becomes flabby. People who are not required to learn gradually lose much of their ability to learn. Therefore, any job in which an individual remains for too long (provided it is not inherently varied and changeable) can eventually become a trap, regardless of whether it was originally set at or below the theoretical limit of his capacities.

In other words, a good deal of the form of competence loss that is a concomitant of rising productivity standards is the result of eroded ability to make a transition from old to new skills. And this erosion is the indirect consequence of not having had to make enough transitions in the past. This clearly works against the long-term interests of anyone who has been highly specialized for any length of time, or who has not been exposed periodically to an opportunity to enlarge his skills or knowledge. This form of competence loss is plainly easier to prevent than to cure; but its prevention demands a continual battle with inertia, tradition, and the perfectly natural tendency to leave well enough alone when the penalty for doing so is remote and unclear.

The problem, in brief, is to *avoid* letting too many people learn their jobs too well. Paradoxical as it may seem, it is contrary to the best interests of both the employee and his employer to let a man become so familiar with his job that he can handle it flawlessly. (Actually, this idea is paradoxical only if we forget that the premises have changed: The crucial ability today is the readiness to acquire new skills, not the burnishing of old ones.) Thus the man who can handle his job "with his eyes closed" or "with one hand tied behind his back" is in danger of forgetting how to learn. If he does forget, only luck can save him from eventual obsolescence. Management policy must therefore be directed toward the preservation of what might be called the "learning attitude"—a disturbing awareness of one's ignorance, a fascination with the way fragments of knowledge fall into place, and a confidence in one's ability to master what is not yet understood. This naïve frame of mind is the best possible preserver of adaptability. But how can it be maintained when the learning process itself tends to reduce ignorance, turn the fascinating into the familiar, and build such confidence in what has been learned that further learning seems unnecessary? Does not, in other words, the normal psychology of a man who has held a job for any length of time work against his ability to learn a new one?

To some extent it does. But it would greatly oversimplify human nature to suggest that the learning process eventually turns itself off or that only the naïve are capable of growing and adapting. Some people manage to keep the spark glowing by themselves, usually in hobbies or interests far removed from their work; others may find that an encounter with some new experience reawakens a taste for learning that they had not felt in years. But management cannot afford to assume that its investment in human assets will somehow preserve itself. It cannot expect to maintain its people in a state of adequate readiness to learn new jobs through good luck and nothing else. There must be a definite policy that creates an environment in which most people will encounter enough experiences of the kind that keep the learning attitude alive or that can rekindle it. Without such a policy, the likelihood that changing productivity norms will eventually make people "obsolete" is more than just a danger; it is very nearly a certainty.

A number of specific programs have helped to maintain this kind of environment. The list offered here is intended to be suggestive rather than exhaustive. In all probability, the list will grow considerably longer as managerial ingenuity comes to grips with the problem in various companies and contexts. One useful technique is what is often referred to as "work simplification." Groups of workers are periodically assigned the task of analyzing their own jobs—functioning, as it were, as their own industrial engineers. They examine the jobs they know better than anyone else for the purpose of making them more efficient. This kind of exercise is usually undertaken primarily for the sake of productivity, secondarily to enlist the support of the workers in implementing any changes in methods that may be agreed to by management. But sessions of this kind, if they occur often enough, can have another result that could be more important, in the long run, than today's productivity and cooperation. By requiring men to think analytically and to look for relationships that may not be apparent, work simplification techniques provide them with invaluable practice in skills that must be in good working order if they have to learn new jobs later on.

Another useful technique is what the British sometimes refer to as "seconding"; that is, periodic assignments to tours of duty in job environments wholly different from the one in which the bulk of one's career is spent. There are many variations on this, but they all have the same effect—to present the individual with the necessity of learning enough about a new specialty to be able to function effectively in it. Some examples are assignments to temporary task forces that are organized to deal with particular problems, such as production bottlenecks; assignments as an instructor, troubleshooter, or consultant; or assignment to a wholly new function (for example, from the field to the plant, or vice versa) .

Still another technique involves formal instruction. There is little doubt that the most important thing gained from most refresher courses is not the material that is taught but the refurbishing of learning skills. Technical updating courses, reviews of recent developments, seminars on related technologies or even on wholly non-job-related topics—all these can provide the needed leavening. Timing is perhaps as important a consideration as course content. Courses that are held too rarely are not much better than no courses at all as far as maintaining the learning attitude is concerned. They may, of course, succeed in teaching exactly what they were supposed to teach; but it is not likely that widely separated courses will deliver any bonus benefits. The problem is to time formal instruction, or any other stimulus, in such a way that future learning is likely to be accelerated. There is no evident formula for calculating how often courses or other teaching methods must be used in order to produce the desired enhancing effect on formal retraining. This apparently depends on many factors, including the adaptability and past experiences of the individual and the difficulty of the material he must learn. In general, some kind of vigorous mental exercise at least once every two years does not appear to be excessive for most people, and even more than that would be valuable for technical and professional workers.

To some extent, exposure to formal training will come whether management intends it as a strategy to facilitate new learning or not. The rate at which jobs obsolesce and the need to preserve employability will see to that. But job-retraining courses are unlikely to be sufficiently close together in time to have a facilitating effect upon each other. The half-life of jobs may be getting shorter, but it is not likely to get so short that retraining acquires the kind of velocity that would be needed for enhancement to occur. Yet performance in formal retraining courses is, after all, what we are trying to enhance. Some kind of additional stimulation between courses, as it were, is therefore needed to help insure that men entering formal training will not be too rusty or too set in their ways. In fact, one can foresee that the investment in retraining (and in all subsequent retraining) will eventually become so great that it would be prohibitively expensive *not* to take steps between training periods that can enhance the payout from training itself.

Other changes can also be foreseen. Industrial education may very well grow to such proportions that a thorough revision of all educational scheduling and funding may be necessary. Many people may receive less education in early life and more education in later life than is common today. The demands on educational facilities and personnel will become so great that a more rational allocation will be needed, and the present tendency to overeducate young people to the relative neglect of the educational needs of older people will have to be corrected. Coping with problems of this magnitude will call for imaginative new methods. But that topic is vast enough to deserve a book of its own; in this book we must return to a consideration of competence loss, this time of the type that results from an actual decrease in what the individual is capable of accomplishing.

Thus far we have dealt with forms of competence loss that are the result of a lack of exercise with respect to learning. In its more severe forms, this can lead to an actual handicap in which the individual becomes considerably less able to adapt to a new occupation than he may once have been. However, these are only potential losses, rather than real ones, until some circumstance comes along that demands learning. If the individual is spared that demand, his loss may never become apparent.

Competence loss can also occur *within* an occupation; that is, where no new learning is required. There are relatively few facts to guide us here, so we will have to feel our way into the subject as best we can by means of some informed guesswork. One reason for the scarcity of facts regarding individual competence loss is that it is quite difficult to establish for certain that it has really happened. We seldom have a suitable "before" measure of productivity with which to compare productivity "after" we begin to suspect that competence loss may have occurred. Many jobs do not lend themselves to simple measurements of productivity anyway; and when measuring *can* be done, it is frequently difficult to determine what part to attribute to the individual and what part to other factors—tools, materials, supervision, and so on.

Despite these difficulties, there is no shortage of opinions on the subject, and sometimes these are so unanimous that they are seldom questioned. Probably the most widespread bit of unsupported "common knowledge" about competence loss is that advancing age brings with it a physical and mental decline which eventually renders the individual unable to compete with younger, presumably more vigorous co-workers.

What little we know about the longevity of abilities indicates that most of them decline slowly, if at all, with age; that wisdom and maturity usually increase with age and can therefore offset—sometimes more than offset—any decline in ability; and above all that there is more variability in productivity *within* any age group than there is *between* any two age groups. The latter is perhaps the hardest fact we have to guide us. It strongly suggests that increasing age, in itself, has only a minor tendency to bring about competence loss. Other causes, possibly including some that we haven't even identified yet, are surely more important.

Most physical and mental abilities seem to continue growing until some time during the third decade of life, after which they remain relatively stable or decline slowly until some time during the sixth decade, when a steeper decline may commence. This is true of visual acuity, hearing, muscular strength and coordination, manual dexterity, verbal intelligence, memory, and reasoning. Somewhat faster declines seem to occur in reaction speeds and in learning complex relationships. Yet for every one of these statements it is necessary to add that they refer to averages, not to everyone, and that there is so much variation around those averages that generalizations are dangerous.

Probably the wisest guess that can be made at present about individual competence loss is that it is *abnormal,* rather than a natural result of aging, and that it is caused either by a failure of wisdom to develop at a rate faster than the rate at which strength declines or by some kind of physical or emotional damage. As for the failure of wisdom to accumulate rapidly enough to offset losses of strength, this may result from a lack of "learning exercise," from a lack of learning motivation (which usually dates from childhood, and sometimes reflects the values of the community in which an individual was raised), or from low intelligence. Physical damage includes not only obvious forms, such as blindness and deafness, but subtler forms—such as cerebral arteriosclerosis, or "hardening of the arteries" in the brain—whose impact on job effectiveness sometimes begins long before the individual comes to the attention of a physician. Emotional damage includes the fairly common "unsettled" periods that occur in midlife when some men must finally face the fact that their youthful ambitions are not going to be realized. These problems are worth a textbook in their own right, but they cannot be pursued here except for one note of caution.

One of the toughest problems a manager ever faces is whether to refer an employee to a neurologist or a psychiatrist. Sometimes, symptoms of potentially serious ailments become apparent in work behavior before they are obvious to relatives or friends off the job. Forgetfulness, tendencies to repeat oneself, inattentiveness, and other early outcroppings of what could become serious problems are all more likely to be noticed on the job than elsewhere, because they can directly affect productivity. But they could also have trivial causes, and indeed it is not easy for most laymen to be certain that a man with whom they work has actually become more forgetful, or less attentive, than he used to be. Further, a man who is in fact going through the early stages of a neurologic or psychiatric illness is likely to be at least dimly aware himself that something is wrong, and more often than not he will be frightened by it. To suggest to such a person that he ought to be examined professionally is likely to produce an angry reaction, because the suggestion only reinforces a fear he is probably trying desperately to deny.

There are plenty of good reasons why managers should not play amateur psychiatrist. On the other hand, when competence loss has occurred management needs to know whether it can be corrected or arrested. For that matter, not only the individual's employment security but his own health and safety may be at stake. So the decision as to whether to seek an examination is always a difficult one. Obviously, there can be no hard and fast rules here. But it does make sense for management to review such cases with competent medical consultants who can at least evaluate the evidence, suggest what else to look for, and then advise about the wisdom or the lack of it in asking the individual to be examined. Of course, the entire problem is obviated in companies that provide routine check-ups for employees above a certain age.

Any action that is intended to remedy individual competence loss must be aimed at the root cause, not just the symptom. Consequently, the first requirement for effective action is an accurate diagnosis. This does not necessarily have to be made by a professional, but it does demand a mind that can deal with subtleties and that has no need to oversimplify. Human beings, even when they are foolish or unsophisticated, are exquisitely complex; therefore their behavior can never be understood by simply labeling it. To say that a man "just can't handle his job any more" is not a diagnosis but a confession of failure to search beyond the symptom for its cause. Diagnosing the reasons for individual competence loss demands a willingness to gather facts and an unwillingness to leap to "obvious" conclusions.

Once a diagnosis has been reached that is a reasonable match for the available facts, a tentative plan of action can be prepared. (It has to be tentative, because until it is tried we don't know whether the diagnosis was right.) If the trouble seems to stem from a lack of learning exercise—that is, if the individual is set in his ways—at least one attempt at getting him to change his ways through retraining is usually worthwhile. This is not because the learning attitude is easy to restore (it is not), but because it *is* easy to overestimate the degree to which someone really is set in his ways.

It must be remembered that any individual who has drifted into the habit of *not* learning for any extended period is probably going to be handicapped with respect to new learning. The man whom the years make merely older—not wiser—is in danger of becoming a psychological cripple who will not be able to function effectively outside his own accustomed environment. He needs special treatment in re-education for the same reason that a physically handicapped person needs special treatment: He cannot learn what he has to learn without it. Specifically, he needs more time, more explanation, and more practice than the person with the same basic intelligence who has been using his more steadily. He needs emotional support too: He should not have to compete with younger or abler trainees, and it should be made clear that the function of his instructors is to teach him, not to pass judgment on him. The judgment, if one is necessary, can come later in the environment where he can defend himself best—on the job. Judgments are passed much too casually about such people, anyway. It is too easy to dismiss them as having brought their inflexibility upon themselves, when in reality their work has been so unvaried and overlearned that the necessity of learning has been absent from their lives for years.

When people are capable of learning, but have not done so because they have not been motivated to learn, the cause may lie in one or both of two circumstances. First, they may have learned, usually in childhood, the advantages of *not* learning. This is paradoxical only to people who grew up in communities where learning was the passport to self-respect and therefore to prestige. In communities where people have learned not to expect to achieve self-respect—where they expect, in other words, to be victimized by their environment regardless of what they do to escape it—learning is a passport to frustration and ridicule. It takes a much stronger character to resist the pressures against learning in a depressed community than it does to accept the pressures for learning in one that is not depressed, which is the main reason successful learners emerge so rarely from depressed communities in the first place.

Second, the lack of motivation to learn may have its roots in private defeats in the individual's own past which are not necessarily the common experience of the community from which he comes. He may, in other words, have had more trouble than he could handle during the years when his attitudes toward the learning process were being formed. For example, he may have encountered disparagement, incompetent teaching, or family tensions that overshadowed whatever the school was trying to teach him. Any of these not uncommon experiences, or a combination of them, could turn a basically intelligent child away from learning if they struck too hard or too often.

No matter how someone learns that it is wiser not to learn—that is, that it hurts less to abandon the effort than to persevere—he is for all practical purposes a badly handicapped person. The basic motivational problem is to find a way to change his perception of learning itself—to have him see it as both possible and worthwhile—if *that* is possible. And it must be said that it isn't always possible. But if the change is to be made at all, it has to be done on the basis of a convincing demonstration. You cannot exhort, promise, or inspire intelligent people to commit themselves to something which their entire experience has taught them to avoid. To be convincing, a demonstration must be dramatic, it probably must be repeated fairly often, and above all it must not fail and thereby reinforce the very resistances that need to be loosened.

It is precisely because the requirements of a convincing demonstration are so exacting that the salvage of people who have learned not to learn is sometimes impossible. Whenever someone learns a way to avoid something he wants very much to avoid, that way—that technique of avoidance—acquires an enormous inertia which at best is costly and difficult to overcome. In short, the cards need to be stacked so heavily *in favor* of the individual that the possibility of failure is very nearly ruled out. Consequently, the rehabilitation of anyone with a learning motivation problem is both expensive and risky, to the point where some may wonder whether the uncertain payoff is worth the sums that have to be gambled. The answer depends largely on the intelligence with which those sums are used.

Basically, the motivationally damaged adult needs a chance to take small steps slowly. This means expensive forms of training: small classes; ample time for repetition and for "hands on" training, if that is appropriate; and plenty of personal attention from the instructor. Such labor-saving educational devices as programmed instruction, or even old-fashioned reading assignments, would probably be inappropriate for this type of person, at least until the back of the motivational problem itself has been broken. This is simply because any technique which requires the individual to provide his own motivation would be self-defeating with a person whose intuitive reaction to study is to avoid it.

Breaking the back of a motivational block can take a long time. In addition to demonstrating to the individual that he *can* learn, it is also necessary to show him that learning pays off. Sometimes this can be done effectively, if not elegantly, by making it clear that failure to make the transition successfully could lead to a downgrading in pay or even to being laid off. But "motivation" that is essentially a threat works best with people who are goaded, not routed, by threats. The kind of person we have been describing is more likely to accept defeats passively, as if they were inevitable, than to make a good hard try to avoid them. This is why motivational problems of this type can seldom be attacked successfully unless job security can, for all practical purposes, be taken for granted. Thus the payoff for learning must consist of something extra, something over and above the mere preservation of employability. Some possible extra rewards would be more attractive or more prestigeful work or the possibility of higher pay. The practical problems of implementing such a motivational policy for costly, high-risk training programs are both obvious and severe. And that is why the scrap heap is where so many basically good minds end up—minds that have been frightened, for one reason or another, of taking on the challenge of learning.

Sometimes wisdom fails to accumulate because the individual is poorly equipped to accumulate it; that is, he is not adequately endowed with that marvelous and ill-understood something that psychologists call "intelligence." Although this faculty that most people (and some other animals too) have for benefiting from their experience has had more concentrated study than any other aspect of behavior, we can still do little more than describe it. We don't really know, except in a gross way, what it is or what causes it. But we do know that it is a potential, in the same sense that the energy of water stored behind a dam is a potential until it is fed into penstocks. There is, in other words, a certain amount of leeway in dealing with intelligence: People are seldom using all they have. The problem, in brief, is to "feed it into the penstocks"—to get people to use more of the intelligence they were born with.

Another thing we know about intelligence is that it has both biological and social roots. Some people are evidently born with more of this potential than others, but the extent to which they actually use it seems to depend largely on the kinds of experiences to which they have been exposed, especially in early life. In addition, there are certain kinds of diseases and injuries which can have the effect of reducing the potential, but these need not detain us here.

To say that a person has low intelligence is actually to make a rather complex statement, and therefore it should never be made lightly. We have to ask, "Low relative to what?" and, "What do you mean by 'intelligence'?" In this case, the only answers that really make sense are, "Low relative to the minimum level at which people can be employed economically in this particular occupation," and, "In this context, intelligence is the ability to minimize errors and maximize productivity on the basis of on-the-job experience." In spite of this complexity, the diagnosis of low intelligence is often made entirely too lightly.

For example, people are written off as "just not having it" (presumably "it" means intelligence) for reasons more often casual than

profound. Thus to fail to grasp a point immediately when it may
have been foggily made, to persist in errors that have never been
clearly pointed out as errors, or to disagree with ideas whose premises have never been clearly spelled out—any of these can lead to the
rather unintelligent decision that a man who is not a mind-reader is
not intelligent. But the "diagnosis," once made, tends to persist, and
for this reason the decision to write off a man's chances of regaining
a satisfactory competence level because he "isn't intelligent enough"
is always suspect.

As with every other aspect of competence loss, the first two stratagems here are to challenge the diagnosis and then, if the diagnosis
survives, to try to minimize its effects by moving the individual
closer to the top of his own capabilities. A sizable number of seeming problems can be cleared up through a combination of this kind
of skepticism and insistence on more-than-ordinary efficiency. But
after both stratagems have had their day, there will still be quite a
few people who are not so easily salvaged, because they really are
limited in their ability to turn their experience into wisdom. And
the salvage of these people rests on the successful redesign of both
the jobs they are assigned to do and the ways in which they are
trained to do them.

Because people who are intellectually handicapped are obviously
unable to handle complex assignments, there is a tendency for management to overcompensate for their deficiencies by assigning them
to work that is well below the limits of even their modest abilities.
But people who are not as bright as most can become just as bored
as most other people when their work fails to challenge them. The
main difference is likely to be a less intelligent reaction to the boredom. Instead of striking at the roots of their problem by trying to
alter the job, they are likely to rebel against it and find ways of
doing it *less* efficiently. Thus they may compound the felony; yet
they were innocent of the felony itself. No solution to problems of
this kind is likely to be lasting if it tries to cope with such people at
their own level—by attempting, in other words, to suppress their
reaction with threats or other pressures.

When it becomes necessary to reassign such a person or to restruc-
ture his job—because, presumably, he has fallen below the rising
level of acceptable competence in his original job—it is vitally important not to commit the felony of underutilizing him. On the

other hand, it is always wise to allow a margin for error in setting the difficulty level of a redesigned job. Thus the question arises as to whether it is wiser to make the first approximation on the high side, so that any adjustments are likely to be in the direction of less difficulty, or on the low side, so that any adjustments are likely to involve increasing the difficulty level. In general, the latter course is probably wiser, if only to avoid the discouragement that a further downgrading could bring.

Training methods for the less intelligent worker should emphasize supervised practical experience, as opposed to classroom teaching and textbook study. The necessity for remembering material that will not be used frequently should be obviated, whenever possible, by eliminating the nonrepetitive aspects of the job. The conditions under which the worker would be expected to alter his routine behavior (for example, to turn off a machine or to summon his supervisor) should be few in number and easily identified. There should be plenty of stress on rote memory and on overlearning—that is, repetition to the point where the correct response becomes almost automatic, requiring little if any memory-search or decision making. Above all, ample time should be allowed for training.

This prescription for training the mentally handicapped worker is in many respects diametrically opposed to what we have been preaching throughout this book: that most people are more effectively motivated when more is expected of them than when their assigned work is well within the limits of what they know they can do. But most people are not mentally handicapped; and right there, in that almost absurdly obvious little truism, lies the crux of one of management's most serious motivational problems. Most jobs should not be designed in ways that minimize the exercise of intelligence. With the exception of those relatively few people for whom mental exercise leads rapidly to overexertion, it is much wiser to design difficulty, variety, and challenge into most jobs. The result will not necessarily be "happy" workers, but in most cases they will be more involved in and more committed to their work than they can be when their jobs are too easy for them.

Sometimes problems which are essentially motivational, rather than educational or intellectual, can bring about a condition of competence loss which is as temporary or as permanent as the motivational problem itself. These range considerably in both variety and severity. Three of the more common types of motivationally induced competence loss are the problem of the chronic "underachiever"; the attitude that there is nothing to be gained by preserving one's competence level; and what might be called "reactive incompetence"—that is, a catastrophic loss of effectiveness resulting from some extreme form of stress.

One of the likeliest victims of rising competence levels is the person who has never been entirely convinced of his own competence in the first place. Any success at all takes such people by surprise, and sometimes success is not enough to erase their own doubts about their abilities. When new demands are placed on those abilities—for example, when their jobs are to be upgraded—they may shrink from attempting it. Or more likely, they may become so well prepared, mentally, for the "inevitable" failure that it seems futile to try very hard to avoid it. By continually discounting their own chances in this manner, such people manage to accomplish considerably less than they are actually capable of.

Sometimes their problem will be obvious, as in the case of the highly trained student who never manages to put his training to productive use. But many other underachievers are unsuspected, because the world accepts their own greatly diminished concept of their potentialities. They seem, in other words, to be properly positioned, and they give no indication of possessing untapped reservoirs of ability. Thus the fact that they are functioning well below the level of their capacity is masked and may not become apparent until they start falling behind the normal pace of growth.

Problems of this kind tend to be chronic, going back a long way into the individual's history. That is why they are very hard to deal with. Professional counseling sometimes helps. For management, the most important consideration is a prompt diagnosis. When this type of person is at the point of failure—that is, when he has been presented with the challenge of growth and has not responded to it—he is commencing a retreat which, if not checked, can turn into a rout. He may be prepared, in other words, to abandon the plateau of competence on which he had been resting and withdraw to a lower plateau, rather than hazard the climb to a higher one. Checking the retreat is primarily a matter of getting some personalized help and reassurance to him in a hurry, before his pattern of overestimating challenges and underestimating his ability has had time to harden. This is easier said than done. That is why, as the pace of technological change continues, many more underachievers will be discovered resting comfortably on competence plateaus well below the level of their real abilities.

Sometimes a man may see little advantage in increasing, or even in preserving, his competence level. This may happen when the penalty for failing to grow is not particularly severe—as, for example, in the case of people whose incomes are protected and who therefore are not dependent on their personal earning power. It may also happen when the reward for increased competence seems too remote. If a man does not really expect to be employed in a particular trade—because jobs are scarce, or because he considers himself unable to compete for them, or because he expects to be victimized by discrimination—he probably won't try very hard to learn that trade. Sometimes, upgrading one's employment also means uprooting one's way of life—relocating, changing hours, or even just submitting to the disciplines of regular employment—and these changes may actually make an upgraded job seem less attractive than an underpaid, underutilized status quo. But perhaps the most important reason why men may profess to see little gain in adding to their competence is rationalization: They are trying to convince themselves that they don't really want the thing they fear they cannot get—or could not accept if they did get it.

Most people in these situations are likely to be considered lazy, and "laziness" is one of those poorly thought-out labels that have acquired the ring of finality. Someone who is lazy is presumably incorrigibly addicted to not exerting himself. But laziness is no more inherent in man than diligence. From the standpoint of motivation, men are lazy or diligent for essentially the same reason—it seems to them advantageous to be one or the other. Both are habits; both are learned. The ease or difficulty of changing them therefore depends on how strong the habits are, and that in turn depends largely on how long they have been habits. Thus the attitude that "there's nothing in it for me" ("it" being a competence gain) is most easily combated in the young or the recently discouraged and is much more difficult to deal with when it has become ingrained.

Sometimes life deals harder blows than a man is prepared to withstand. When this happens—especially when a number of these misfortunes occur more or less simultaneously—it may trigger a decline in productivity. This is especially likely when one of the blows was dealt by the job itself, as in the case of a demotion or a dismissal. The essential motivational message of such an event is that somebody in the environment does not have confidence in you. If that kind of message reaches a man whose own confidence has already been shaken—perhaps by events in his private life—the combination may be enough to disorganize his customary ideas about himself. He is then compelled to seek out a less demanding role for himself, one that can be more easily sustained than the one which his experience had invalidated. The result is likely to be a more timid and tentative approach to work. In all probability, his productivity will fall away sharply.

Whether this sort of reactive incompetence is temporary or permanent depends on whether the man's original self-concept can be restored, or to put it more simply, on whether he can regain his original confidence. The best guarantee that he will is the possession of a basically strong character that can reknit and rebuild itself once an abnormal period of adversity has passed. Since not everyone is built that way, the next best guarantee of recovery is a management that can deliver a blow to a man's ego without shattering it. What is needed, in other words, is a sufficiently open relationship with a man to allow for telling him convincingly that, while the action taken against him was justified, it by no means precludes a re-advancement if he is determined to earn it. However, management of such quality is rather rare, and for that reason the most common approach to reactive incompetence is to leave the individual to work his own way out of it as best he can. Unfortunately, he may only work his way more deeply into it. That is why it is so important, whenever a man's effectiveness declines sharply after some kind of blow to his self-esteem, to reassure him that his future performance has not been prejudged. Failure to do that—and to mean it—is tantamount to writing off an asset that might otherwise have had considerable value.

Chapter 9

Money for Membership

THE BEHAVIORAL SCIENTIST HAS HAD SURPRISINGLY LITTLE
to say about the motivating power of money. This is not because he
considers it unimportant but rather because he has not yet defined
this power to his own satisfaction. This puts him in the unique position of knowing that he does not really know precisely how and why
money affects the motivation of working people. On the other hand,
nearly everyone else "knows"; that is, they know the standard folklore about money which has endured, largely unquestioned, since
the dawn of the Industrial Revolution. By this reckoning, money is
supposed to be the main reason, if not the only one, that most people have for working at all. Hence motivation is supposed to consist
largely of knowing how to dangle money as artfully as possible before the eyes of one's subordinates.

The behavioral scientist knows that the folklore about money
cannot begin to explain the facts. But until recently he has addressed the problem of money only as a side-issue—something tan-
gential to his main interests. There are encouraging signs that the
long-overdue research assault upon the problem of money is now
beginning in earnest. If this happens, we will be able to analyze the
motivating power of money with considerably more certainty and
precision a few years from now than we can today. But as of now, we
have to be guided by a few scattered facts, some researchers' insights

that have the ring of truth, and as much common sense as we can muster.

Perhaps the first bit of folklore we should dispose of concerns the behavioral science position on the importance of money. This has sometimes been misinterpreted as suggesting that money doesn't really matter, or that management can "buy" motivation at a lower price by adroitly manipulating other needs. What the behavioral scientists have actually said is rather complex, as befits the nature of the subject, but they have in no way relegated money to a minor role in motivation. In saying that the myth of monetary omnipotence is just that—a myth—they have not suggested that money is impotent. On the contrary, money appears to have considerable untapped motivating power, chiefly because it is not often administered as an effective motivating tool today.

It has been shown repeatedly that when managers are asked to rate the various factors that motivate their subordinates, money will nearly always be at or near the top of the list. When their subordinates are asked to rate their own motives, on the other hand, money is usually ranked below such factors as job security, job interest, and agreeable workmates. The question as to which is "right" is neither answerable nor important. Both groups are reporting the reality they choose to see.

In the manager's case, he may hear complaints about wages, but he is considerably less likely to hear complaints about, say, job interest. Accordingly, his experience tells him that employees are interested primarily in money, no matter what they may say to a researcher. Further, the manager usually has more control over an employee's income than over, say, the social aspects of his job; and it is natural that he be more impressed by a tool he actually has at hand than by esoteric matters he can hardly influence at all. In the employee's case, the implication that a man may have a "price" at which he would sacrifice his self-respect or peace of mind is not likely to jibe with his favorite ideas about himself. Since he is seldom faced with an actual choice between money and some other value, he reports truthfully that some of those other values seem more important to him than money.

If importance is only a matter of what people *say* it is, they are clearly free to contradict each other, and therefore *both* managers and subordinates are right. But if we choose to interpret importance in terms of the visible consequences of a reward upon people's behavior, it quickly becomes apparent that money's importance is quite complex; that is, it is an influencing factor in many areas, and its importance is greater in some areas than in others. We will explore that complexity in some detail, but we should note that there are no simple, factual answers to questions on the importance of money. Simple questions seldom have simple answers in the behavioral sciences; mankind just wasn't designed that way.

We ought to begin by defining the terms that will have to be used frequently in exploring the motivating potentialities of money. Much of the existing misinformation is traceable to the use of different terms interchangeably, especially the terms "satisfaction" and "motivation." We happen to know considerably more about the former than we do about the latter. This has sometimes led to the comforting illusion that the answers to management's questions about the motivating power of money have already been filed away in the behavioral scientists' notebooks. They haven't.

There is nothing correct or official about the definitions we will propose here. They are simply the key to our private code—that is, we are stating what these two terms will refer to in the remainder of this discussion. The semantics will be disposed of as briefly and painlessly as possible. Alas, it is quite necessary to go into them. Without clear definitions, any analysis of how money can best be applied to motivation is likely to bog down quickly and irretrievably.

For our purposes, *motivation* will refer to any influence that causes an individual consciously to select a course of action for himself other than one he might have chosen in the absence of that influence. Thus a motivator is something that changes the balance of forces affecting an individual's decisions. It makes a difference; its presence is felt. Something that is done for the purpose of altering someone else's behavior, but that does not have the intended effect, would not fit our definition. It may be a distraction or it may be no more than a futile gesture, but it would not in any case be motivation.

By insisting on this strict definition—that motivation has to make a visible difference in behavior—we can avoid a good deal of need-less and perhaps meaningless argument. True, we have taken a certain liberty with ordinary language—which after all permits words to carry a variety of nuances—by restricting this word to only one of its several meanings. We have deliberately excluded a great many factors to which the individual is exposed, but which are too subtle or too unimportant to produce a change in his overt behavior.

We will use *satisfaction* to describe events that lead to subjective feelings of relief or pleasure which can be reported by the person who experiences them, but which cannot be observed directly by anyone else. A satisfier, then, is something that makes people feel better than they would feel without it, but does not necessarily change their outward actions. Of course, some experiences can have both effects; that is, they can both satisfy (produce subjective plea-sure) and motivate (change behavior). Perhaps this inconvenient bit of reality should compel us to take another liberty with the lan-guage and coin some hybrid term like "satisfier/motivator" to de-scribe experiences having both effects. The language would then be much the worse for our efforts, but we would at least have separated phenomena that cannot be known in the same ways. (It is a pity that in order for our psychology to get better, our rhetoric some-times has to get worse. But since this book is for managers more than it is for psychologists, we will compromise the language no fur-ther.)

Now, armed with our new definitions, what can we say about money to the manager who is interested in managing by motiva-tion? The answers may at first be rather disappointing. Monetary re-wards, as they are typically used by most organizations, are not very effective motivators. The behavior they affect is more likely to con-cern *membership* in the organization than contributions to its effec-tiveness or profitability. That is, money is used chiefly as an induce-ment for people to join an organization and to stay in it. They, in turn, may choose to leave the organization because of monetary op-portunities elsewhere or to take a kind of partial leave of it (by means of strikes or slowdowns) when they are dissatisfied with their incomes.

Management's typical strategy with regard to money is designed to keep the organization adequately manned, rather than to make optimal use of the talents and potentialities of its manpower. Implicit in this strategy is a key assumption about the sources of productivity which has never been tested adequately. This assumption is that growth in profits or efficiency comes chiefly from improvements in equipment or in the organization of work and only secondarily, if at all, from the increased contributions of people in the organization. People are regarded as a necessary and costly but on the whole static and unimprovable factor in productivity. Not many managements would subscribe to this statement, yet few administer their pay programs in ways that are inconsistent with it, either.

In most organizations, money is distributed more with an eye to keeping the peace within the corporate household than as a device for encouraging efficiency. Witness the emphasis that most compensation programs place upon equitability: Job rating and wage surveys are, in the last analysis, devoted to justifying any one individual's pay relative to any other individual's. There are sound reasons for doing this, and we will explore some of them presently. But for the moment, let us simply note that organizations are constrained in their pay practices by considerations of equitability, with the effect that pay motivates joining, staying, or leaving to a considerably greater extent than it motivates individual or group productivity. The point we hope to prove, or at least support, is that it is not equitability but management's underlying assumptions about the potential contribution of people that limit the motivating effect of money upon productivity. Let it be clear that what we are finding deficient is not the motivating power of money itself but rather the ways in which it is usually employed.

Before attacking the question of motivation, which will have to be done somewhat speculatively, it would be wise to devote the remainder of this chapter to a review of what is known about the relationship of money to *satisfaction*. We are on a firmer factual basis here than we will be in discussing motivation. There are two reasons why this is so: First, because of management's preoccupation with adequate manning and the hard lessons it has learned about the effects of dissatisfaction, there has been ample support for research in this area. Second, behavioral scientists themselves have tended to give more attention to satisfaction than to motivation because measurements of satisfaction are much easier to obtain, and perhaps also because of a tendency to assume—incorrectly—that attitudes are inevitably translated into actions. We will consider three major aspects of monetary satisfaction: the tendency of dissatisfaction to recur, equitability, and secrecy.

Satisfaction from money results primarily from an *increase* in income, not from income itself. Most people are, in a sense, ingrates. They regard their current income level as something they have already earned, rather than as something to be especially savored or appreciated. Thus the fact that an employer may pay his employees quite well relative to the outside labor market will not, as a rule, make his employees feel particularly grateful. It may motivate them to stay, however, and that is often more important than gratitude. But it is the *experience* of an earnings increase that provides them with satisfaction—and perhaps even with some temporary feelings of gratitude as well. It is the *anticipation* of an increase that provides them with excitement and perhaps even with an incentive to help it happen through conspicuous effort or diligence. It is the *lack* of an increase, when one is expected, that causes dissatisfaction.

The expectation of an earnings increase tends to recur. This is a stubborn and extremely important fact of life for the organization's compensation manager. The expectation recurs periodically, almost regardless of income level, effort, or accomplishment. Pay increases interrupt the cycle, but only temporarily. Many people therefore spend more time being dissatisfied with their incomes than they spend being satisfied with them. Even people who are relatively well paid, in terms of objective indices, will spend a significant part of their careers in a state of relative dissatisfaction with their pay.

We don't really know very much about the reasons for this recurrent dissatisfaction. One explanation that probably does *not* hold water is the notion advanced by some marketing strategists that man has an insatiable appetite for upgrading his standard of living. No doubt there is always more that one could ask for; but the more one has the more it takes to seem like more. The size of the income increase needed to produce a notable improvement in an already high standard of living is, in other words, improbably large.

Probably the best guess that can be made now about the recurrence of dissatisfaction with pay is that it is primarily a psychological rather than an economic phenomenon. To be sure, inflation can reduce purchasing power, and a rising income can bring an individual within buying range (especially through the use of credit) of goods he had not previously aspired to. But dissatisfaction with income recurs even in the absence of inflation or rising purchase aspirations. Its causes must therefore be sought primarily in the inner workings of the individual, not in the inner workings of the economy.

The recurrence of income dissatisfaction is probably related to the fact that money tends to take on various nonfinancial meanings for most people. That is, in addition to representing a medium of exchange, which is ostensibly its only purpose, money can also become a symbol of other values. Intrinsically, money is nothing more than a symbol. Even its economic function is to represent real goods or services that cannot be carted about as easily as money can. Because its function is only symbolic to begin with, there is almost no limit to the variety of *other* symbolic meanings money can acquire. To some people money seems to represent social respectability; to others it may mean recognition for achievement; to still others it stands for worldliness, materialism, and "the root of all evil." The important point is that, since money can represent so many other values, a periodic heightening in the individual's need for any of them can serve to create dissatisfaction with current income.

Even if money is inherently without a meaning of its own, it is tangible. On the other hand, the various values it tends to symbolize are intangible. Since most people are not very introspective they focus their attention on the tangible symbol rather than on the intangible reality. When they feel insecure, for example, they seek money to make them feel secure again; but what they *experience* is not a lack of security but a lack of money. The memory of past satisfactions is not, for most people, a particularly attractive substitute for current satisfactions. Hence the various intangible needs represented by money tend to grow gradually more acute as the memory of past satisfactions fades. As people thus grow less secure, less certain of their prestige, or less convinced that their efforts are appreciated—indeed, as *any* need which has become symbolically tied to money grows stronger—satisfaction is sought through the symbol.

So monetary dissatisfaction tends to recur, with or without valid economic arguments regarding purchasing power or equitability with the pay of others. Even if this tendency does not have economic roots, it has pronounced economic consequences. Unless productivity can keep abreast of wage increases, profits erode or prices rise—or both.

The recurrence of income dissatisfaction is such an obvious and uncomfortable fact of life that it has tended to obscure the potentialities of income as a motivator. Managements tend to accept the notions that pay functions chiefly as a dissatisfier and that the main purpose of compensation policy should be to minimize frictions and damp down the passions that arise whenever pay dissatisfactions become acute. They accept these notions because their own experience has confirmed them. But this is tantamount to concluding that the patient is incurable and that we should be content with suppressing his symptoms instead of trying to restore his health. In other words, pay policies that are designed to still the tumult of dissatisfaction do not, in themselves, provide an adequate test of man's ability to respond to positive financial motivation. To emphasize equitability (satisfaction) to the effective preclusion of incentives (motivation) is simply to create a self-fulfilling prophecy. If you pay people to keep them from becoming too unhappy, rather than to direct their efforts toward selected results, money will function chiefly as an antidote to chronic monetary dissatisfaction.

Although many pay programs include a consideration of performance or "merit," the actual fraction of total pay that is clearly attributable—in the recipient's eyes—to his own efforts tends to be too small to have a practical effect on his behavior. The great bulk of his pay tends to be determined by his entry level and the number, not the size, of the increases he has received since then, and he knows it. Later we will return to this question of influence ratio—that is, the proportion of total pay which an individual believes himself able to influence—because it could have considerably more significance than may at first appear. For the moment, suffice it to say that most employees probably regard their pay as the price they can command for remaining in their organizations, not as an inducement to excel in their work.

The principal reason why pay is administered in a manner that pacifies rather than motivates is that organizations find it necessary to maintain equitability. This is a somewhat complex concept, having roots in both economics and psychology, and not too well understood in either. From an economic standpoint, employers who compete with each other for various forms of labor create what is, in effect, a market; and this market is subject to price movements similar to those of most other markets. Thus the employer whose pay scale is below the prevailing rate must be satisfied with marginal employees, whereas the employer who raises the price he will pay above the prevailing scale can probably skim the cream from the available supply. In the process, he will probably force other employers to follow suit, provided he can continue to pay the higher price. Others will follow suit because their own employees would feel, otherwise, that they were being underpaid. Perhaps they were content with their pay before the disturbing element—a higher price paid for similar work by another employer—was introduced. But, human nature being what it is, they are unlikely to interpret the new price as an overevaluation of their services by the other employer. Instead, they are likely to see it as proof of an underevaluation by their own employer.

This is why employers follow each other's pay practices as closely as they do, and it is also why the range of pay scales for comparable jobs tends to become compressed. In effect, the need to maintain equitability between different organizations produces a sort of standardization of pay. The exceptionally capable man probably can always command a somewhat higher price elsewhere if he wants to, and the exceptionally labor-hungry employer can probably always detach a few people from other organizations by offering them a high enough premium for joining him. But for the great mass of employees, the monetary advantages that may be gained by changing employers tends to be marginal; and *that is exactly what the system is designed to accomplish.*

From a psychological standpoint, equitability is more likely to be related to comparisons between individuals than to comparisons between organizations. Pay, as we have noted, serves to symbolize important needs. It also happens to be issued in precisely measurable units—dollars and cents—which make it an extremely handy (even if spurious) way to compare people according to any of those important needs. A man's income is hardly a reliable index of his worthwhileness as an individual, but it is a convenient index of that and of any other value one may care to measure. Therefore it is used as a way of establishing where one stands relative to other people. Pay comparisons have a considerable impact on self-respect; although this fact may be lamentable, it is a fact nonetheless.

As a consequence, pay comparisons that the individual finds difficult to reconcile with his own favorite ideas about himself can arouse some of his most powerful, most goading emotions. What is at stake for him, in brief, is not merely a few dollars but his ability to live comfortably with himself. It would be entirely natural for most men to run risks for the sake of preserving this ability, even if their defensiveness is triggered by some trivial difference in pay. Indeed, it would be rather unhealthy if they did not. Thus even an individual whose financial needs are being met, in the sense that the standard of living he can afford is acceptable to him, may still become dissatisfied—even acutely, angrily dissatisfied—with his income. This is most likely to happen if he feels inequitably paid *relative to someone else.*

Much of what we know with any certainty about the processes by which people decide whether their pay is equitable derives from a group of studies which J. Stacy Adams did for the General Electric Company.[9] According to Adams, there is a rather pronounced tendency for industrial workers to select people whose pay is *higher* than their own for standards of comparison on pay. In other words, most workers tend to rate their own jobs more highly than the job-rating system does, and this results in rather widespread feelings that one's own pay is inequitable. There is no reason to believe that this tendency to equate one's job with others at a higher pay level is peculiar to General Electric. On the contrary, it seems to be a normal, if difficult, characteristic of human nature.

In equating one's own job with those at a higher level, what is really being asserted is a denial that one is less deserving than those who seem to have been given somewhat better treatment. To feel otherwise would call for considerably more humility than most people can muster. Theoretically, the seeming inequity could be eliminated by reducing the pay of the higher-paid group or by holding it constant while the lower-paid group is allowed to catch up. But this is not only administratively difficult; it would also be psychologically unsatisfying. Once the invidious comparison has been made, it constitutes a sort of wound in each offended person's ego. Such a wound is healed, not by wounding someone else's ego (through wage reduction), but rather by giving the "wounded" party the same treatment as the person with whom he feels unjustly compared. This not entirely rational bit of perfectly normal psychology is at the root of Adams' finding that most people compare upward—not sideways or downward—in trying to determine whether their own wage is fair.

The consequences of comparing upward can be serious. For example, Adams has shown that employees who feel there is an unfair discrepancy between their pay and that of the group they select for comparison have a quit rate about double that of employees who either see no such discrepancy or do not regard it as excessive. In unorganized plants, those who consider their pay inequitable relative to some higher-paid group are much more likely to favor unionization than are employees who perceive no such inequity. Indeed, one has only to examine the history of wage negotiations in recent years to see the disruption caused when one craft union breaks through to new wage levels, and other groups react by trying either to catch up or to reassert a previous position of superiority over the breakthrough group.

However, Adams has evidence to show that the concept of equity is not entirely capricious. It does seem to have an underlying logic of its own. Briefly, what seems to occur is a rough comparison of "ratios" between, on the one hand, one's own pay to the value of one's services, and on the other hand, the same ratio for the person chosen for comparison. In most cases, this comparison is of course *very* rough, since neither the pay level nor the nature of the work being done by the other fellow is likely to be known accurately. But despite its inaccuracy, this kind of ratio seems to serve as the basis for most people's attempts to assess the fairness or equity of their pay. Obviously, if there were a way to rate the comparative value of jobs that everyone would subscribe to, questions of equitability would long ago have ceased to be of particular importance. But there is not, and perhaps there never will be, such a method. The reason lies not so much in the limitations of various methods of job evaluation as in the unwillingness of most humans to concede that the value of what they do is less than that of people whom they choose to consider their peers.

Before passing from this consideration of equitability, we should note that one behavioral scientist has hit upon a way of relating jobs to wages that may, eventually, at least partially disprove what we have just said. He is Dr. Elliot Jaques, an English psychologist whose work with Glacier Metals Company has led to the concept of "time span of discretion." [10] Briefly, Jaques has found that most jobs can be rated in terms of the maximum period of time that is likely to elapse before it could be established by an employee's superior that his subordinate's work was less than satisfactory. The employee's "time span," then, is the period during which he is for all practical purposes on his own. In lower-level jobs, the time span may be only a matter of minutes; in professional or executive jobs it may run into weeks or even years.

By following some six dozen employees of Glacier over a period of many years, Jaques has arrived at two conclusions about time span which are potentially very important. First, although time span tends to increase as the individual grows older and presumably wiser, it has different rates of growth for different people. This is evidently correlated in some way with ability. That is, those people who are entrusted with relatively long-time-span jobs at an early age tend to move into longer-time-span jobs at a more rapid rate than those who, at the same early age, were entrusted with comparatively shorter-time-span jobs. Or to put it more simply, the sooner a young man proves himself able to shoulder responsibility, the more quickly is he likely to be given more of it and the greater the load of responsibility he will ultimately be able to carry. The theory is intriguing, especially since it seems to fit in with the biographical studies of managers reviewed in an earlier chapter. But it obviously needs to be tested in a wider variety of companies, and even countries, before we can lean upon it as a guide to action. This is what Jaques is now attempting to do. But the growth rate of time spans is not the point that is most crucial to our consideration of equitable payment.

Jaques' second and, for our purposes, more crucial finding is that when people are asked to estimate the level of pay which they would regard as equitable for the job they are doing at present, their answers tend to be highly correlated with time span. In other words, as time span increases, so does the level of pay which the job-holder regards as fair for his particular job; and the *rate of increase* of both time span and equitable pay is about the same. Thus Jaques has been able to plot both time span and equitable pay on a set of coordinates, from which he has been able to estimate the *earnings progression* that the individual would presumably consider equitable. This means that if a man's level of responsibility grows at about the rate that Jaques, knowing the man's time-span history to date, would project, and if it can be assumed that any pay adjustments resulting from cost-of-living changes would be distributed so as to leave everyone in the same position relative to one another, then the level of pay which that man will regard as equitable at any future point in his career may be calculated in advance.

The implications of Jaques' theory, if it can be verified, are a bit chilling. But that in itself is not a valid reason for rejecting them. It may turn out to be true that—if equitability is to be the only, or at least the chief, criterion of what a man should be paid—his lifetime earnings potential may be estimated once we know how quickly he is able to take on increased responsibility for the management of his own work. But assume, for the moment, that Jaques is right: How much leeway is then left for the operation of money as a motivator? (Remember our definition of a motivator: Something that affects an individual's overt actions.) The answer depends on how large a role is assigned to equitability in determining pay. It is clear that if the overwhelming emphasis currently given to equitability continues, money (assuming Jaques is right about equitable pay being tied to the growth of time span) will do scarcely any motivating at all. Indeed, one could argue that it is not really doing very much motivating now.

The pressure for equitability is likely to constitute a more or less permanent constraint upon management's policies with regard to pay. This is hardly to be questioned, and therefore the practical question facing us is not whether to lament this fact, but whether it leaves us any leeway. In other words, can we, without violating the principle of equitability, administer pay in ways that will give it a significant motivating effect with a significant part of the employed population? I think we can, but it will be *very* difficult to do; so difficult that we are unlikely to attempt what must be done unless we ourselves are strongly motivated to try it.

As a small contribution to acquiring that motivation, let us consider four likely effects of continued undiluted emphasis on equitable pay:

    1. A general compression of wage rates, and with it an increasingly marginal pay advantage of one level of respon-

sibility over another. This means that the motivation to qualify for advancement will have to come largely from nonfinancial sources. In a sense this is already true in many firms, especially at higher pay levels. But as money becomes progressively less significant as a motivator, fewer people will be reached by whatever motivators remain and at least some of them will be reached less effectively.

2. A tendency of wage structures to move more or less simultaneously, so that the relationships between jobs change little if at all. Pay levels will tend to move in lock step, with whatever inequities and inflexibilities may be retained becoming more or less permanently fixed.

3. A great deal of difficulty in upgrading the relative pay position of groups which may, in the future, be recognized as making more of a contribution than they did in the past. This in turn will make it harder to divert manpower —especially scarce or highly talented manpower—into occupations for which there may be an increased economic need. (Consider, for example, the difficulties in attracting a sufficient number of men into the teaching profession.)

4. Difficulty in introducing new occupational groups at pay levels that are noticeably out of line with those of traditional groups. We must assume that technology will continue to generate new occupations; the best recent example is computer programmers. Attracting enough qualified manpower into such new professions is difficult enough when the wage market functions so as to permit an economic motive to operate. It would be that much more difficult without one.

Altogether, then, the long-range effects of continued emphasis on equitability, to the relative exclusion of individual variation in performance, are likely to be inflexible pay structure, an impeded flow of manpower into and between occupations, and a relatively inefficient use of the dollars paid out in salaries.

This is not to say that people whose pay is determined primarily by equitability will not be motivated to work efficiently. It is only to suggest that if they are so motivated, it will not be because of money. Further, among those who display no such motivation to be productive, it may be that at least some of them could be reached by the prospect of a clear-cut monetary pay-off. Elsewhere we have given considerable attention to nonfinancial motivators, and rightly so. But they will not become less important if money can be administered in a way that makes it more important as a motivator. On the contrary, the strongest and most enduring forms of motivation are found when several motivators—both financial and nonfinancial—can interact and reinforce one another.

There has been considerable controversy in recent years about another aspect of pay satisfaction: secrecy. Most organizations that are not compelled by law or by contract to publish their pay schedules do not do so. On the contrary, they often go to considerable lengths to keep these schedules secret. An individual's pay is regarded as a confidential matter between him and his company; and while the fact that ranges exist is not denied, neither their parameters nor the classification of any given job is likely to be revealed. In these circumstances, it is usually considered a breach of etiquette to inquire about someone else's pay.

Various defenses have been advanced for pay secrecy. One is that what a man earns is really no one else's business and that he has a right to expect his employer to protect his dignity by not revealing his pay to anyone. (The obvious exception is the Internal Revenue Service, whose discretion in these matters is if anything more rigidly enforced than industry's.) It is also held that publishing pay rates simply invites invidious comparisons and that management would inevitably lose all flexibility in trying to administer a merit pay program if it continually had to justify every rate and every increase. No one doubts that the invidious comparisons occur anyway, but it is felt that they are at least muted sufficiently by secrecy to permit some semblance of a merit system to operate.

The principal critic of pay secrecy has been Edward E. Lawler III of Yale University.[11] His research has demonstrated a tendency for employees in companies that maintain pay secrecy to *over*estimate the pay of their peers and subordinates and to *under*estimate the pay of their superiors. In other words, the individual whose only sure clue to what other people earn is his own pay tends to assume a greater compression of pay levels than actually exists. On the one hand, overestimating the pay of those at equal or lower levels creates a suspicion of inequity and makes the individual less satisfied with his own pay. On the other hand, underestimating the pay of those at higher levels may decrease the apparent desirability of advancement. That is, the added responsibility and exposure of a higher-level job may not seem to be compensated adequately by what the individual *thinks* the differential in pay amounts to.

Lawler concludes from these findings that pay secrecy actually causes more trouble than it is worth. He notes that pay serves, or can serve, as a form of feedback; that is, pay can establish the relative worth of the individual's services within the organization as a whole. Lawler reasons that to deny the individual access to accurate feedback is to cut him off from a potentially effective motivator. In fact, he argues that the principal undemolished argument for maintaining pay secrecy is simply that actual pay distributions—as distinguished from the "structures" of ranges, midpoints, and so on, to which most companies try, theoretically, to adhere—would often be hard to justify. The number of people above and below their assigned ranges, the assignment of jobs to ranges, and the differences between ranges would all be open to scrutiny if secrecy were to be abandoned. Lawler suggests that these are often in such disarray that management would prefer to avoid the embarrassment of explaining them.

The charge of disarray is perhaps justified in too many cases. But even where it is not, the comparative advantages and disadvantages of open and closed pay systems need more analysis. Behavioral scientists have learned not to dismiss traditional managerial practices too lightly; they sometimes contain a kernel of what the late Douglas McGregor used to call "unconscious wisdom." It may be, in other words, that regardless of how objectively equitable a pay distribution may be, opening it to public view would be like opening Pandora's box. The pressure for apparent equitability could easily lead to "homogenized" pay rates—a trend that is already evident when the scales that are incorporated in various union contracts are published. It can also be questioned whether feedback as to one's relative standing in a pay hierarchy is likelier to motivate striving for advancement or carping with the hierarchy.

Probably the best-known example of published pay rates is the Civil Service. However, it is difficult to draw any firm conclusions about effects of open pay systems on the motivation of civil service employees. Other factors, such as a high degree of job security and the fact that government pay is usually lower than that for comparable jobs in private industry, help to obscure the effect (if any) that published pay rates have by themselves. Further, the very inflexibility of the system—the knowledge that government executives are restricted by the pay schedules and can do relatively little to change any individual's pay—may serve to prevent a good deal of felt dissatisfaction from erupting into open complaint. Thus all that can be said for the largest single example of a nonsecret pay system is that its motivational advantages over secret pay systems are difficult to demonstrate, if any exist at all.

The dilemma, then, is how to avoid the real compression of pay rates that publication would probably bring, while at the same time avoiding the perceived compression that Lawler's research reveals in companies that keep their pay rates secret. (It should be clear that when people *think* they are part of a compressed pay structure, they will *behave* as if it really were compressed—even if it isn't.) Perhaps, as Lawler suggests, some form of partial disclosure would be the answer. But before experimenting with such systems, it would be well to examine some of the other motivational effects of secrecy.

It is rather unfashionable nowadays to suggest that secrecy, with its archaic and undemocratic overtones, may have its positive aspects. Yet it may very well have some. (We might have dodged the problem by using some more innocuous term, like "confidentiality." But "secrecy" is the term Lawler uses, and, more important, it calls a spade a spade.) What, then, are the motivational benefits of pay secrecy? More precisely, what dissatisfaction does secrecy avoid, and what motivational effects does secrecy permit, that are less likely to occur in an open pay system?

One effect is illusion. Lawler has shown that certain illusions can dissatisfy (believing subordinates' pay to be higher than it is) and that others can demotivate (believing that superiors' pay is lower than it is). But there are other illusions, and to date research has not yet catalogued or evaluated all of them. For example, there are merciful illusions, such as the belief that someone who is considered a peer, but whose job may actually be rated higher, is paid as a peer. And there are also motivating illusions; for example, a salesman may know, or should know, that the odds against closing an order larger than a certain size are very long, but he may still drive hard to earn the commission that such a sale would bring. All illusions, by definition, insulate people from reality; but when that reality is harsher than the individual is built to endure, a bit of self-deception is neither harmful nor unnecessary.

This point is easy to misinterpret, but it is too important to leave unsaid. There can be no quarrel with the idea that frankness and clarity are desirable in all human relationships; but it is also a fact that few people can tolerate *complete* candor *all* the time. This is why psychological defense mechanisms—the various tricks of emphasis and interpretation that we all play on ourselves at times to help make reality more palatable—are so common. It is also why societies invent customs or institutions that blur distinctions between people which might otherwise be too harsh for them to accept. Perhaps pay secrecy serves as one such custom. The important point here is that the existence of ways of obscuring reality—and the need for them—is one of the coldest, hardest realities with which we must deal.

One final point about secrecy in pay policies: Whether they are accepted by the people whom they affect depends at least partly on the degree of confidence and trust within the organization and on whether overall pay levels are considered competitive with outside levels. Under these circumstances management is usually given the benefit of the doubt, or at least the doubts the employees have about equitability do not gnaw at them very severely. But to the extent that trust is absent or that outside pay comparisons are not satisfactory, suspicions about equitability can become severe. Secrecy is then intolerable, because employees feel they need some means of monitoring management's pay practices in order to protect themselves against favoritism. The relevance of the argument against secrecy is thus at least partially dependent on what might be called the state of organizational credibility: the degree to which employees believe that their pay is, and will continue to be, determined largely by the value of what they contribute to the company. We will explore this concept further in our discussion of organizational climates.

Chapter 10

Money for Motivation

THE OVERRIDING FACT THAT MANAGEMENT MUST GRASP IF it is to approach money motivation realistically is that the capitalist system has entered a new historic stage in which earlier assumptions about employee motivation are no longer valid. At one time, the preservation of any income at all may have been enough to make people work harder, simply to retain their membership in a company. That is seldom true today. In brief, current income has become solely an economic factor, rather than a mixed economic/psychological factor. Current income operates like a price mechanism to distribute the labor supply among employers, but it does *not* affect job performance in any lasting or significant way. Once this point is grasped—that the history of the past three decades has changed the rules of the motivational game—we can make some progress toward discovering newer, perhaps better ways to use money as a motivator.

We can get an important clue to what must be done to make pay an effective motivator by examining the problem of wage-related turnover. We noted earlier that an employer who is willing to raise the price he pays for labor above prevailing rates can nearly always detach a few employees from other companies' payrolls and add them to his own. This is, of course, a fairly common practice, especially during periods of labor shortage or with occupational groups that are in chronically short supply. There can be no airtight defense against tactics of this kind. One reason is that if an attempt were made to build a monetary wall around a few "exposed" employees—that is, employees who are attractive to a competitive employer—equitability would eventually compel an exorbitant general increase. A more realistic defense is based on the psychology of the exposed employee. This strategy concedes some losses, but concentrates on raising the price that the competitor must pay to a level that effectively minimizes the losses.

A man who is employed by Company A, and who is being sought by Company B, will ordinarily make some kind of rough calculation of the difference, or gap, between what he knows about life at A and what he thinks he knows about life at B. He knows that A has a certain mix of satisfactions and dissatisfactions for him, and unless he is a fool he will realize that there must also be some sort of mix at B. But A is the devil he knows, and B is the devil he does not know. Therefore the gap between A and B must be decidedly in B's favor before he will consider it seriously. In other words, B must offer some kind of clear-cut advantage to offset the uncertainty, inconvenience, and bother of adjusting to a new employer. The more favorable the mix of satisfactions and dissatisfactions at A, the larger the gap must be before the employee will think seriously about B. The obverse is also true: The less favorable the mix at A, the smaller the gap need be to be tempting.

This simple principle lies at the root of most successful campaigns to entice employees away from other companies, as well as most successful strategies to minimize such losses. A company with a relatively unfavorable mix is an easy target for another company that would like to help itself to a few experienced employees. On the other hand, a company with a relatively favorable mix is a formidable opponent. To make the gap attractive to the employees of such a company, the "raiding" firm is compelled to raise its bid (of money or other bait) to levels that quickly become uneconomical. A wise management knows that it is not necessary to match every offer in a tight labor market in order to succeed in containing a threat of turnover. What *is* necessary is a level of overall satisfaction high enough to make it uneconomical for another firm to offer enough inducements to be tempting.

What motivates the employee to stay or leave, when he finds himself in a seller's market, is the *apparent relative increment* in the mix of satisfactions and dissatisfactions between his present employer and his would-be employer. We have to speak of "apparent" increments because in most cases the employee doesn't really know what life in Company B would be like. But he usually knows that he doesn't know, and the value of that uncertainty is directly related to his current satisfaction. If he likes working in Company A, it would cost a lot to offset the uncertainty; but if he doesn't like A very much the uncertainty could be paid for cheaply. We have to speak of the "relative" increment because the size the gap must reach to be an inducement increases as the current level of satisfaction increases. Most important of all, we have to speak of an "increment"—a net gain—because it is only when this exceeds a certain critical level that *temptation is likely to be translated into action;* in other words, that the gap becomes a motivator.

What can be learned about money motivation from this brief analysis of turnover? Simply this: Money can motivate—that is, influence action—only when the *increment* that is in prospect is large enough relative to existing income. Most salary increase, bonus, and profit-sharing plans and many commission and incentive pay plans do *not* provide an increment that is large enough to motivate any action other than the purely passive action of staying in the organization. They are not usually large enough to motivate extra effort, extra creativity, or any other kind of nonroutine performance. That kind of motivation demands increments of a considerably greater order of magnitude than are usually available.

At this point it is only fair to note that we have now departed from subjects in which our statements could be supported by facts and have ventured into theory. The statement that monetary increments are not ordinarily available in sufficiently large sizes to produce significant changes in job performance is a deduction, not an established fact. There are not, in other words, an adequate number of *very* large increments in use to permit a valid test of the idea. However, not only is the deduction defensible, but it can and should be tested.

The main reason why large increments are so scarce is that management is caught between its own budgetary disciplines and employee pressure for secure, nonvariable income. Incremental income of all kinds is therefore added to a large, relatively stable base. Once management has paid for that base, the relative number of dollars that are left in the compensation budget for increments is not likely to be large. Consequently, most compensation dollars are assigned the job of *satisfying* the employee: They pay his bills and help him to feel tolerably secure. In effect, these dollars buy his membership in the company. Relatively few dollars are left over for motivation; and because the necessary dollar gap between current and prospective income is sizable, those few dollars left for motivation are usually inadequate. So one reason why money seldom motivates is simply that not enough of it is available for income increments.

We can thus suspect, on the basis of management's dilemma with regard to pay, that the *scale* on which increments are paid is seldom large enough to be effective. In fact, we seem to be headed toward a rather paradoxical conclusion: It costs a lot more money to use money effectively as a motivator than is ordinarily spent. Money may well turn out to be the costliest motivator of them all, which in itself is an excellent argument for giving more stress to nonfinancial motivators. But money may also prove to be the most potent motivator of all, at least in certain circumstances and when used on a sufficient scale. Therefore the central question about money motivation is its cost/effectiveness—that is, the price of productivity when money is used to its greatest motivational advantage—and there are simply no available answers to that question. Money has *not* been used to its greatest motivational advantage by organizations, at least not on a scale that would permit a valid test of its effects.

Our analysis of how money *might* be used to motivate productivity more effectively will carry us into new, largely uncharted territory. Therefore it would be best if the reader had a rough guide of where we are headed. The argument to be presented in the remainder of this chapter and the next chapter will be roughly as follows: First, we shall consider the concept of an increment more closely, especially the size an increment must reach in order to operate as an effective motivator. We shall note that there are some severe practical restraints on the large-scale use of effective increments and that some form of rationing is therefore necessary. This will lead us to the next major question: Just which individuals should we attempt to motivate by means of adequate increments? Third, we shall consider the specific ways in which we can expect increments to influence behavior. This turns out to be more a matter of channeling effort into particular kinds of activities than of increasing overall effort levels. Last, we shall consider ways of dealing with a crucial problem that underlies all questions related to compensation and nearly always subverts the motivational effectiveness of pay plans: the fact that nearly everyone who works for an organization, regardless of his pay level, is economically dependent on that organization.

Let's begin by taking a closer look at what an *increment* is. In our illustration of wage-related turnover, we spoke of an apparent relative increment. This phrase is a highly condensed description of the motivational aspect of all pay increments, not merely those affecting turnover. But the phrase is unwieldy, and we will simply have to remember that when we use the term "increment" in the remainder of this chapter we will mean a change in pay having three characteristics.

First, an increment always carries a heavy load of *subjective* freight. It can never be described in an entirely objective way, even when its dollars-and-cents value is known precisely. Whatever symbolism money has for the individual and whatever presumptions or illusions he has about how added income would affect the way he lives are as much a part of the increment for him as is the money itself. Consequently, equivalent increments for two or more people are not necessarily equivalent at all in terms of their actual effects. The importance of an increment is as much in the eye of the beholder as in its monetary value.

Second, an increment is not only partially subjective, it is also *relative*. The absolute number of dollars involved gives little indication of how the individual may be expected to react. That depends on his existing income, his net worth, his history of income growth and capital ownership, and his own estimate of the marketability of his services. In general, the more a man has or is accustomed to having, the more of an increment is required to impress him as really being more. This is one reason why it is easier to attract the sons of lower-middle-class fathers with corporate salaries than it is to attract the sons of upper-middle-class managers and professionals.

Finally, an increment is always something extra, in the sense that it is *added to* the income that is already guaranteed or expected. It cannot be overemphasized that current income motivates nothing but membership, if that; it does not motivate out-of-the-ordinary performance. An increment that is large enough to motivate more than membership must be of at least a certain size—that is, it must reach a certain "critical mass"—or it will merely be more money and not a motivator. Critical size is determined by the individual's estimate of the cost of a *safe but radical change in his financial condition.* This is a complex concept that requires more explanation.

Critical size is based on an estimate which is seldom informed or precise. Since most people have no precedent on which to base such an estimate, their thinking will necessarily be murky, approximate, and—not unlikely—unrealistic too. But the effective gap for any individual can usually be estimated by what amounts to a bargaining process. An example of such a process is found in the attempt of a company to lure a basically satisfied employee from another firm. Although the luring firm cannot afford to make an unnecessarily extravagant offer, neither can it afford an offer that will be regarded as only marginal. A gap that faces the individual with a difficult decision—in other words, one that is large enough to be interesting but not large enough to be decisive—is not large enough to be an effective increment. An individual who is likely to be plagued by second thoughts about the wisdom of his commitments is not an effectively motivated individual. Liberality is therefore essential in determining effective increments. This does not mean unrestricted access to the corporate treasury, but it does mean providing a margin for error in the individual's favor. The sum he is offered must be clearly out of the gray area of indecision or uncertainty.

Further, critical size is concerned with an estimate of cost. This is more than just the price of a new standard of living or of a new financial status. It also involves offsetting uncertainties, discomforts, and anxieties. The most common uncertainty about high income is whether it is sustainable. The most common discomforts are greater commitments of time and effort to the maintenance of the new financial position. The most common anxieties involve a change in role; that is, the necessity of loosening old social ties and forming new ones. All these intangible considerations may enter the individual's calculations on the debit side of the ledger. They represent what he thinks he may be asked to sacrifice in exchange for the in-crement. The more he values what he fears he may lose, or the less certain he is about what he may have to lose, the greater the cost of the increment will appear to be, and accordingly, the higher the fig-ure that must be set to offset this cost. In fact, it is not sufficient merely to offset the psychological cost of agreeing to a sizable incre-ment. There must be a clear, sizable net gain.

It would be easy to argue that no monetary price can be set on in-tangibles such as uncertainty or anxiety. But that really depends on the individual's values. If he prizes something that money can buy, or if he values something that money can symbolize, a sufficiently liberal increment *can* offset his anxieties. In other words, some people—perhaps most people—do have a price, and there is nothing necessarily dishonorable or reprehensible about that. What is "sold" in these transactions is not necessarily honor; it is more likely to be immunity from worry and the luxury of inaction. Indeed, one could argue—again, depending on his values—that such "sales" are consid-erably more ennobling in their effects on the human spirit than are the no-sale effects of inertia, indifference, and lack of commitment.

Returning to our analysis of critical size, it involves the cost of a *safe* change. Safety in this sense refers to protection against getting less than one had bargained for, either because of some unforeseen hazard or because the new arrangements somehow fail to work the way they were supposed to. An increment would be a bad bargain indeed if it failed to materialize, or fell short of promised levels, or proved to demand much more of the individual than he had been led to believe it would. Precisely because an increment has to be big to be effective, it is likely to encounter skepticism. Consequently, it has to include some form of "insurance," either in the way it is paid or in the traditions of the firm that offers it. We will return to this point later; for the moment let us note that the greater the apparent hazard in accepting the opportunity to earn the increment, the greater the increment has to be in order to motivate effectively.

Finally, critical size requires a radical change in the individual's financial condition. The change must be more than one of degree; that, after all, could be expected to occur eventually anyway, at less hazard and at lower cost. It must be a change in order of magnitude. It must make possible things only dreamed of ordinarily. Unless the increment is princely, it is unlikely to excite the imagination or whet the appetite. It must do more than just raise income; it must change the individual's capital position. It must enable the traditional debtor to get out from under his debts; it must enable the man of no means to acquire at least some degree of real wealth. In short, the income must be large enough to change the individual's basic attitudes toward money. That obviously requires *a lot* of money. Make no mistake about it: Effective motivation with money is no piker's game.

Note that we spoke of guaranteed or expected income as the base which motivates only membership, not productivity. This is where most wage and salary programs run into difficulty. Because of the normal tendency for monetary dissatisfaction to recur, the increase budget is in effect continually chasing the moving target of employee expectations. Further, it does not take a mathematician to project, on the basis of past history or a union contract, approximately when increases will occur and how large they will be. The pressure for equitability, or perhaps management's reluctance to run the risk of arousing that pressure, turns most merit-increase programs into a close approximation of a general-increase program. The actual variation in the size of relative increases between individuals is not likely to be significant. For all these reasons, it is rare for employees to be surprised by the timing or the size of their pay increases. They may be disappointed, but they are seldom surprised.

Consider the psychological effects of this predictability of income increases. When the time at which the increase is expected is still remote, the prospect of the increase serves to motivate membership, provided the expected increase is considered to be equitable. (Note that when pay secrecy operates, illusion can serve to set the expected increase at satisfactory levels, thereby avoiding the unpleasant necessity of looking around for another job.) As the time when the increase is expected comes nearer, the main things it motivates are curiosity and alertness for confirming signs that it will indeed occur. If the increase has not occurred on schedule, that fact will generate disappointment, feelings that the system is unjust, and perhaps—if the delay is considered prolonged—a search for another job. Or the individual may be motivated to complain, not necessarily about money alone, but about all the petty annoyances he is ordinarily willing to tolerate. He may even feel compelled, as a matter of pride, to *reduce* his performance level to a point that is commensurate with his now "inadequate" income—to escape, in other words, from a pay/work exchange that he now regards as exploitative.

Consider also the effects of the *size* of the increase, once it becomes known. If it is less than the individual expected, he may very well feel that he has been deceived. It is easier to live with this feeling, after all, than to acknowledge that *he* has been unrealistic in his expectations. This sense of disillusionment will not necessarily lower future expectations, however. It is more likely to make the individual cynical about his company and mistrustful of what it attempts to tell him. On the other hand, if the increase is about equal to what the individual expected, the company will simply be seen as having purchased his continued membership at a fair price. The experience will also reassure him that the system to which he is attached is fair and responsive. But these reassurances only satisfy; they do not motivate.

Finally, if the increase actually exceeds the employee's expectations—and this does happen, sometimes—then either of two reactions is possible. There is some evidence that when certain people feel that an increase results in overpay for their jobs, they will actually increase their output to a level that justifies their new earnings level. Other people, however, are less interested in justifying their perceived overpay than in protecting it. They are likely to develop various restrictive practices which have the effect of monopolizing their overpaid jobs. Both reactions have the same underlying psychology: that this is too good to last, and therefore *something* must be done to keep it from being found out and changed.

With the single exception of one of the two reactions to an underestimated increase, the motivational effects of *expected* increases are very small indeed. For all practical purposes, an expected increase is already the property of the individual who expects it. Psychologically, it is already incorporated into what he regards as his earnings base; it is not "something extra." Therefore *expected increases are not increments in the motivational sense*. When they materialize, they are a cost increment to the organization—a necessary, unavoidable cost increment—but they are not a motivational increment.

Now we can begin to see why compression of wage and salary scales works against motivation and helps to make most compensation programs basically satisfiers or dissatisfiers, not motivators. By reducing the monetary gap between pay levels, compression also reduces the likelihood that an increase will be sizable enough either to motivate action before it is granted or to motivate "justifying performance" after it is granted. By reducing the relative size of increments, compression has the effect of making the base by far the most sizable part of compensation. This means that money is channeled almost exclusively into motivating membership, to the relative exclusion of motivating performance. Especially undesirable is the fact that compression reduces the organization's ability to provide higher-management personnel with "insurance" for the risks they incur in accepting heavy responsibilities.

Responsibility and exposure increase together. The greater a man's responsibilities, the less the organization can afford to tolerate ineffective work and the greater the possibility that he may have to be relieved, perhaps precipitately, of those responsibilities. To compensate a man for accepting that risk, the proportional dollar gaps between executive salary levels should be greater than the gaps between lower-management pay levels. To the extent that compression prevents the gaps at higher levels from being large enough, executives may find themselves in the position of having to ask whether it might not be wiser to decline a promotion in order to preserve an already high income at an acceptable risk level. That is, they may decide that their ratio of income to personal cost is already at its maximum level and could only worsen if they accepted a modest increase in pay and a sizable increase in risk, discomfort, or any of the other elements of personal cost. If too many executives begin to regard promotion as a bad financial bargain, top jobs may go by default to imprudent risk takers—exactly the kind of men who should not be given high-level responsibilities.

Thus pay increments *must* be large enough to excite the imagination, or to change fundamental attitudes toward money, if they are to have any hope of motivating extraordinary performance. But increments of that order are quite inconsistent with compression of pay scales. So compression would appear to cost more than it is worth. Before accepting this conclusion, it is legitimate to probe the consequences of liberal increments a bit further. After all, they may have unwanted side effects that negate their benefits. Specifically, we have to ask whether increments that are large enough to be motivationally effective would also be economically feasible, and also whether they might not motivate something other than productivity—such as complacency or even a cavalier disregard for responsibilities and obligations.

Effective increments are *not* economically feasible on a large scale. They cost too much. If they are to be used at all, they must be rationed; and this raises the ticklish question of exactly who should be singled out to receive them. Generally speaking, effective increments should be offered only to people who are susceptible to them—that is, are likely to respond, for whatever psychological reason, with the desired action—*and* who are also capable of some singularly important contribution to the organization, something they would be unlikely to attempt unless they were unusually motivated. The key word in the preceding sentence is "and"—that is, both susceptibility and capacity must be present. Thus the field of potential receivers of large increments is greatly narrowed to begin with, because relatively few people fit this description. Further, there would be little point in paying a premium for performance that would probably be attempted even without extra pay. Consequently, it is also a relatively rare type of task that lends itself to effective increments. The task must include risks, discomforts, or difficulties that would ordinarily preclude attempts to accomplish it. So the field is narrowed still more. In fact, the combination of men and jobs for which effective increments are appropriate is quite rare.

This does not mean that such increments could not be used to good advantage. There are at least two circumstances in which they would be indicated. First, some men are capable of leading the way into "breakthrough" areas which change the whole mission or strategy of the organization. The classic example is the story, possibly apocryphal, told about the late Charles P. Steinmetz, whose inventions practically created an industry for General Electric. Steinmetz is said to have been compensated rather ingeniously. GE, according to one legend, gave him a checkbook and told him it would make good any drafts he signed.

One does not have to reach the towering stature of a Steinmetz, however, to qualify for effective increments. Creative work in such fields as product development, organizational analysis, and investment or acquisition analysis are examples of jobs that could, in the right circumstances, qualify for the large-increment treatment. Doing jobs of these kinds properly sometimes demands more than just skill: It may demand courage too, because the consequences of a mistake can be so horrendous that the individual's reputation is at risk along with his security. But it is plainly in the organization's interest to have decisions of these kinds made solely on the basis of capable men's judgments, undiminished by any fears for their own future. Thus an increment large enough to overcome their natural tendency to play it safe could be more than amply repaid by the results. Whether this would or would not be a gamble for the organization depends entirely on the wisdom with which the man, the job, and the increment itself were selected.

Some men are capable of developing their managerial abilities faster, and ultimately further, than others. But to do so requires, above all, exposure to heavy doses of responsibility—often before the individual really feels ready for them. Increments that are liberal enough to pave the way to a wholly new financial status could be an effective way of encouraging such people to accept the risks of moving ahead rapidly. The game, in other words, should be worth the candle. Some companies already recognize this principle by tying the compensation growth rate of selected young "high potential" men to an estimate of that potential rather than to current job level.

It is worth noting at this point that heavy responsibility is not, in itself, a justification for large increments. Responsibility is continual and must therefore be paid for continually, in the form of salary. Large increments make sense chiefly when the challenge to the individual is finite; that is, when one can say at any given point that the challenge has, or has not yet, been met. This means in effect that top executives will not necessarily be the most logical recipients of large increments, despite the fact that they currently receive nearly all the increments that could be classified as effective in a motivational sense. Depending on the needs of the organization, effective increments may be used more appropriately with scientific or professional personnel, or even with junior levels of management, than with executives.

The most obvious objection to large increments is that they could destroy the incentive to work, since work would no longer be an economic necessity. That particular objection can be disposed of briefly. There is little evidence that the acquisition of wealth decreases the motivation to work. What it evidently does decrease is the individual's tolerance for work he does not like. Wealth makes people more selective about the work they do, but it seldom makes them less interested in occupying their time constructively. Perhaps this is more true of people who have had to work for their wealth than of the legendary idle rich; but in recent years many rich men have been conspicuously un-idle. It would appear that meaningful work is not inherently distasteful to most men, at least not the kind of men who are likely to accomplish something worthy of being paid for by large increments.

There is another, subtler reason why certain men should deliberately be made wealthy. There is a certain paradox in the relationship between the people who pay the bills (stockholders or taxpayers) and the people on whose success the fortunes of the enterprise may depend (those who may qualify for large increments). To put it another way, it is very much in the interests of the organization to be able to rid itself of an individual in a hurry if it becomes evident that he is not going to accomplish what he was asked to do; yet it is equally in the organization's interests that certain men may be undismayed and uninhibited by that ever-present possibility. Independent wealth is one way to resolve that dilemma.

There can be some serious problems associated with the rapid growth of income when the job for which the income is paid is not sufficiently satisfying to the individual. At one end of the income spectrum, there is a tendency for some workers in relatively repetitive, unchallenging jobs to demand wage increases that bear little relationship to the contribution of their work to profits or to the growth, if any, of their productivity. They tend to demand whatever the traffic will bear and to support militant union leaders who will press management for the largest possible wage settlement. The result, sometimes, is that their income eventually approaches uneconomical levels. Yet they can hardly be said to be motivated by their incomes or by the prospect of income gains, at least not in the sense of deliberately producing at a higher-than-usual rate. Money seems to serve a function altogether different from motivation for them. One behavioral scientist, Chris Argyris of Yale University, has suggested that the real psychological purpose of money in such cases is a sort of "revenge" against management, a way of hitting back at an adversary where it presumably will hurt most. The tendency to see management as an adversary has less to do with feelings of inadequate pay than with feelings of alienation; that is, the feeling that one doesn't count for much in the system of which one is a part. The devil is more likely to find work for idle minds than for idle hands, and the "work" he finds is quite likely to involve fault finding, resentment at being ill-used, and a search for ways of hitting back.

At the other end of the income spectrum, some young men experience such a rapid rise in income that they may become surprisingly blasé about the prospect of further increases. (This is what happened with the salesmen of metering equipment who were described in Chapter 1.) This too-much-too-soon phenomenon is more complex than it may at first appear. For one thing, it is likely to occur in the context of jobs that have been tolerated largely for the sake of money—jobs that have been regarded as a temporary and expedient means of arriving, more rapidly than would otherwise have been possible, at a position of financial comfort. Once such jobs have fulfilled this purpose, they may no longer be so easy to tolerate—unless, of course, the men who hold them have in the meantime discovered some sort of intrinsic interest in the jobs which they had not anticipated when they began. Further, these young men are not entirely disenchanted with money, even though they are sometimes willing to accept a modest financial sacrifice to switch to jobs that are more to their liking. Their basic motivational problem with regard to money is that their base has grown so large that the prospect of an increment large enough to motivate them to stay in their present jobs has become quite remote. Once this happens, the bloom can come off the monetary rose very quickly, and men become more responsive to nonfinancial motivators than they had been. Finally, when income seems to exceed what the job is worth, the excess is of course welcome; but it does not motivate. That is, overpay does not necessarily lead to higher sustained output than equitable pay, *if* the job itself does not seem to deserve the extra pay. The job, not the money, is the limiting factor.

It follows from this that effective increments are possible only in the context of certain kinds of jobs. Specifically, large increments make sense only when the individual is—and knows he is—capable of exerting a substantial influence on the results he attains. This influence can vary all the way from very little (as in the case of a worker who tends automatic equipment or whose job is to respond to inputs he cannot control, such as a telephone operator) to a great deal (as in the case of a research scientist or a playwright). Unless the individual can deliberately make a substantial difference in the results of his work, the monetary reward that can be tied to that difference will not be large enough to matter to him. That is, his "influence ratio"—that part of his income which he feels he can affect through his own efforts—will not be large enough to reach whatever constitutes his own "critical size." What we have referred to here as influence ratio is probably related, but not identical, to what Jaques calls "time span of discretion."

The effort required to make the difference must be extraordinary: the sort of thing that could not reasonably be expected of a man at ordinary levels of pay or simply for the joy of accomplishment. The cost of the action to the individual must be roughly proportional to the increment. That cost could be represented by a heavy, prolonged commitment of time or by a sizable risk to the individual's reputation, career, or peace of mind. In other words, not only must the game be worth the candle, but the candle must also be worth the game.

By now it is clear that the actual number of situations in which motivationally effective increments can actually be used is quite small. Even so, they are not by any means used widely enough. When increments of the type we have described are applied at all, it is nearly always in the form of profit participation by a relative handful of key executives. Our analysis suggests that a wider application is desirable, not only at the executive level but at the professional level as well. Arguments against the broader use of very large increments usually boil down to the notion that few people, if any at all, are really worth that much to their employers. In this view, effective increments are a colossal and unnecessary waste of the stockholders' or taxpayers' money. And that objection reveals the heart of the problem of money motivation.

We have argued that to use money effectively as a motivator, it must be used with discrimination, but on a princely scale. It must be used to make men wealthy. But we have to face the fact of a considerable resistance to the very idea of deliberately making certain men wealthy. This comes not merely from socialist and egalitarian trends in society as a whole but, more important, from certain biases common to management itself. The fact is that most of the great productivity increases in recent memory did not happen because individuals resolved to do more. Rather, they resulted from the introduction of new tools, new products, and new processes. These in turn reflect the coordinated efforts of very large groups of people, rather than a few individuals. This fact has focused management's attention upon managing large groups, which in turn means keeping peace in the house through equitability, and the consequent use of money as a buyer of membership.

In other words, the nonmotivational use of money traces back to the assumption that individual effort really doesn't count. Now, it may be a bit heretical to admit this, but that assumption is often true. Our main point is simply that there are enough *exceptions* to make them well worth seeking out. In those few cases where large increments can make a difference, they can make an enormous difference. It cannot be overemphasized that increments large enough to be effective make no sense at all unless the potential benefit to the company is huge. Managements should therefore continually seek out opportunities for benefitting their companies hugely by deliberately making certain individuals wealthy.

We are now ready to consider how this might be done.

Chapter 11

Making Men Wealthy

It is not equitability but management's underlying assumptions about the potential contributions of people that limits the motivational effect of money upon productivity. We must now ask why the potential value of the individual contributions are so often underestimated. One answer lies in the common experience of management: There have been very few Steinmetzes, Ketterings, or Lands to put the GE's, GM's, or Polaroids on the map. The conclusion drawn from this experience is that genius must be an extremely scarce commodity. So most management strategies assume that one had better not wait for a genius to show up, and that instead the job of management is to harness the efforts of ordinary men in the most practical ways available. From that point, the equitability-compression cycle takes over almost inevitably.

But the logic in that strategy rests on the rather tenuous assumption that genius needs no encouragement, that it will somehow come storming through in spite of itself. In other words, much current thinking about the proper role of money rests, at bottom, on the hero fallacy. But not all geniuses are self-motivated, obstacle-ignoring heroes, and that is precisely why most of the potential geniuses in this world remain only potential geniuses. Those few men who accomplish exceptional things are, to be sure, considerably brighter than average men; but they are not necessarily more gifted than, say, the top 5 or 10 percent of the population, most of whom accomplish nothing really extraordinary in a lifetime. There is, in other words, an enormous reservoir of relatively untapped genius—that is, the capacity for exceptional accomplishment—which existing systems of motivation have failed to reach. Even a small penetration into this reservoir could be hugely rewarding. We are suggesting here that the judicious use of effective increments may be capable of at least such a small penetration.

Another reason why the potential contribution of individuals to their organizations is often underestimated is that it is seldom in their best interests to be as productive as they could be. Thus there are few glimpses, so as to speak, of what that potential really is. The main reason why most people function far below their capacity lies in the essentially dependent relationship of any individual to the organization that employs him. When a man is financially dependent upon the continuity of his paychecks, he will be more interested in preserving that continuity than in inflating the next check.

This is most familiarly and dramatically seen in the tendency of production workers to restrict their output, even in the face of incentive payments. Their usual rationale is that to exceed a certain level of production would invite management to increase their quotas, or that it would create intolerably divisive strains between the more efficient and the less efficient workers, or that management would profit so disproportionately that it would be tantamount to letting themselves be used for someone else's advantage. Whatever the reason, the effect is the same: to limit productivity to levels that appear to be safe. The fact that considerable capability remains unused because of these attitudes is widely and tacitly understood. It may be deplored, bargained over, or jealously guarded, but it is seldom questioned.

Something quite comparable occurs at higher organizational levels. It is equally against the interests of the executive to rock the boat by disagreeing with the opinions of his peers or superiors, or to take risks whose payoff is uncertain, or to make decisions that could be difficult to explain. Thus the executive's productivity may be limited by his own concern for security and the continuity of his income. Elsewhere in the organization, the ambitious youngster learns the wisdom of not outperforming his peers by too wide a margin, since they have their own ways of making him regret such action. In all these cases, men of heroic proportions can and do resist the pressures and sometimes accomplish great things. But they have also been ignominiously defeated, and that is one reason why heroes are too scarce to be counted on.

It is important to realize that an organization confronts the individual with realities of its own. These alter his situation considerably from that of a genuine entrepreneur. (In modern organizations of any size, hardly anyone, including the top executives, is a genuine entrepreneur.) The situations of an organization member and an entrepreneur are profoundly different, and consequently they see things differently and behave differently. These differences have led to stereotyped notions that still persist; for example, that workers are lazy and want something for nothing, or that employers are venal and interested only in money. Both are perfectly normal misperceptions which result from looking at the other fellow as if he were in your situation. These differences in situation have also led to countless attempts to "sell" employees on the free enterprise system, when what they needed to be sold on was not the system itself but rather their position within it. The point is that organizations do not normally motivate their members to function the way an entrepreneur functions, because it does not seem *to them* to be in their best interests to work at their peak levels.

The basic problem in elevating performance levels is to eliminate dependency somehow, or at least to reduce it greatly. A fundamental fact of life must be changed, and that is of course no easy task. But dependency, in the last analysis, is subjective; there is no way to measure "real" dependency or to say that one man's situation makes him more or less dependent than another's. A man is as dependent as he feels and acts. (A hero, by this definition, is simply a man who doesn't feel dependent enough to be deterred by fears of losing a supposedly essential relationship.) Thus the problem narrows to finding those people who would *feel* independent if they were given suitable financial treatment. We have to find people who are already predisposed to acting independently and provide sufficient financial support to help them step over the line. If we must change facts of life, it is best to begin with small ones.

It is too seldom recognized that it is very much in an organization's interests to place its fortunes in the hands of men whose fortunes are *not* tied to the organization's, men who work because they want to work rather than because they have to. This is not merely for the sake of risk taking and nonconformity. If there is any single quality that is required of a man of higher management levels, it is *credibility*—the ability to make unpopular or unwelcome points without being suspected of masking the truth for some ulterior motive. A credible executive can protest, for example, that a production target is impossible, without being suspected of merely bargaining for an easier goal. He can warn his superiors as dramatically, or if need be as annoyingly, as they must be warned in order to convince them that a projected action is dangerous, without fearing that he will lose their esteem. A credible executive is one whose inputs to the management decision process are listened to, not discounted; and for that reason his impact on the fortunes of his firm is much greater than that of dozens of peers who are, if you will, "incredible."

There are many ways to become credible, and undoubtedly the best of these is through demonstrated good judgment and ability. But when a man has done that, he is still not necessarily free of the consequences of his dependency. Here is a subtle but extremely important point: Even if he is in fact undeterred by his dependency, he is not freed of the suspicion of being deterred. So he will find himself bargained with and fenced with in an endless attempt to estimate the "truth" behind his words, in spite of the fact that he may be concealing nothing. To be credible, a man must have more than just ability: His motives must be unquestioned. He must have nothing to gain or lose except his pride; and it must be apparent to those who deal with him that the desire to be proved right, not gain or safety, is his real motive. Thus credibility can hinge, in the last analysis, on independence, and *credible* independence hinges on wealth.

This principle is not new. It is already recognized in the role of the "outside director"—a man whose financial stake in the organization is usually small, but who is brought into the corporation because of his wisdom and his independence. The outside director is expected to take the long view and to represent the long-range interests of the stockholders. Their best guarantee that he will do this lies not in the discipline they can exercise over him—unlike the inside director, he is under practically no financial restraints whatever—but rather in his demonstrated integrity. The system obviously works, and we must therefore conclude that integrity can be a very powerful motivator—more powerful than money or security—*for certain men under certain circumstances.* This powerful motivational tool is underutilized in most current compensation systems. That is one reason why the full motivational power of money has not yet been revealed.

Money can motivate exceptional accomplishments in two ways. First, it can motivate through the *prospect* of becoming wealthy; that is, of a radical improvement in one's financial circumstances. Second, it can motivate by becoming irrelevant, by *freeing* the individual of both real dependency and the tendency of others to suspect him of the tactics of dependency. Thus money can be a liberator of potentialities and an unlocker of nobler, more enduring, more fruitful motives. But the process is not automatic: Witness men of substantial wealth who are timid or inflexible or even venal. If men are deliberately to be made wealthy in order to increase their effectiveness, it must be done selectively, not indiscriminately. The technique for making these selections has not been perfected, which makes this a priority target for the applied behavioral sciences.

If some men are to be singled out for wealth, it is vitally important that measurements be found to determine whether the treatment is deserved. Not only must an extraordinary investment be carefully audited, but a convincing demonstration of the equitability of the investment must also be available. Otherwise, the effects of this treatment upon those who do *not* receive it could be costly and troublesome enough to cancel out whatever benefits the recipient produces. (Remember Adams' formulation of equitability; it is based on the ratio of what a man contributes to what he receives.) To be perceived as equitable, an effective increment must be tied to a much-larger-than-usual contribution—larger than the one expected from someone with similar preparation and operating at a similar job level. Thus the question of effective increments brings us into a confrontation with the problem of performance measurement, a problem that plagues compensation planners for all levels of jobs, but is especially demanding in cases where performance must justify wealth.

A motivationally effective performance measurement system must be based on three realities: the effects of monetary incentives upon performance, the limits of performance measurement itself, and the organization's optimum long-range interests. When any of these three realities is ignored, the resulting system is very likely to sink of its own weight—which has been the fate of all too many performance appraisal systems.

We noted earlier that one of the principal functions of performance measurement is to motivate. For most people, the knowledge that measurement of their work will affect their pay does motivate them—but not always in the direction of productivity. Here indeed is one of the most important and widespread fallacies in the compensation field: Measurements do motivate, but only in the same sense that a traffic policeman motivates drivers. The effect of measurements is to direct energy into channels that will cause the measurements to register at satisfactory levels. This is usually accomplished by draining energy from other channels, not by increasing the total energy expended. Thus it is imperative that the measurements themselves be chosen wisely. To make this choice has proved to be quite difficult, because it is not so much their *direct* effects as their *unintended side-effects* that determine whether the behavior they motivate will, on balance, advance the cause of the organization that uses them. We are still learning the difficult arts of applying performance measurements wisely. They have by no means been reduced to an exact science. In fact, a long and sometimes costly period of trial and error still seems to be required in order to install such systems properly.

Today it is increasingly popular to use "management by results," a system of measuring an individual's performance solely in terms of specified results achieved by the resources he directs, relative to some predetermined standard. Much of the confusion about the applicability of the management-by-results doctrine stems from the fact that although its underlying theory is appealingly simple, its practical application is appallingly complex. On the one hand, the idea that most men are motivated by the challenge of having to make their own day-to-day operating decisions is amply supported by both research evidence and common experience. On the other hand, the selection of specific results targets is fraught with danger, for three reasons: First, if an individual works as part of a group it is very difficult to tease out that part of the group's results which represents his own unique contribution. Thus to measure his performance by what the group achieves can easily lead either to crediting him with more than he deserves or to blaming him for failures that were not really his fault. Second, the specific actions that are clearly attributable to one individual, and to no one else, are often trivial. Thus the results that an individual clearly "owns" may reveal little about his personal impact on the organization as a whole. (There is a significant loophole in this argument, to which we shall return presently.) Third, and most important, results seldom occur simultaneously, and they seldom become static or final.

This is perhaps best illustrated by the effects of what might be called a coercive approach to cost reduction; that is, imposing severe restrictions on operating expenses without permitting the affected people a voice in deciding whether or where the cuts should be made. Actually, there are several results of such an action (as there are to any significant management decision), but some are obvious and others are subtle. What is more important, they develop over time at different rates. One result is financial: Since there is almost always a certain amount of unused capacity in any organization, the immediate financial result of coercive cost cutting is likely to be an increased cash flow.

So far, so good. But meantime a subtler result is also occurring, usually at a slower pace: an erosion of whatever loyalty the affected people may have had to the company. Their attitudes change more slowly than financial results, but as their loyalty erodes it becomes progressively less important to them to do their work properly. The company's action has revealed it as indifferent and unresponsive to them, and they retaliate in kind with waste, absenteeism, grievances, and turnover. This leads to yet another result, which usually shows up only after attitudes have deteriorated: a gradual lowering of skill levels, efficiency, and productivity. These operational changes penalize the organization's financial results, eventually reducing cash flow and perhaps even leading to a worse crisis than the one that precipitated the original cost-cutting campaign.

Thus the adequacy of results as a performance measurement in this case would depend entirely on which results we chose to observe and the point in time at which we chose to observe them. Results never really stabilize; they are always evolving in one direction or another, and consequently the assessments we make of them at any given point in time are nothing more than samples. Whether they are relevant or misleading depends, among other things, on both the wisdom and the luck of the people who are doing the assessing.

Similarly, the action that would be motivated by a management-by-results system depends on the results selected for measurement and on the timing of the measurement. If the criterion of effectiveness is a fast turn-around of declining cash flow, there is likely to be little if any negotiation about the imposition of budget cuts: They will be sudden, steep, and arbitrary, and the devil take such niceties as morale. On the other hand, if the criterion of effectiveness is a balance of improved cash flow and improved morale, a consultative approach to finding ways of saving money is a more likely tactic. The point is that behavior—in this case, management's behavior—is not entirely a matter of personal style; it can also be strongly guided by the method of evaluating personal performance. Thus the effect of performance evaluation is to emphasize certain kinds of action and to de-emphasize others; this is at once its greatest strength and its most glaring weakness. Measurement is, in fact, an extremely powerful motivational device, so powerful that it can produce vast organizational dislocations if the full consequences of the chosen measurements are not foreseen.

Thus we are always playing with fire, at least potentially, when we introduce performance measurements; and when in addition we tie those measurements to the possibility of earning very large pay increments, the situation is indeed incendiary. But effective increments can be justified only by carefully selected measurements. These would not necessarily be stated in precise terms, since they could require a break-through into uncharted areas where no measurements as such exist. What may be required, for example, could be the successful development of a new product or successful entry into a new market; and success in such cases is difficult to specify in advance. But there must also be parameters or boundary conditions to the success measurement. The desired result should not be obtained at the expense of profit, legality, or loyalty. Further, because the goal must be both large and somewhat imprecisely stated, the judgment of whether the goal has been reached must necessarily be somewhat liberal.

All performance measurements have certain limitations, two of which are very important with respect to effective increments: the motivation of the rater and the selection of factors to be rated (which provides the loophole we referred to earlier).

Even with the best of intentions, it is difficult to be entirely objective when rating the performance of another person. The reason usually has less to do with favoritism or bias—most managers are above that—than with a conflict between the immediate needs of the rater's job and the long-range interests of the organization. The manager who knows that his own success will hinge at least partly on the continued dedication and effort of another man will be more interested in motivating him than in measuring his work precisely. Thus the bias in such a case is often in favor of generosity and overestimating performance. This is of course a serious hazard when not only large sums of money, but organizational morale as well, ride on the judgment of performance. The best defense against this tendency is to specify the components of acceptable performance in advance, so the rater's job is to *testify* that certain events did or did not occur, rather than to estimate that a man's work was above or below average (whatever "average" means) or that it merited some slippery adjective like "imaginative" or "aggressive."

But which components should be specified? Which factors in performance should be rated? Historically, most performance rating systems have been designed through a common sense approach, including a variety of factors which summarized the job description in rather general terms. Despite their common sense origins, these systems are usually, and rightly, regarded as unworkable or irrelevant or both. They are unworkable because they require the rater to make diagnoses of which he is hardly likely to be capable (of personality and attitude, for example). They are irrelevant because most factors are stated so generally that the rater can respond only generally and therefore approximately. What is more, they are irrelevant because they attempt to summarize all the things a man does on his job; whereas in reality *only a very few of those actions really matter very much*—and the ones that matter are usually not specified because they have not been identified.

This last point is extremely important and is well worth dwelling upon briefly. There are few singular events in any job. For this reason, fine distinctions between the performance of one man and another are seldom really possible. Instead, gross distinctions can be made between the large mass of performances which are adequate or satisfactory and those few at either extreme which are either unacceptable or literally extraordinary. Thus most people spend most of their working time attending to the ordinary things they are paid to attend to, and they seldom get an opportunity to do anything exceptional. Ordinarily, their performance levels are quite difficult to distinguish from each other, because *their performance is in fact determined more by the job itself than by themselves.*

It is only in those occasional moments when an opportunity to do something critical—or at least unusual—arises that the man himself is tested. It is only in the out-of-the-ordinary circumstance that he does something that really matters, something that can distinguish his performance as unequivocally better or worse than that of his peers. These opportunities to do something that matters much more than everything else are neither random nor excessively rare. They can be isolated for most jobs by means of a well-established technique—the "critical incident" method—which in effect distills from a job those few events which weigh far more heavily than all the rest. This is not to suggest that day-to-day performance can be neglected; obviously, it cannot. Rather, it suggests that because day-to-day performance is *not* likely to be neglected, differences in day-to-day performance are not likely to be great. The sharp, reliable, meaningful differences between one man's performance and another's are more likely to be detected in certain highly specific nonroutine events.

We noted earlier that most of the events which can be attributed specifically to one man rather than to the combined efforts of several men are trivial. Precisely because of this, most jobs do not really lend themselves to the use of effective increments: A suitable measurement of extraordinary achievement cannot be found. In those exceptional jobs for which specific, critical, *and* exceptionally important actions can be isolated—actions that set the individual's achievement apart from all others and radically affect the fortunes of the organization as a whole—large increments are probably the best guarantee that the action will be taken effectively. (Note that whereas most jobs have their moments when differences between individual capabilities are tested more sharply than they are in routine performance, those moments are only rarely crucial to the organization as a whole. It is only when both elements are present—when an event is singular and has a massive impact—that it can be used as a yardstick of whether effective increments are justified.)

Thus the measurement of whether wealth has been earned is likely to be highly specific; more exactly, it is likely to consist of a *series* of highly specific, objectively verifiable goals which determine both the rarity and the impact of the actions that have been taken. And this leads to another implication about the limits of effective increments; namely, the kind of organization that can use them. If the measurement that determines whether the increment is to be paid is based in part on the magnitude of the *impact* which specific actions have upon the organization, it follows that effective increments are appropriate only in an organization that *wants* to be heavily impacted —that wants, in a word, to change. Effective increments are really quite incompatible with maintaining the status quo, if only because there would be no effective answer to the charges of inequitability or of needlessly squandering the stockholders' money. On the other hand, effective increments are very well suited to the needs of an organization that wants deliberately to change its products, markets, size, profitability, or any other basic dimension. It is an incentive worthy of the challenge to remake an organization.

We now turn to the mechanism for payment of effective increments. The objective of a program of effective increments is to produce a fairly rapid, quite drastic increase in a man's assets, as distinguished from his income per se. Once the program has begun, it should proceed to its conclusion by relatively quick steps; say, in five or six years. The quicker the man's capital position changes, the quicker his attitudes are likely to change in the direction of broadgauge, long-range, independent thinking. Further, a too-distant goal has relatively little motivating power. Once the financial target has been reached—that is, once the man has been made wealthy—subsequent income need not be exceptionally high.

The increment must be conditional, of course, but in a somewhat unusual way. Ideally, there should be two conditions, each with its own increment. One would be for accepting the risk of the project itself, the other would be for attaining it; and the ratio between them should probably favor the latter, but not too strongly. (Until there is a body of experience to guide us, trial and error will have to prevail; but common sense suggests something in the range of 1:2–2:3). The risk component would be paid out regardless of whether the project succeeds or fails; it is therefore a joint risk, since the organization may lose its investment as easily as the individual may lose his reputation and his job. (Those who feel that the burden of risk in such an arrangement falls more heavily upon the organization than upon the individual would do well to ponder Shakespeare's lines: "Who steals my purse steals trash . . . but he that filches from me my good name robs me of that which not enriches him and makes me poor indeed." Shakespeare was an excellent psychologist.) Besides, the risk is real, since, as we have already noted, there would be little point in offering such a reward for tasks which are fairly certain to be accomplished.

Both increments should be paid out over a period of years. But since the risk may be accepted long before the task itself is accomplished, the payments will not coincide and indeed may not overlap at all. (This is one reason why the risk component of the increment should not be too small, relative to the accomplishment component.) The reason for spreading both payments over several years has less to do with taxes (about which more will be said shortly) than with psychology. The man whose income could suddenly dry up is likely to be considerably more conservative than one who knows he will have substantial income for a reasonable period, even if he is without a job. Boldness, not conservatism, is needed to accomplish the kind of goals that are large enough to justify effective increments. But the boldness must be calculated, not brash; and that is why the accomplishment payment should loom even larger than the risk payment. It should, in effect, make the difference between becoming well-to-do and becoming wealthy.

The steeply graduated income tax is of course an immense barrier to the use of effective increments. The cost of transferring a suitable "estate" from the corporate treasury to the individual would be vastly greater than the cost of the estate itself. In effect, the government would become a far more favored beneficiary of the individual's achievements than he would himself. Thus it is only realistic to conclude that, under existing tax laws, effective increments would usually be prohibitively expensive. Even the small opening that effective increments could create for the motivational use of money is therefore greatly narrowed.

One could argue that the income from at least the accomplishment component should be treated, for tax purposes, as a capital gain. The goal could be registered and, if need be, certified in advance as one which, if achieved, could add significantly to the organization's wealth-producing power. Some kind of favored tax treatment for bona fide increments of this kind is clearly desirable, and for exactly the same reason that a tax credit on investment in capital goods is desirable: It would enhance the capability of the economy to produce, employ, and compete.

The most common wealth-building mechanism is the stock option. There is an important, if subtle, reason why this is *not* the method of choice for paying effective increments—entirely apart from changing forms of tax treatment. The effect of the stock option is to tie the recipient to the company, since he might forfeit a fortune by leaving. Even after the option is exercised, the bulk of his wealth will usually be his equity in the organization that employs him. But it is not necessarily in the best interests of the organization that he feel *constrained* to stay. The pressure to make one's compromise with the status quo, for the sake of tolerably comfortable relationships in the future, could weigh heavily on a man who feels he has no financial alternative but to stay. Paradoxically, commitment to the organization—when it is imposed by self-interest rather than generated by satisfying experience—can reduce the effectiveness of a man whose job is to alter the status quo. Stock options *do* motivate: They motivate people *not* to do something (leave the organization). Whether they also motivate men to attempt to accomplish things they would not otherwise accomplish is a moot point.

Because of their favorable tax treatment, stock options will probably be the most practical means of conveying wealth. Therefore, despite their defects as motivators, they will probably be used more often than cash. It should be clearly recognized, however, that this is an accommodation to the tax laws, not to psychological laws. A man with cash in his pocket is considerably more independent—more able to make unfettered decisions and therefore to function at the peak of his abilities—than a man with a stock certificate in his.

The question of the size of an effective increment is very difficult to deal with, yet deal with it we must. In general, the amount of money which would constitute a "psychological estate," and therefore modify attitudes toward money, probably varies with the individual's experience with money. The less he has had, the less it takes to seem like a lot. Thus to someone who has never been able to accumulate money in excess of what he needs to live, a sum equal to twice his yearly income may seem to be a fortune. The ratio probably increases as prior experience with owning capital increases. It may go as high as ten times annual income for people of substantial means. This too is an area which demands more research than it has received.

Most of the space in the last three chapters has been given over to a consideration of how money might be used as an effective motivator. Our analysis has indicated that this can be done, but probably only with a relative handful of people. It now remains to consider what an intelligent policy would be for the compensation of that vast majority of organization members for whom money is *not* likely to be an effective motivator. (Again, at the risk of being repetitive it is important to recall our definition of a motivator: something that influences action.)

The main motivational purposes of money, when applied to the vast majority of organization members, can only be to attract and hold employees and to provide suitable ways of differentiating the status of people at different levels of responsibility. Money motivates by attracting, by competing with other monetary attractions, and by flattering. Its motivational effect upon productivity is seldom substantial or prolonged except in a few circumstances. Rather than lament the comparative weakness of money as a motivator, it is best to use it as carefully as we can for the few purposes to which it does lend itself and find other means to prompt the kinds of behavior which money does not motivate. Before turning to those other means, let us briefly consider some exceptions to the principle that money is not an effective motivator of productivity.

Money can be an effective motivator for people who expect it to make a substantial difference in their lives. The young professional, usually possessed more of ideas than of wealth, usually is quite responsive to opportunities to earn more money, because he expects to use it to pay his way into the upper-middle-class way of life. Once he gets there, he will not become averse to money, but he will be less willing to *exert* himself for it; he may even prefer to let his money make money for him than to make it himself. Similarly, younger skilled workers will usually respond to opportunities to increase their incomes with considerable vigor, although this too tends to diminish as their standard of living gradually stabilizes at a level they find acceptable.

While younger professional and skilled workers could be classed as temporarily poor, there is also a large group of what may be called permanently poor people, most of whom are unskilled and likely to remain so. Whether they respond to income opportunities with vigor or lethargy probably depends on whether they expect money, in the amounts they are able to earn, to make any significant, lasting change in their lives. A good deal of poverty is probably the result of expecting to be poor, or more precisely, of assuming (perhaps with good reason) that poverty cannot be climbed out of by one's own efforts. If some means could be found to change these expectations—and that could be done only by changing the reality, not by exhortation—the response of the poor to earnings opportunities would probably be quite strong. As it is, however, money is not a particularly effective stimulus to sustained productive effort for those people whose need for money is most desperate.

Some people are evidently insatiably money-hungry. The main difference between them and people (such as the younger professional) whose lust for money eventually runs its course is that theirs does not. Regardless of their earnings level or capital position, they are continually eager to increase both. They are therefore quite reliable in their response to income opportunities. This particular motivational pattern is evidently associated with certain types of personal background rather than with skill levels or with ethnic groups.

But these are the exceptions: the temporarily money-motivated, because they expect to put their money to their own uses; and the permanently money-motivated, for whom money evidently feeds some insatiable symbolic (not social or economic) need. What about everyone else?

For everyone else, the main motivational significance of money is undoubtedly its role as an indicator of equitability. (This assumes, of course, that basic economic needs are being met; but for the vast majority of Americans in the second half of the 20th century, they *are* being met.) Money is primarily a means of dispensing justice, and this is why a continual process of internal and external wage comparisons is essential. It is also why wage settlements that change the traditional relationships between jobs should be made only when there is clear proof that the job in question is being underpaid relative to its comparative importance. (We might note, parenthetically, that the tendency to use coercive bargaining power is *not* proof of underpayment.)

The only motivational value of equitability, despite all the difficulties of attaining it, is that it motivates people *not* to leave, complain, strike, restrict production, or waste material. Thus for most people, effective motivation is primarily a matter of nonfinancial rewards. Understanding how these rewards operate requires a large view of the way in which organization, communication, and leadership interrelate with one another. In the remaining chapters of this book we will consider how these can be used, and misused, for purposes of motivation.

Chapter 12

Organizational Climate

We have had a good deal to say about organizations in this book; but since in the remaining sections we will focus upon them quite intensively, it behooves us at this point to define what we are talking about. For our purposes, an organization is any deliberately associated group of two or more people whose actions, when coordinated, lead to a planned result. It does not matter who did the deliberating; for example, a platoon of draftees is an organization (if its drill sergeant has it under control), even though it is hardly a voluntary association. What does matter is coordination. Thus two research laboratories in the same corporation, each engaged chiefly in thinking of reasons why a project should not be assigned to the other, are not an organization; they are opponents in a game. On the other hand, a worldwide network of manufacturing plants, each producing parts which are ultimately assembled into one line of finished products, is an organization—in a highly developed form. The term "organization" is meant to apply equally to privately and publicly owned groups involved in just about any kind of activity.

Some organizations create conditions in which it is easy for their members to collaborate, keep each other informed, and maintain a steady rhythm of work; and others do not. It is important to recognize that merely because a group of people may occupy the same building or may be included in the same payroll, they do not necessarily *function* as an organization. In this connection it is useful to

compare the behavior of working groups, most of which are intended
by their managers to function as organizations, to the behavior of
crowds at a sporting event. The behavior of the crowd changes radically from that of an informal but highly coordinated organization
during the game to that of a disarticulated, self-frustrating mob immediately afterward. During the game the spectators stand, sit, cheer,
and groan in a rough sort of unison, coordinated by their common
attention to events on the field. When the game ends they disperse,
get in each other's way, and create mutually exasperating traffic jams.
During the game they are, in effect, an organization of sorts. But the
game itself is the unifying force, and when it ends they deteriorate
quickly into a mere crowd. Thus in the space of a few short minutes
they illustrate the extremes of organization and disorganization.
Working groups, which are nominally organizations, can function at
any point between these same extremes.

Organizations exist to do things that individuals, opponents, and
crowds cannot do. Some organizations do their jobs wonderfully well,
while others perform only indifferently. The reason for this variation
very often lies in the way an organization is organized; and that diagnosis is not as redundant as it sounds. There is a vital, if still dimly
understood, difference between an organization that functions like
one and the organization that is one in name only. The search for
this essential difference has preoccupied behavioral scientists for
more than four decades. It is a slippery quarry, but it has been
glimpsed fairly often in a variety of settings. Among the behavioral
scientists who have studied organizations, there is now a consensus of
sorts on the question of why some organizations function badly and
others function well. But as we shall see in the next chapter, there is
no consensus at all on the more practical question of how to help the
faltering organization. However, there is plenty of activity and even
some research in the area, and we may hope that out of all this ferment some tangible progress will emerge.

The behavioral scientist's diagnosis begins with the way in which
organizations have been structured traditionally and with the reasons
for it. Most organizations, even today, are built on the assumption
that *authority* is indispensable—that unless someone gives a command that someone else feels constrained to obey, nothing really
happens. It follows, then, that some people must be clothed by the

organization with the right to issue commands and the power to enforce them; otherwise (theoretically) the organization will not function. Hence the process of designing a traditional organization is largely a matter of distributing authority to certain people—in a way, one hopes, that insures it will be exercised in a coordinated manner. According to this concept, "organization" itself can be thought of as a process of imposing reason and discipline on what otherwise would be a mere crowd.

The behavioral scientist finds this concept of organization doubly deficient: First, it does not describe reality; second, it does not work.

To begin with, the premise is wrong. Both individuals and groups can get a great deal accomplished without anyone telling them what to do. Sometimes, in fact, authority merely gets in the way. The real role that authority plays in an organization's life is highly complex, despite its theoretical simplicity. Authority undoubtedly can get things done; but it usually gets a great deal *more* done than it was ever intended to do. This "excess" accomplishment results largely from the ways in which organization members come to grips with two emotions that are by far the most common reactions to the experience of living in an authoritarian system: dependency and frustration.

Some people learn to live with authority simply by surrendering to it. That is, they cease trying to understand or modify their work (if they ever did try) and turn instead into rote, unquestioning compliers. This makes them easy to manage and even, in many cases, contented; but it also deprives the organization of whatever capacity they may have had for creative improvements to their work. Their productivity is therefore almost entirely a function of the abilities of management—which is all right provided management has a near-monopoly within the organization on both technical insights and ingenuity. This of course it seldom really has. Further, people who are dependent upon the directions of their managers become attached to familiar ways and rather fearful of change. Thus dependency exacts its price, in the forms of inefficiency and rigidity, for the questionable advantage of making it more convenient to manage people.

As for frustration, people who are either incapable of surrendering their habits of thinking for themselves or unwilling to do so inevitably find an authoritarian management hard to take. They may remove their discomfort by simply leaving the organization, or if for some reason that is not feasible they may "leave" it mentally by finding outlets for their creativity away from their jobs. Or they may grumble, agitate, and even watch patiently for "safe" ways to sabotage the plans of what is, to them, an unresponsive and therefore undeserving management. Once again, the loss of such people may be no loss at all to management if it has no need for fresh ideas or for a hard, critical surface against which to sharpen its own ideas.

On balance, it seems fair to say that authoritarian management works well enough in organizations which are not subject to change and which have mastered their technologies to a degree that leaves little room for improvement. There still are organizations that fit that description, but of course the whole thrust of current history is tending to make them rarer, and by the same token it is making increasingly obsolescent those management styles that rest primarily upon authority. For organizations which do not fit the description, authority exacts a price for relying upon it, and the price is often exorbitant. To the behavioral scientist, the most alarming aspect of this price is its subtlety. The consequences of an inappropriate managerial style accumulate gradually, so gradually that they often appear to be merely a part of the local economic landscape rather than outgrowths of an allegedly "common sense" policy. Thus if an organization finds itself unable to exceed its historic profitability levels or unable to rid itself of recurrent strikes, slowdowns, or inefficient work practices, it is seductively easy to shrug and say, "That's just the way we are . . . ," without ever questioning whether the organization had in fact inadvertently made itself that way. The price, in other words, is too often deducted from the profit side of the ledger without management's even being aware that it is taxing itself.

What matters is whether management's style of managing creates a conducive climate for its people to operate in—conducive in the sense of encouraging behavior that ultimately benefits the organization—or an inhibiting climate that either prevents effective behavior or encourages people to act in ways that ultimately damage the organization's interests. Managerial style is largely a function of the *assumptions* managers make about themselves, their jobs, and the people they manage. Like everyone else, managers act in ways that make sense to them in terms of the kind of world they *think* they are living in. The crucial variable, then, is what managers think about the nature of management. It is perhaps not too uncharitable to say that most managers don't really think very much at all about the process in which they are involved, not because of any particular deficiency on their part, but rather because the process of managing seems so deceptively obvious as to require little or no analysis. The *need* for thinking hard, deeply, and utterly without sentiment about management becomes apparent only after a thoughtful exploration of behavioral theory and research data. That, indeed, is part of the problem!

The word "assumption" is not really a good description of what the behavioral scientists now regard as the crucial variable—the main determinant of what an organization's working climate will be like. To speak of assumptions is to imply more of a conscious, deliberate process than actually takes place. Most people do not think out their basic attitudes toward work, people, and themselves. Instead, they come into these attitudes unthinkingly, absorbing them, as it were, from the behavior of people around them and seldom questioning whether they have interpreted the behavior correctly or, indeed, whether it was appropriate in the first place. There are, in other words, large areas of life to which we are educated in casual, almost accidental ways. These include, not only the entire arena of work (which occupies so sizable a share of our days upon this earth), but most of our relationships with other communities and other nations. It always comes as something of a shock to realize that we teach sewing to girls and baseball to boys with infinitely more care and design that we teach them—or rather permit them to learn what they can—about the dynamics of living and working with each other.

Because assumptions themselves are learned in such a random, unplanned way, their very existence is unclear to many people; and consequently their power to control and influence behavior is greatly enhanced. It seldom occurs to us that we could become captives of our own overly casual and unexamined ways of thinking. But to the extent that we govern our lives by means of assumptions which we have not examined or tested, we are not really free-willed at all. Instead we are mindlessly and predictably following a program—a program that was accumulated rather than planned and that entrenches itself instead of policing itself.

Assumptions are like roadmaps which we follow faithfully, almost without regard to the real topography we are driving through. So, for want of a better term, we will continue to refer to these unvalidated ideas as assumptions, primarily to indicate that the ideas of which we speak are the products not so much of experience as of guesswork and generalization. They are seldom entirely fictitious; but their danger lies less in their inaccuracy than in their tendency to resist the inroads of reason and of experience itself. To the extent that they insulate the individual from the implications of his own experience, assumptions—even more or less realistic ones—place him in peril of tilting with windmills.

The longer an assumption goes unchallenged, the more obvious and self-evident it seems to be; and therefore the less evident the need to examine it. In this manner, ideas about one's self, about one's work, and about other people which would shrivel in the light of day not only are able to persist but can quite literally control a man's thinking on these subjects. This is not to suggest that assumptions are necessarily false or unworkable; obviously, life would be utter chaos if they were. The important point is that assumptions— unexamined beliefs—are part of the mental baggage we all carry around with us; and unless we can somehow contrive to examine them dispassionately they will largely determine what we think we see in our experience. In that case, the lessons we distill from our lives will only be further "proofs" of our assumptions, rather than insights into our lives. Thus we have the too familiar phenomenon of persons who go through life finding reasons for saying, "I told you so," because they are unable to interpret anything that happens to them as being more than just a confirmation of their assumptions. At their best, assumptions are tentative theories to be held lightly until more plausible explanations come along. At their worst, they are convenient devices for preventing life from teaching us anything new. Assumptions are therefore able to assert a sort of tyranny of their own, simply because it is not *evident* that the ideas have become masters of the man, rather than vice versa.

Thus a factory worker who encounters work measurement may see in it a confirmation of what he "always knew" about management: that it entrenches its power with costly, sophisticated instruments and that it presses the individual into a tighter, ever more demanding mold. Or an executive who encounters a budget may see in it a confirmation of what he "always knew" about the financial staff: that they are oblivious to the everyday realities of running a business and that they blindly milk the business to produce this year's profit at the expense of long-term growth. The mental process in both cases is essentially the same: A previously formed assumption, initially supported by little more than suspicion or folklore, is hardened by experiences which, had they been analyzed, might have taught an altogether different lesson. The all too natural tendency is to treat experience not as an opportunity to learn but as a support for what is already believed; and in that sense much of our experience is wasted upon us.

Everyone who works in an organization brings assumptions with him in exactly the same way that he brings his knowledge, skills, and abilities: They are built into him through the normal processes of living. But the assumptions of managers, and in particular those of managers at high levels or of managers who participated in the formation of the organization, have a much stronger effect on the development of organizational climate than those of the rest of its members. This is so because managers design the *architecture* of the firm—what shall be done, and where, and with what, and by whom—and they *regulate* its operations in the sense of setting standards of acceptable and unacceptable performance. Thus they create an environment, partly visible and partly invisible, in which the rest of the organization works. While it is true that nonmanagerial employees develop subordinate styles of their own which reflect their assumptions and guide their behavior in much the same way that a manager's style guides him, these subordinate styles are not, as a rule, as important in the aggregate as managerial styles. Organizational climate is the product of all its component styles, but within that potpourri the influence of managers, and especially top managers, is disproportionately heavy.

It is all too easy to speak of management style within a company as if it were essentially the same from manager to manager, or even (in large companies) from division to division. This of course is not true. Indeed, it is precisely because there are usually some maverick managers or maverick divisions that the possibility of organizational change, for better or worse, exists. (In fact, a good prescription for initiating change in a stagnant company is to make a maverick out of one of its parts.) These mavericks are, in effect, managing an experiment in alternative ways of managing for their companies. As long as such experiments are tolerated, there is always a possibility that they may influence the style of the majority. Over a period of several years—say, a decade—the gradual incorporation of maverick philosophies into the mainstream of management thinking has in fact changed the organizational climate of many companies. For example, the behavioral sciences were themselves rather exotic and even suspect in managerial circles a decade ago, whereas today they are very much a part of both managerial thinking and managerial practice.

Despite mavericks, however, there will ordinarily be a mainstream or typical managerial style which characterizes, at least in an approximate way, the actions of most managers in an organizational unit. The differences *between* units, in other words, will tend to be greater than the differences between managers *within* units. This reflects a natural tendency toward what might be called "organizational homogenization," which a previous generation of observers lamented as conformity and which we know today is simply the result of the ways in which managers are selected and their facility in learning the ropes (that is, absorbing their predecessors' beliefs) . If a unit is new, or has had a recent change of management, or is in the throes of some serious internal conflict, this homogenization will tend to diminish. On the other hand, if a management team has been in office as a team for quite some time and has learned to work smoothly as a unit, the managerial styles of its members will tend to be quite consistent with one another.

Management style is, in other words, complex and fluid. It is much too slippery to be adequately captured by so indefinite a phrase as management style. Nevertheless we will continue to use that inadequate term without further qualification, both for the sake of simplicity and for the lack of a better term. With that caveat behind us, let us briefly explore the ways in which management styles affect organizational climate and the ways in which climate in turn affects productivity under various conditions.

Regardless of the beliefs (if any) which management proclaims or publishes about its job, it will do that job *as if* its underlying assumptions were true. Yet these assumptions do not necessarily correspond to its overt statements. (This is not hypocrisy but perfectly normal human blindness to one's assumptions and to the disparity between them and the values to which we overtly subscribe.) Management's assumptions are revealed not so much in what it proclaims, or even in what it does, as in the *way* in which it does things. Managerial style is essentially qualitative and therefore very hard to measure: It is more a matter of emphasis, nuance, and interpretation than of particular actions or policies. We evidently communicate considerably more to each other with gestures and tones—a lifted eyebrow, a subtle pause that emphasizes the next few words, a well-timed cough—and even with things left unsaid than we ordinarily realize. At any rate it is out on the fringes of behavior, in those added touches which are perhaps less subject to deliberate control, that assumptions have their principal impact. We reveal ourselves when our guard is down. Again we must stress that while we are focusing this discussion upon management, the same analysis could be made of *anyone's* behavior. We single out managers, not because they are peculiar, but rather because their perfectly normal behavior has such weighty consequences for the organizations they direct.

Generally speaking, two kinds of assumptions have considerably more weight than others in forming a managerial style. One concerns the *competence* of the other people in the organization, and the second concerns the degree of *commitment* to organizational goals which they are capable of developing. A manager who assumes that his subordinates are capable of exercising sound, reliable judgment when they encounter situations not covered by instructions is likely, for that very reason, to issue fewer instructions and to do less policing of their work. On the other hand, a manager who assumes that his subordinates are, at best, capable only of following instructions is likely to try to cover every eventuality with detailed directions on what to do. Similarly, a manager who assumes that his subordinates could, given the proper incentives, become wholeheartedly devoted to the attainment of group goals is likely to concentrate on creating those incentives. A manager who assumes that his subordinates are working only because they must is more likely to be interested in ways to prevent loitering, pilfering, and infractions of work rules than in ways to create positive commitment.

The important point is that *assumptions* regarding ability and motivation—the two principal subjects of six decades of behavioral research—largely determine both the selection and the implementation of managerial tactics. Because of the way in which most assumptions evolve, these are very often at variance with the findings of research. That, in a nutshell, is why it is the behavioral scientist rather than the cost accountant or the engineer (both of whose battles have already been won) who is currently on the leading edge of the ferment, controversy, and change within management. But it is important to note that the behavioral scientist came into management because management itself saw the need of having him there and invited him in; indeed, there would be no behavioral science movement of any consequence within management today if this had not happened. Although the relationship is certainly reciprocal, it exists chiefly because some managers had the vision to foresee that a crisis would soon be upon them, and accordingly they called in the most sophisticated help they could find. That crisis was a progressive deterioration in the effectiveness of traditional methods of managerial control.

The old reward-and-punishment system was (and is) breaking down. People with access to rewards were grumbling, complaining of esoteric frustrations, and quitting; people under the threat of punishment were organizing, striking, flouting rules, and restricting production. Some other means of getting people to work together within the framework of some overall coordination was needed. The first breakthrough came in a re-examination of the nature of control itself. The behavioral scientist does not quarrel with management's need for a mechanism that makes behavior at least partially predictable, but he does find that traditional concepts of how control could be accomplished have become woefully unrealistic. Even today, control is too often thought of in a largely mechanical sense, as if men could control other men in the same inescapable, unvarying way that a piston controls a driveshaft. Not only is the manager who has his organization "under control" supposed to know where his cash is going and what his inventory consists of, but he is also supposed to know exactly what he must do to make his subordinates punctual, diligent, loyal, and even (if need be) inventive.

But of course no organization, not even a chain gang, is ever under such absolute control: It always retains a considerable amount of internal direction. This is the end result, not of political trends or of democratic ideology, but simply of a normal human tendency—the tendency to protect oneself by controlling, to the extent possible, the environment in which one has to work and live. Because of this tendency, managerial control in any absolute sense is neither possible nor necessary. What *is* necessary is an understanding of how to work with, not against, man's natural insistence on maintaining a sizable share of control over his own actions. If control can be achieved at all, in other words, it will be achieved through some kind of sharing; and this will become increasingly true as the labor force becomes populated by better-educated and more mobile workers than it has absorbed in previous generations. History, in our era, is not on the side of tradition. As the late Douglas McGregor once put it, "We can improve our ability to control only if we recognize that control consists in selective adaptation to human nature, rather than in attempting to make human nature conform to our wishes."

McGregor was the leading spokesman for the behavioral science approach to organization, and a few words about those of his ideas which are pertinent to the question of organizational climate will be appropriate here.[12] We will consider his concept of how control could actually be achieved and his famous distinction between contrasting sets of managerial assumptions, which he labeled Theory X and Theory Y.

McGregor's analysis began with the observation that traditional control methods not only did not "work" but actually tended to produce what they were intended to prevent:

> Pressure for compliance in a climate lacking in mutual trust and support leads to the perception of threat. The reaction to threat is hostile, defensive, protective behavior. Attempts to correct control systems designed on the basis of conventional strategy by increasing the accuracy of measurement, by audits or by tighter controls simply serve to increase the threat. . . .[13]

In other words, as long as management persists in the assumption that the failure of people to act as it wishes them to act is due either to some moral failure on their part or to its own inadequate policing, it will inevitably dig itself in deeper and deeper. A control system that is *perceived* (regardless of what it is intended to be) as a slur on an individual's integrity motivates him to strike back against the source of the slur. In this sense many conventional methods of auditing behavior (time cards, budgets, quotas, higher-level concurrences, and the like) literally encourage a search for ways to counteract or even to undermine the audit itself. How many office managers, for example, witness the daily 50-yard dash from the parking lot to the time clock, followed by a considerably more leisurely 15 minutes in the powder room or over the morning paper? How many production foremen witness the rapid build-up of production to the minimum daily output quota, followed by an hour or more of scarcely concealed relaxation?

But merely to do away with control mechanisms is no answer, even though many of them probably cost more, in the long run, than they are worth. Reducing controls would probably reduce resistance, but it would not *of itself* bring the typists to their desks on time or lift production above the minimum quota levels. To do that, you need a mechanism for enlisting what McGregor called "commitment": a determination to achieve one's own part of an organizational goal for the sake of personal pride, for the inherent satisfaction in achievement, or even for the sheer enjoyment of it. To many managers, McGregor's call for commitment seemed at first like a pipe dream. Their experience with conventional control systems offered little encouragement for the notion that people can work effectively because they want to rather than because they have to. But some organizations had actually achieved that, and to McGregor the implication was plain: Whatever "magic" enabled those organizations to create commitment in their members had to be identified and then either reproduced or, if necessary, synthesized in other organizations.

To McGregor, this process of identifying the sources of commitment and learning how to transfer them was *the* essential task of the behavioral sciences. His great contributions were his demonstration that commitment was possible, and not necessarily on a restricted scale, and his persuasion of some managers that the behavior they had witnessed in their companies was perhaps not so much "inherent" in human nature as it was a product of the conditions under which employees were required to function. The source to which he traced both the commitment-generating climate and the apparently control-demanding climate was what we have referred to here as assumptions. The study of how assumptions form and of how they might be changed was the principal preoccupation of McGregor's later career. In the next chapter we will review sensitivity training, which he regarded as perhaps the most promising method for modifying assumptions; for the moment let it be noted that he was too much of a scientist to develop premature enthusiasms for techniques that were (and still are) insufficiently researched themselves.

Theory X and Theory Y were not, as is commonly supposed, simply courteous devices for sidestepping the issue as to which managerial approach was right and which was wrong. They were not even opposites. McGregor designated as Theory X the more or less traditional set of assumptions about human nature on which management practices had been built since the Industrial Revolution: that work was not a natural activity for most people, and that intelligent cooperation within an organized system was equally contrary to most men's instincts. But since industry required both work and cooperation of its employees, a means had to be found for exacting them from people, and this means was developed (said Theory X) primarily through various ways of manipulating the economic dependence of the average employee upon his employer. To compensate for the employee's inability or unwillingness to make sensible decisions in the best interests of the organization, management imposed explicit rules from which the employee was not to deviate, and it also provided a means of auditing (first through supervisors, later through reporting procedures) to insure that he did not deviate.

McGregor regarded the assumptions underlying this Theory X approach as a rapidly antiquating, if perhaps previously justified, view of mankind. He recognized that there were circumstances in which these assumptions were perhaps the most realistic that could be made, and he did not dispute the appropriateness of Theory X tactics under those circumstances. What disturbed him was the inertia of Theory X—its near-universality despite the rapid change of employee populations. McGregor was not advocating a "soft," automatically trusting approach to management any more than he advocated a "hard," automatically suspicious approach. What he pleaded for was an *appropriate* approach, based on an examination of organizational realities rather than upon automatic reactions of any kind. That was the essence of Theory *Y:* an insistence that managerial strategies be based upon examination, not assumption, and that there were *no* eternal verities upon which management could rely so faithfully that a close examination of its own organization became unnecessary. The defect in Theory *X* lay not in its assumptions but in its rigidity: its tendency to suggest that other approaches would not be appropriate, even in other circumstances.

Unfortunately, many of McGregor's readers (including both sympathizers and others who were not so sympathetic) saw Theory *Y* as simply the opposite of Theory *X*. Perhaps, to some of them, Theory *Y* suggested some sort of longed-for millennium when all men would be made responsible simply by treating them as if they were. In fact, part of McGregor's otherwise well-deserved popularity among managers may have been based on this misinterpretation of Theory *Y*. It provided a sort of intellectual defense for managing more sentimentally, less demandingly, than they were accustomed to. No one was more sensitive to this misinterpretation than McGregor himself. His final book, *The Professional Manager,* was clearly his attempt to correct what he regarded as an overreaction by his own more zealous supporters.

McGregor's stress on *appropriateness*—on fitting managerial style to the realities of an organization's members and its situation, rather than to the habits or assumptions of its managers—is crucial to our examination of styles and climates. To oversimplify a bit, it is possible to conceive of four combinations of managerial style and what might be called organizational "readiness"—in this case, we refer to readiness to accept a permissive managerial style in a mature, responsible manner. To avoid compounding the misinterpretation of Theory *Y*, we will describe managerial styles in two extreme forms: coercive and permissive. A coercive style relies entirely upon management action, typically involving various restrictions and sanctions, to motivate people to work; a permissive style relies largely upon the employees' own willingness, especially when they are suitably supported and rewarded, to take whatever actions are required of them. It need hardly be said that such "pure" forms as those we have described here probably do not exist. Most organizational units, however, could probably be placed with reasonable precision at some point between the two.

A coercive management style would be quite appropriate to a condition of extreme unreadiness. It would, in fact, be about the only style through which management could expect to accomplish very much. On the other hand, to the degree that the organization approximates a higher degree of readiness, coercive styles become increasingly inappropriate. In fact, beyond a certain point they become destructive in the sense of generating so much opposition that the organization functions far less efficiently than it would under an alternative style. On the other hand, permissive management in a condition of unreadiness is simply an invitation to abuse and costly, inefficient operation. (We are clearly implying here that people who have not been prepared for responsibility will *not* become responsible if they are merely treated as if they were.) But permissive management in a group that is ready for it is not only appropriate; it is also the most effective prescription we know for organizational growth and productivity.

What matters most, then, is not managerial style per se but management's ability to diagnose readiness accurately and to stimulate and enhance it. Both are *very* difficult questions to resolve in actual practice, which is of course part of the reason why the problem of organizational climate continues to generate considerably more heat than light. But our analysis thus far compels us to express a bias, which is that wherever research data can be collected and analyzed, the results are likely to be a far more reliable guide than *anyone's* assumptions. Recognizing the ubiquitous nature of assumptions and the futility of debating about conflicting assumptions, let us examine three sets of research data for the clues they offer on the effects of managerial styles upon organizational climate. Although the findings themselves come from widely differing sources (Dutch manufacturing plants, the U.S. Department of State, and a cross-section of American industry), there is a significant degree of consistency among them.

G. H. Hofstede, a Dutch psychologist, conducted an unusually thorough study of the effects of budgetary control systems on lower levels of management.[14] Working in six Dutch plants of five companies representing the printing, food processing, metal products, textile, and electronics industries, Hofstede held detailed interviews with some 90 line and 50 staff managers, all in the first three levels of management. His objective was to discover how and why they reacted to the way in which operating budgets were administered in their companies. (Capital budgets were not considered.) He was therefore able to correlate the companies' budgetary practices both with the subjective feelings of the managers they affected, on the one hand, and with their overt performance measurements, on the other. What emerged was some particularly valuable insights into the ways in which organizational climate is affected by financial controls.

There is, of course, a good deal of managerial folklore about the effects of budgets, and there is also some relevant research on the subject. Budgets are regarded as either tyranny or salvation, depending largely on the side of the organization from which you look at them. Further, various research studies have indicated that budgets tend, at least under certain fairly common circumstances, to result in opposition to the staff by the line, conflict between departments, fault finding, and parochialism—to mention just a few of their more deleterious effects. For all that, budgets are an indispensable tool of financial management. Hence they are usually regarded, at least by those who have to live with them, as a necessary or at least unavoidable evil.

Hofstede's study calls into question whether there is an *inevitable* conflict between organizational requirements for control and individual needs for autonomy. True, that very kind of conflict is evident enough much of the time; but under certain (too rare) conditions, budgets seem able not only to motivate superior performance but actually to make the job seem like fun as well. In some of the departments Hofstede studied, budgets seemed almost to create a "game" spirit: they were a challenge accepted as much for the joy or sport of trying to outperform a standard as for their inevitability. To find the antecedents of the game reaction and to differentiate them from those of the more common reactions to budgets became, for Hofstede, the principal objective of his research.

Notwithstanding the negative or demotivating aspects of budgets, which are real and serious, it is apparent that budgets can, under certain circumstances, have a positive motivating effect: They can lead to a sustained improvement in performance. According to Hofstede, the first and most important circumstance is that the budget itself be fair and relevant. Since these are both essentially subjective considerations, it is vital that some mechanism exist through which fairness and relevance can be negotiated, if necessary, so that some kind of consensus can be reached. But genuine consensus, as distinguished from mere acquiescence to the inevitable, is attainable only when the parties are able to bargain, so to speak, as equals. This means that the company's financial officers must *in practice* be open to influence from the line. If budgets are negotiated through mutual staff-line consultation, rather than imposed by fiat or presented on a take-it-or-try-your-luck-on-an-appeal basis, the likelihood that they will engage the line manager's *personal* motivation is greatly enhanced.

There are a number of reasons why this is so. The most obvious is the effect of participation in the decision to set the budget at its specific levels. The line manager's own judgment and trustworthiness are on trial precisely to the extent that his judgment and his persuasiveness have influenced those levels—no more and no less. If the budgetary standards turn out to be too loose (too easily attained), he will be revealed as at best an incompetent estimator and at worst an unprincipled scoundrel; if they turn out to be too tight, he will be revealed as a fool. His pride, reputation, and ego will all be involved in the rightness of the decision, and for precisely that reason he will *work harder to make the decision right* by operating effectively within the limits of his budget than he would if he were not so involved. The enlistment of his ego will, in other words, tap reserves of effort, determination, and ingenuity that are not ordinarily called upon.

On the other hand, if the line manager feels his budget is really the product of someone else's judgment, he will have no particular stake in *making* it turn out to be realistic. Except for minimum compliance and whatever sense of loyalty he may have to the firm, he will have no reason to regard the tightness or looseness of the budget as a reflection on anyone but the financial department. If his operations are restricted, he can rationalize by saying he is understaffed. He will consider the fault to rest with the staff, not with him; and about the only additional effort he is likely to show will be to make it clear to everyone that his difficulties are entirely attributable to his budget.

However, subtler and potentially more powerful motives can be triggered when budgets are, in effect, negotiated. Hofstede calls attention to the possibility of tapping the "achievement motive" when budgets are perceived as fair and relevant. The importance of the achievement motive would be difficult to overestimate, since it is apparently insatiable and operates so as to produce continual striving for accomplishment *largely for its own sake*—that is, with comparatively little reference to external rewards. What we know about the achievement motive suggests that it is especially likely to be aroused under certain conditions; specifically, when the task in question is regarded as significant (intrinsically worth achieving), difficult but still attainable, and measurable (in the sense of providing more or less prompt feedback on progress toward the target). A budget which the individual has helped to set *can* have all these characteristics for him; at least, it is much more likely to have them than is one which was simply presented to him. Of course, some people will be more responsive to such opportunities than others. The important point is that a *realistically challenging* budget is much more likely to tap whatever potential for achievement motivation is present than either a budget that appears to be scarcely attainable at all or one that appears to be absurdly easy to reach.

Hofstede observed that actual performance against standards tended to be best when the line managers regarded their relationship with the financial staff, and with the budget itself, as a sort of game—in the sense of an opportunity to match wits in a friendly contest where the prize for winning is simply a boost to one's ego, and the penalty for losing is largely a matter of being disappointed with one's own performance. In other words, budgeteering can become a skill which is practiced largely for the enjoyment of playing the game well, much as golf, bowling, or even market speculation is practiced because playing it well can be fun. Hofstede also notes that whether such a game spirit is actually aroused, or whether the budget simply plays its usual role as a bone of contention between line and staff, can depend to a considerable degree on the *tactics* of the staff.

Tactics follow more or less directly from assumptions. In this case, Hofstede draws a distinction between financial staffs that assume it is their role to teach, advise, and provide expert assistance, on the one hand, and those which assume it is their role to police, to measure, and in the last analysis to judge the performance of the line, on the other. When the staff has the first concept, the line is evidently much more likely to react to a budget the way an inveterate golfer reacts to par. But when the staff has the second concept, the line managers are more likely to feel that the staff can look good only by making them look bad. They will therefore tend to assume that some sort of malevolence or arbitrary whim lies behind the staff's every action. If the first set of assumptions obtains, tactics will tend to be employed that have the effect of putting more control of financial performance in the hands of the line. For example, Hofstede notes the use of periodic sampling rather than constant measurement of every manager or cost center, as well as the use of variance limits (a range of permissible plus or minus deviations from target figures) rather than precise limits.

Another characteristic of effective budgetary motivation, according to Hofstede, is open communication. The communication that customarily takes place with respect to budgets consists of investigations and requests for reports, on the part of the staff, and of concealment or at least a certain lack of candor by the line. This is obviously unproductive, but it is also entirely natural if the staff conceives of its job as keeping the line honest. The line will then understandably become both self-protective and more motivated to comply than to cooperate. If the staff understands and accepts the necessity to share its power—for example, by refraining from arbitrary rejection of budget-increase requests or from across-the-board (rather than selective) reductions—it is more likely to win line cooperation. It takes tangible behavioral evidence like this, more than mere protestation, to convince the line that the staff is prepared to meet it halfway.

Hofstede's observations make considerable sense, both in terms of motivation theory and more particularly in terms of the behavioral scientists' concept of the effects of organizational climate. Basically, he has confirmed the theory that assuming that people in organizations need to be controlled by agencies other than their own self-control makes for less profitable operations in the long run. Further, he substantiates the idea that assuming that most people are capable of adequately controlling their own activities leads to more profitable operations. The actual chain of events is, of course, more complex than that. It leads from assumptions to a choice of tactics, which in turn affects the perceptions of those who are affected by those tactics, which in turn leads to the selection of tactics in response to the first tactics, which then affects the perceptions of the people who started the chain, *ad infinitum*. The important point is that organizational climates can and do affect efficiency, and that the principal variable affecting those climates is the way in which people in positions of power *think* about the requirements of their jobs and the capabilities of the people who are available to help them get their jobs done.

In 1965 the U.S. Department of State invited Chris Argyris, a behavioral scientist at Yale University, to explore the question of how the department might cope with some of its organizational problems. This led to a series of seminars in which some 60 Foreign Service officers met with Argyris and undertook a candid review of the unwritten codes by which they worked and lived (which Argyris refers to as the "living system"). This in turn led to a program in which the State Department has attempted to foster its own organizational development, much as many private companies have done. It also led to the publication of a short essay which provides one of the most revealing glimpses into the inner mechanics of organizational climate ever published about *any* organization, public or private.[15]

Before reviewing the findings of this study, it is important to place them in their proper context. The State Department has been the butt of so much journalistic and political criticism, as well as of a widespread contemporary folklore, that it would be easy to look upon the results of this investigation as a condemnation or as just one more proof of how bad things really are in Washington's "Foggy Bottom." It is neither. First of all, the very fact that the department could undertake a study of this kind on its own initiative bespeaks a much higher degree of realism and determination to come to grips with tough internal problems than most organizations, in or out of government, have yet shown. Second, while the State Department, like all organizations, has its own peculiar codes of conduct and its own distinctive climate, there is no reason to believe that other organizations would look any more rational or less self-defeating if they were exposed to the same kind of examination. In fact, the State Department study revealed it to be remarkably similar to most other large, relatively old organizations in all the fundamental aspects of its internal climate. The differences are largely matters of detail that reflect the department's history, the nature of its business (diplomacy), and the character of its "ownership" (the executive branch and, to a considerable degree, the legislative branch of the Federal Government). Third, the department asked Argyris to concentrate on what was wrong, so that its problems could be isolated and attacked; therefore, the study did not focus upon the many strengths of the organization. Let what follows be understood, then, not as an attack upon the State Department but as a diagnosis of organizational climate not unlike that which has emerged from similar studies of other organizations. (It is also probably not unlike the findings that would emerge from a study of any organization that had as much courage to look itself in the eye as did the State Department.)

A living system, as Argyris uses the term, consists of the ways which the people within an organization have evolved for getting along together. It is the accepted code of conduct, the usually unwritten and seldom articulated rules and traditions that govern the behavior of members toward each other. Some kind of living system is both natural and necessary within any organization. Without one, each member's behavior would be unpredictable or even incomprehensible to every other member, and the organization could scarcely function in an organized way. The living system seldom corresponds exactly to an organization's published statements about itself, and it is seldom the result of deliberate planning. Instead, a living system results from a history of compromises through which the purposes of both the organization and the people in it have managed to be served.

One of Argyris' major premises is that most living systems tend to gravitate toward organizational ineffectiveness. Any organization is essentially an information-processing machine in the sense that it exists chiefly to provide data for decisions, to implement the decisions, and then to provide feedback data on the effects of the decisions. Its effectiveness is therefore a matter of the appropriateness, timeliness, and clarity of the information it provides. To the extent that information is blocked or distorted, is provided inopportunely or too late, or is obscured or resisted, the organization is functioning inefficiently. Argyris has found that the living system of any organization tends to produce one or more of these inefficiencies, because the people who comprise it learn to be self-protective. More importantly, Argyris points to a tendency on the part of management itself to behave in ways that bring out the worst in many and the best in few—an unintentional and usually unconscious effect. It is an ironic but nonetheless well-documented fact that managers often induce behavior on the part of their subordinates to which the managers themselves object. This is not because managers are lacking in vision but rather because they are caught in the same living system as their subordinates and are, in effect, charged with enforcing it.

The living system of the State Department—or more precisely, of the high-level Foreign Service officers who participated in this study—included a number of elements which had the long-term effect of rendering its information flows sluggish and of insulating the department against the effects of viewpoints and attitudes that were different from its own. One of these was a tendency for these officers not to "level" with each other; that is, to avoid expressing themselves candidly and to withhold some of the information that was available to them (including information as to their own judgments and attitudes). While an inclination to play one's cards close to the vest is by no means peculiar to diplomats, it gets considerable reinforcement in a profession where negotiation—which in the diplomatic context is the art of winning as many concessions as possible in exchange for as few as possible—is so critical to success and so frequently used. (To avoid confusion, let it be understood that the term "negotiation" will be used in the sense just defined in this section only. Elsewhere in this book it denotes a process through which the people who may be affected by a decision can influence it.)

Apparently these officers carried the tactics of negotiation over into their relationships with one another. That is, they tended to withhold certain information from each other for the purpose of advancing whatever internal cause they had espoused. This, too, is not at all uncommon in industry. In the State Department, however, negotiation was so firmly rooted in the traditions of the organization that people not only were disposed to use the tactics of negotiation much of the time but also recognized when other people were negotiating with them and even recognized when other people recognized that they were negotiating. The charade persisted, however, for the reason that people who were good at it tended to do well in the organization and those who were not tended to leave it.

Another aspect of the living system revealed by Argyris' study was a tendency to regard overt displays of competitiveness as uncouth and to react to them by becoming icily correct and bland. This, too, had its origins in the world of diplomacy, where above all else it is important to preserve an atmosphere in which further talking is both possible and likely to lead somewhere. But it also tips a man's hand. When some of the officers detected that stiff politeness in another officer's bearing, they knew perfectly well that he felt they had violated the rules of the game and that he was now for all practical purposes inaccessible. Consequently, a great deal of effort went into avoiding such impasses by side-stepping confrontations and by preserving enough ambiguity to permit opposing viewpoints to coexist. This made it possible for the various factions to work together. But it also had the effect of postponing decisions, encouraged behind-the-scenes campaigns instead of open debate, and led to studied attempts to keep relationships impersonal—and, to that extent, less than genuine. That the system itself was indirect and wasteful was generally acknowledged; but overcoming it required more force than any individual could muster. This was so because any attempt to change the system through individual intervention would have appeared to be an attack, and the system would simply have closed itself against the maverick. It became, in other words, a sort of self-perpetuating code, quite impervious to anyone's frustration with it or dislike of it.

This living system thrived on deference, on movement by slow and carefully measured steps, and above all on a tendency to let the system itself dominate the individuals within it. The last point is a very common observation in organizational studies of this type. In other words, what is wrong with most organizations is not so much the caliber of the people in them as it is the system of relationships on which their behavior toward one another is predicated. In the State Department, the tendency of the living system to encourage discretion, circumspection, and conformity was greatly reinforced by the essentially ambiguous position of the Foreign Service within the government as a whole. That is, no officer could ever be certain that the policy guidance he received from his superiors would not be countermanded by forces outside the department. He worked in an uncertain environment, in which to pin one's hopes too fondly on a particular program or policy was to court disappointment. The predictable result was a certain detachment: Officers learned not to become very involved in their work and to resist any cause that was pleaded with too much fervor.

The "selection out" system, by which officers whose efficiency ratings remained consistently low were encouraged to leave the service, had the effect of homogenizing the behavior of those who stayed. People who were prone to violate the system's norms—for example, to state opinions too bluntly or to press for a decision which, if made, would hurt a particular group—tended to receive low ratings. (This was not, of course, the only reason for low ratings.) The effect was to eliminate those who did not abide by the system and to retain those who had learned to make their peace with it. This homogenization is of course very common in organizations that have existed long enough to establish well-defined living systems of their own and that have a growth rate slow enough to prevent the consolidation of different systems. The only difference is that in the State Department a formal mechanism exists which accomplished the standardization of behavior; in other organizations it usually occurs more subtly, through attrition or promotion policies.

The reward and punishment system operates in such a way as to perpetuate the living system, even when the living system progressively incapacitates the organization with respect to its main "outside" mission (in this case, implementing the foreign policy of the United States). Further, the living system operates so as to make the members of the organization introspective—that is, preoccupied with the internal mechanics and politics of making the system work—to the detriment of the external matters that constitute their business. Finally, the living system operates so as to protect itself from both internal and external assault, even when those assaults are designed to make it more effective with regard to the organization's main mission—its *raison d'être*. The "instinct" of most living systems is to survive by insulating itself, not by adapting itself. This is why anachronistic organizations sometimes survive for a time, even after they have ceased to be relevant to the purposes for which they were created.

It cannot be overemphasized that only the details of the preceding discussion are peculiar to the State Department. The essential realities of organizational climate just described can be found in almost any organization inside or outside the government. During the long, slow evolution of organizations to their present size and complexity, the tendency for internal climates to outlive their original reason for existence, thereby rendering the organization irrelevant to its external realities, was seldom a serious problem. This was because outside changes occurred slowly enough to permit even ponderous adaptations to keep pace. Today, those organizations that tend to be in the forefront of change, actually creating change and handsomely benefiting from it, are likely to be both young and rapidly growing. For these reasons they are unlikely to have firmly entrenched traditions. Instead of having a characteristic managerial style they have a loosely knit collection of styles, enabling them to exploit a variety of potential opportunities. The organizations which have had to work hardest to keep up with change, and which to a certain extent have been damaged by it, tend to be older and to have grown at rates slow enough to permit the reward-and-punishment system to operate faster than the rate at which "new blood" has been infused. They are, in other words, organizations with entrenched, relatively static traditions. Does the era of accelerating change handicap the older, slower-growing organizations to the advantage of the younger, faster-growing ones? Evidently it does, *if*—as is often the case—their organizational climates are such as to make them inefficient information processors and at the same time impervious to changes in outside realities.

The implication of Argyris' study, and of related investigations in private industry, is that some kind of overhaul is needed to enable organizations to make better use of their own information-processing potentialities. The requirements of this overhaul are that it overcome the natural resistance of living systems to being changed, that it reorient the living system toward current and anticipated outside realities, and above all that it build adaptation rather than insulation into the system for the future. We will review some contemporary attempts to accomplish these purposes in the next chapter.

The most comprehensive set of investigations yet undertaken of the relationship between managerial styles and organizational effectiveness is contained in the continuing research program of the Institute for Social Research at the University of Michigan. By now its studies have been extended to literally hundreds of companies in a wide variety of industries. This work constitutes the largest available foundation on which to erect some major generalizations about organizations and the internal factors that tend to make them function well or function poorly. Yet even this massive accumulation of data yields only tentative, not conclusive, implications for management. The reason lies in a discovery that is, in fact, one of the Michigan group's most important contributions to the scientific study of management.[16]

This discovery is the "time lag"; that is, the time that elapses between the introduction of a change in management style and the detection of the full results of that change. Apparently it takes considerably longer for these causes to develop their full-blown effects than had been assumed. About two years, or possibly even longer in some cases, seems to be required before changes in management style yield their full consequences in organizational performance. One effect of this discovery is to raise the question whether most other behavioral research programs have lasted long enough—whether, for example, studies that revealed no particular results would eventually have shown significant changes, or whether studies that showed changes in one direction might eventually have seen them shift in another direction, had they been extended far enough across time. A definitive answer may take years. Meantime, piecing together bits of evidence from various sources, Rensis Likert (director of the institute) has developed a theory of how the time lag evidently affects organizational climate.

According to Likert, if management tactics change in the direction of becoming more demanding and coercive (for example, by introducing stricter work measurements, reducing budgets, and adopting a take-it-or-leave-it attitude with regard to employee complaints), the *short-range* effect upon operating results will tend to be an improvement. The *long-range* effect, on the other hand, will tend to be a serious, prolonged decline in operational efficiency. If the change in management tactics is in the direction of becoming more supportive (for example, through delegation, job enrichment, two-way communication loops, and so on), the short-range effect upon operating results will tend to be either no change or even, under certain circumstances, a decrease in efficiency. But the long-range result will tend to be a lasting, significant improvement in profit or any other index of organizational efficiency.

In order to understand why this happens, it is necessary to distinguish among three kinds of events: managerial actions, attitude changes, and operating results as revealed by orthodox financial measurements. It is the slow, hidden effects of management styles upon *attitudes* that reverse the original trends and then go on to produce lasting changes in the quality of organizational performance. Because these changes occur subtly and only gradually, and because they are likely to precede changes in financial measurements by months or even years, Likert believes that regular measurements should be made of employees' attitudes toward relevant aspects of the organization. These measurements should then be assessed along with accounting statistics in order to determine the full momentum and direction that management tactics have produced.

What evidently happens is this: In the first case (a shift toward control by coercion) unused physical capacity will be utilized quickly and overhead costs will be reduced, thereby producing a rapid, sometimes even dramatic improvement in operating statistics. There will seldom be nearly so immediate a response on the part of employees; they will frequently appear to have simply accepted the new tactics passively. (Actually, they are likely to be a bit bewildered and still wistfully hoping that the "good old days" will soon return.) Management may thus conclude that whatever fears it may have had of an employee backlash were groundless, and it may congratulate itself for having brought off such a marked change so painlessly.

At this point, and for a period of several months, management is almost literally living on borrowed time. Whatever reserves of goodwill its employees had for it, whatever willingness to give management the benefit of the doubt and to tolerate its minor or temporary deficiencies, is being rapidly depleted. However, most managements are still inclined to assess employee attitudes with such relatively crude indicators as turnover statistics or grievance submissions, both of which tend to reflect fully (rather than partially) deteriorated morale. Lacking a reliable early-warning mechanism of the kind Likert advocates, management may in effect be congratulating itself while the foundations of its profitability are being rapidly eroded away. One ironic and not infrequent result of this time lag is that the executives who produced the improvements are likely to be promoted before the longer-term consequences of their policies become apparent. Someone else reaps the whirlwind; and likely as not he is blamed for it as well.

Meantime, the employees will be progressively discovering that what has happened is not temporary and that the new "regime" is not to their liking. It is *not* the demand for higher productivity, but rather the resort to thinly veiled threat and the implication that management considers them unmotivatable except by threat, that produces the dislike. The simple fact is that coercive tactics which stress sanctions against the individual if he does not comply, and which minimize his potentialities for responsible self-management, are seen as an insult by most adults. Once the full implications of the insult become clear—that continued employment in this environment will be demeaning and degrading—several chains of events are begun which all lead, inevitably, to organizational ineffectiveness. The time lag is largely due to the fact that this realization generally comes slowly and is even resisted for a time. It is no more welcome to the employees than its eventual consequences are to management.

The simplest and most damaging of these chains of events begins with the decision to leave the company. This is much more likely to be taken by highly competent people who are assured of a warm reception elsewhere, or by specialists whose skills are in short supply, than by run-of-the-mill or marginal employees. The sophisticated personnel man knows that conventional turnover statistics can conceal several kinds of turnover, and that this kind is much more serious (even at relatively low rates) than the turnover that merely flushes out transient or nonessential employees. Top-quality people are hard to replace at any time and even harder when the word gets out (as it will) that this company has become a less attractive employer than it used to be. As a result, the average levels of skill, competence, and experience within the organization will go down. The human organization's potential for productivity is diminished, and management is left with less to work with. Indeed, it finds itself in much the same bind it would be in if it had destroyed a scarce and expensive piece of capital equipment—with this difference: Money alone may suffice to replace a ruined machine. It will not suffice to restore competence. Inevitably, a deterioration in competence leads to lessened quantity and quality of production.

Those who cannot or will not leave are not without recourse for dealing with their changed environment. From a psychological standpoint it is quite necessary that they fight against it. This is another of those easily misunderstood points whose significance to management would be difficult to overestimate. The various forms of employee resistance to management—such as slowdowns and work stoppages, restriction of output and high scrap loss, selection of militant union leaders, and the rest—are usually a *normal* response to an unsatisfactory organizational climate. They are seldom simply the result of obstinacy or outside agitation. Most workers who actively undertake to penalize and sabotage management do so because they feel they have been attacked; and they counterattack in any way they can that appears to be appropriate and safe. To fail to do so, given the premise that management's policies are insulting or exploitative, would be sick; it would be tantamount to accepting a drastically lowered estimate of their manhood and their personal worth as human beings. Consequently, coercive managerial tactics, even when they are intended only to tighten up inefficient operations, inevitably invite retaliation. That retaliation in turn exacts a continuing toll on costs, quality, and output that eventually destroys—in fact, "overkills"—the initial gains of such tactics.

On the other hand, a change in tactics in the direction of control by motivation (harnessing latent potentialities for personal commitment and self-control) may also produce bewilderment and skepticism at first. Many employees will wait, with the "wisdom" born of cynicism, for management to tire of its flirtation with new fads and revert to type. Those who are willing to involve themselves in decisions affecting their work may stumble and make mistakes at first. Management itself may move awkwardly in its initial efforts to build commitment. The entire process, in other words, is likely to begin unevenly and to proceed by fits and starts. Hence the statistics that measure performance may show no gain at first and may even decline.

This initial period of ambiguity puts management's faith in its philosophy to a severe test. Most managers are accustomed to being measured on performance over comparatively short periods—monthly or quarterly, or at most annually. To adhere steadfastly to a program that does not move the trend line in the desired direction for several months in a row is at best difficult. This is why understanding and support at the highest levels are essential to give such programs their maximum chance of success. Interestingly, Likert notes that managers who have successfully implemented such programs *without* top-level support tend to be situated in cities far removed from corporate headquarters, where their activities are not so closely scrutinized.

But in time enough employees are won over to begin producing a difference. The company holds its better people and improves its ability to attract more of them (which incidentally relieves the strain on its selection methods). Lateness, absenteeism, "sickness" days, and other forms of time loss decrease. Quality goes up and scrappage goes down. Slowly the organization's productivity record builds toward new heights. Technological or organizational changes cause relatively little disruption because they are viewed as the decisions of a management that is competent and benevolent, not malevolent.

In reviewing a very large number of studies that compare management style with operating results, Likert has observed that the styles of consistently high- and low-producing groups tended to be quite different in many respects. In general, the low-producing units follow what we have described here as a coercive approach. They do not deviate from it because they consider it a necessity. To do less, they feel, would be to invite their employees to take undue advantage of their liberality. The high-producing units tend to enlist the pride and self-satisfaction of employees in their work to the extent that they can. They do this not by telling them that their work is important but by making it important. That there is a significant lesson in these findings for managers—especially those who would practice management by motivation—can hardly be doubted.

We can now try to summarize the rough consensus that has appeared among behavioral scientists who attempt to define the factors that make the crucial difference between organizations that function effectively and those that do not. To the extent that these differences reflect the internal workings of the organization itself, and not some external factor such as market conditions or availability of credit, they are due to differences in assumptions by managers regarding the human potentialities of their respective organizations. More specifically, the difference seems to be due to the ways in which managers conceive of the capabilities of their available manpower resources to develop both technical competence and emotional commitment to work. These assumptions are the direct antecedents of managerial tactics, and especially of the intensely communicative nuances of *how* tactics are applied.

What we have referred to as organizational climate is essentially the pattern of behavior which the managers and the managed learn for dealing with each other. It has its roots in their assumptions about each other and in their interpretations of each other's behavior. All too often, both sets of assumptions are essentially unvalidated ideas which have never been examined and which entrench themselves by interpreting experience as confirmation of the assumptions. Relatively little effective communication is possible in these circumstances. This is one of the major reasons why most organizational climates are *not* conducive to maintaining a high level of motivation for productivity.

However, effective motivation is clearly possible in some organizational climates. Indeed, the climate itself, rather than any particular component of it, seems to be the principal reason why those groups which consistently outstrip the average attainments of comparable groups are able to do so. The whole organizational climate, so to speak, is greater than the sum of its parts. The same generalization seems to be true with regard to ineffectively motivated groups: the deadening climate is more of an inhibitor than any of the particular tactics or policies that have helped to produce it. The problem, then, is to find practical ways of coming to grips with organizational climates that make less than optimal use of available human resources. The potential payoff is enormous, but the problems of finding the right methods and making them work are severe. But the important point, as we shall see in the next chapter, is that the battle has been joined. What we perhaps euphemistically call organizational development is—in terms of its aims if not yet in terms of its achievements—the premier managerial challenge of our times.

Chapter 13

Organizational Development

THE PROPER FUNCTION OF AN ORGANIZATION IS TO ORCHES-trate the application of its members' skills and energies to the solution of larger problems than any of them could handle separately. "Orchestration" in this sense implies that the total contribution of all the individuals in the organization is made greater than its mere sum. If an organization does not multiply, at least to some extent, what its members could achieve severally, there is no reason for it to exist. But to orchestrate implies more than just producing more. It also means that skills are blended and optimized. An organization justifies itself by applying its skills deftly, not just massively.

The concept of organizational development rests on two assumptions: that this orchestration is seldom accomplished with as much deftness or effect as the organization is potentially capable of achieving; and that many older styles of orchestrating have been invalidated by changes in the environment. (The question whether they were ever really effective in the past is thus academic.) Most behavioral scientists would not quarrel with either of those assumptions.

The problem, in brief, is to optimize the effectiveness of groups. We are concerned here with the extent to which organizational climate can have an enhancing effect upon their accomplishments. Organizational climate is best understood as a pattern of mutual expectations which largely governs the ways in which organizational members, both those who manage and those who are managed, deal with one another. This climate, and more precisely these expectations, are the targets of organizational development. The underlying theory is that if these expectations can be made more realistic, the people in an organization can learn to enhance each other's effectiveness. This demands that people's assumptions about themselves, their jobs, and each other be examined and, if found deficient, discarded and replaced.

The examining, discarding, and replacing can be done only by the organization members themselves, since it is their own thinking that is subject to change. But to suggest that thinking is awry and in need of redirection sometimes arouses cries of manipulation or brainwashing. Actually, organizational development is no more manipulative than a course in algebra. It is an attempt to teach an orderly approach to matters that are usually left undefined. However, there can be no blinking the fact that organization development calls into question one's own behavior and its antecedent assumptions; and in that sense it demands, for most people, an unprecedented confrontation with reality.

To the extent that we let our assumptions govern our behavior, we are all at least potentially unrealistic. But to concede this in more than just an intellectual way, and to go beyond that and put one's own assumptions to the test of open exploration, is no easy task. It is therefore legitimate to ask whether this kind of exercise is really necessary, whether the same purposes could not be accomplished more easily in some other way. The answer is complex and not entirely clear.

In the modern organization, with its dependence on appropriate response and feedback, we seem to have a set of requirements for which our experience has not adequately prepared us. That is, we get little if any practice in examining our assumptions or our reactions to other people's behavior, such as our tendencies to filter what they say or even to "turn them off" if we do not like what they say. As a result we are all somewhat handicapped, so to speak, with respect to the requirements of membership in an effective organization. To function effectively, an organization requires that its members transmit needed information to one another at the right time and with ample clarity; and the plain fact is that life prepares few of us to function as efficient message-switching mechanisms. Precisely because the requirements of large, information-dependent organizations are unprecedented, some kind of supplementary education is often needed to prepare people for effective membership within them.

The real problem is not so much with organizations as with ourselves. We are prone to lead relatively lax intellectual lives; we do not demand enough proof of our casually acquired but firmly held ideas. Just as the computer required management to rethink and rationalize its internal systems and procedures, eliminating illogic that had not been noticed previously because nothing had compelled attention to it, so the modern organization demands a certain degree of intellectual housecleaning on the part of those who are genuinely committed to managing it effectively. Thus managers, along with that increasing corps of professionals and specialists whom Peter Drucker calls "knowledge workers," find themselves in an unprecedented, somewhat disconcerting dilemma: It appears that to maximize their effectiveness, they must contribute *more* than just their technical abilities. They must also learn a few skills for which ordinary life offers little preparation: how to examine, and if need be how to discard, ideas one has probably never questioned. Not to do so is to leave organizational climate at the mercy of assumptions, which the behavioral scientists tell us is precisely what has been wrong with many foundering, inadequately motivated organizations. Let's consider one example.

At a monthly staff meeting, a plant manager observed that it might be wise to have a stand-by plan drawn up for deferring the purchase of certain vendor-supplied parts. This plan would be put into effect in the event production did not rise to forecast levels as quickly as had been hoped. After he made this remark, a debate began among his lieutenants as to whether such a plan was really necessary. Some of them were quite optimistic that the planned production levels could be attained, in which case the extra workload and disruption caused by drawing up the plan would have been wasted. However, others were skeptical, and they pointed out that actual production had been lagging behind the planned rate for some time and had only recently shown signs of accelerating.

After listening to both viewpoints, the plant manager said he was encouraged by the recent increase in production, but in itself the increase was no guarantee that planned levels would actually be reached soon enough. There he let the matter rest, turning to other topics. His implication, he assumed, was clear enough: He wanted his staff to provide for the contingency of continued inability to produce at planned levels. However, no plan was drawn up, since his staff assumed that he had merely raised a hypothetical point and that he was persuaded by the recent increases that no deferral of purchases was necessary. On the one hand, he had not been entirely explicit; and on the other hand, his staff had read its own opinions into his remarks. Both had failed to verify their interpretation of what the other was thinking, since it seemed abundantly clear that they already knew. The result was an excessive inventory of parts and a shortage of working capital, both owing not so much to a lack of foresight as to a lack of ability to escape the bounds of assumptions.

To begin the process of organization development with some hope of tangible success, it is more important to have a strategy than to become prematurely concerned with tactics. The choice of tactics (which consist mainly of various educational procedures) really depends largely on strategy anyway. In general, what is being sought is not necessarily a "hard" or a "soft" management style, not a so-called Theory *X* or Theory *Y* approach, but an *appropriate* management style—appropriate to the problems and potentialities of the organization. The critical skill is really diagnosis, not therapy. What organization development demands above all is a clear view of the organization's strengths and its weaknesses. Questions of who shall be trained and how are secondary until the more fundamental questions are addressed: What are the organization's real resources? How well do they function relative to their capabilities? Only then can decisions be made about an appropriate management style, and only then can existing styles be compared with a meaningful standard.

Learning to assess an organization's capabilities is at once the prerequisite to developing those capabilities and its most difficult and crucial aspect. It is also, perhaps, the most frequently overlooked aspect. What is called organizational development too often begins with a choice of the treatment to be applied, instead of a determination of the specific strengths and weaknesses of the organization as an information-processing system. For the lack of an appropriate basis for selection, the treatment is frequently chosen on the basis of irrelevant criteria—because it is currently in vogue, or because someone has already tried it and found it stimulating, or because it has been promoted effectively. When programs selected in this manner actually do benefit the organization, it is due more to luck than to wisdom.

What is required for an accurate diagnosis is primarily an attitude. Techniques themselves are secondary, and indeed they can be applied effectively only in the context of a conviction that the relationships between people and between groups in an organization are both legitimate and necessary subjects for managerial examination. Relationships need to be audited for much the same reason that assets and operations need to be audited: because they can affect the performance and ultimately even the survival of the firm. Once management becomes committed to the concept of examination as a regular organizational discipline, and not just as an experiment or as an occasional remedy, it will have taken the longest single step toward full utilization of its available assets. It will also become interested in making these diagnoses in the most reliable and economical (that is, cost/effective) ways. This interest is its best defense against fads or other inappropriate methods of organizational development.

The organizational development process probes into the tacitly unprobed and the typically ignored aspects of communication between organization members. It does so because of a conviction, supported by a considerable body of data, that here is where the principal barriers to effective communication lie and that the fact of being unexamined gives these barriers their power to do mischief. But there are some subtleties here which may appear to raise ethical issues. Does an organization have the right to probe into the private opinions of its members, even if such probing could make the organization more efficient? The answer is clearly no; but of course that really depends on what is meant by "private opinions." Organizational development, at least of the type that is focused on building group effectiveness and not on mere social voyeurism, has no need to expose feelings that anyone does not wish to disclose. Its purpose is to permit self-discovery of ideas which cannot stand the test of examination and are therefore valueless or even handicapping. It needs to expose these ideas to no one but the man who holds them.

There is, unfortunately, a certain enthusiasm in some quarters for public frontal attacks upon people who are supposedly retarding group effectiveness.[17] However, there is no reason to believe that anger or humiliation is an effective teaching tool, even when the victim *is* holding back the group. Within the broad movement that is collectively known as organization development there are certain practices which seem to lose sight of the distinction between organization development and group psychotherapy. Organizational development is concerned with the working relationships between people, not with "problems" that they may or may not harbor, individually, within themselves. On the other hand, group psychotherapy is a collective attempt by people who do have handicapping emotional problems of their own to help each other to cope with them. Wherever this distinction is lost, the value of the program for increasing the group's working effectiveness is, to say the least, dubious.

If the learning in organizational development often takes place in groups, that is because a group happens to be a good place for certain kinds of self-examination, not because real development has any need for accusation, confession, and other forms of unbridled self-expression. For these reasons, questions of invasion of privacy do not really arise in the context of *effective* organizational development. To the extent that it succeeds in revealing assumptions for what they are, and in opening the individual more fully to the implications of his own experience, organizational development actually increases his command of himself. In that sense it is the very antithesis of the invasion of privacy.

There are two basic ways to diagnose the information-processing capabilities of an organization. One is to let its people talk about it and the other is to let them write about it. Talking could take place in contexts ranging from the familiar interview, through guided "group interviews," all the way to training groups (popularly known as T-groups), in which the subject of discussion is not so much the recent history of the organization as the immediate, then-and-there events within the training group itself. (T-groups are usually thought of as an educational or, if you will, a therapeutic instrument, rather than as a means of diagnosing organizational strengths and weaknesses. However, their efficacy as revealers of what is right and wrong with the information processes of a company is much easier to demonstrate than their ability to rectify them.) As for writing, it is a much less communicative medium than speaking for most people. Consequently, its use for organizational diagnosis is usually confined to groups that are uneconomically large for the speaking approaches or to groups which tend to be neither articulate nor outgoing.

The fundamental question to be answered during the diagnostic phase of an organizational development cycle is not whether developmental steps are needed (they usually are), or which ones are needed (that comes later); rather, it is the organization's *readiness* for development. Not much is going to be accomplished with any group or person who feels either that an examination of his own assumptions is unnecessary or valueless or that it is personally offensive or morally wrong. Some kind of preparation or warm-up is usually desirable to enable the members of the group to benefit more fully from the exercises to which they will be put. This should involve some kind of demonstration that a communication problem exists and that it is at least addressable by available techniques. One of the problems common to all educational programs—and organizational development is no exception—is that the people who have the greatest need of it are likely to get the least out of it, and vice versa. The more effective an organization has already become in its internal communication, the more ready it is for further development. Merely getting the group to a point of optimum readiness can be more of a battle than learning the disciplines of examination themselves.

For the purpose of laying the intellectual foundations for organizational development, a review of behavioral research and theory can be useful. However, it seldom provides more than a foundation. Most people need to be confronted with a dramatic illustration that a principle is actually at work in their own bailiwick before it loses its abstract quality for them and becomes instead a practical problem demanding *their* attention. One of the most common reactions to a long recitation of research results is that it was interesting and made a lot of sense, but it wasn't directly applicable to *my* organization because my organization is unique in a number of respects. *All* organizations appear to be unique to the people in them; their similarities are harder to recognize. Yet the fact remains that until research data, or at least some convincing cases, can be generated from within a particular organization, its members will be inclined to feel that "This research is all very interesting, but it doesn't apply to us because we're different." Therefore the wise manager of an organization development program will not try to develop readiness solely on the basis of textbook examples; he will do a little research of his own as well.

Once the intellectual groundwork has been laid, the next problem to be addressed in developing readiness is candor. The group must learn to look at events, rather than policy statements or principles, as the only meaningful basis for measuring itself. This is much harder to do than it may seem, especially for managers who may feel that any failure of an organization to live up to high standards is in some way an indictment of their stewardship. It is not an indictment at all, but simply a variance from a standard; and what matters is not whose "fault" it was (frequently it really cannot be pinned on anyone) but, rather, why it happened and how it could be prevented in the future. Once this diagnostic rather than juridical frame of reference is established, the way is clear to begin determining what management's style and the group's climate really are and how these affect the organization's operations.

The basic dimensions of managerial style are the assumptions managers make about the competence and commitment of other people in the organization, including their fellow managers. The basic dimensions of organizational climate are the timeliness, appropriateness, and clarity of information flow, as well as access to wanted (not just needed) information and the sources from which information is normally obtained. In every case, what needs to be established is what actually happens, not just what should happen. Neither does it suffice to pin a label on a person or group. To say, for example, that a department is run according to Theory X or that a manager has confidence in his men really says very little. Both are summary statements which do not lend themselves to appropriate action. That is, Theory X may be appropriate in the specific context of one department and confidence may be inappropriate in another. In any case the terms do not describe what *happens;* they are merely someone's shorthand for events which others might not label in the same way.

The raw stuff of an organizational diagnosis consists not of labels but of behavior itself; that is, the things that people in the organization actually do. Actions are the only tenable basis for inferring assumptions; and assumptions can *only* be inferred, not disclosed or stated. For all these reasons, an organizational diagnosis calls for a searching look at what actually happens as the organization functions. For a while, at least, its members must attempt something not unlike standing outside themselves in order to watch themselves in action.

At some point, however, the introspection must cease and a description of managerial styles and organizational climates (there may be several of both, depending on the size of the organization) must be attempted. The description is intended neither to compliment nor to criticize, but simply to summarize the behavior that has been examined and to essay a few hypotheses (not conclusions) as to the kinds of assumptions that may lie beneath them. The underlying hypothesis of this step is that all behavior is intelligible and justifiable to the behaver. Consequently, trying to classify a man or his actions as benevolent or malevolent is useless, and what we really need to know is the assumptions that guide his behavior. To the extent that the actions and assumptions revealed by this analysis act as handicaps to the organization, in the sense of limiting its ability to use its available talent and information effectively, plans can be made for corrective action. In other words, we can then begin to pinpoint the assumptions that need to be brought out into the daylight, examined, and perhaps modified.

It is at this point, *and only at this point,* that a meaningful organizational-development plan can be designed. But one of the most significant steps will already have been accomplished: The group will have been introduced to the process of self-examination, which must become a habit if organizational development is to have a chance of lasting success. We referred earlier to organizational-development cycles, because the diagnostic phase just described should be repeated periodically (perhaps biannually). The more often this is done, the more skilled the group will become and the greater the likelihood that its deficiencies as an information-processing unit will be remedied. The objective of all this is nothing less than a self-evaluating, self-diagnosing, self-correcting group that has no need of outside resources or outside motivation for accomplishing these functions. In practice this goal is seldom attained, because both the composition of groups and their assigned missions tend to change. But even partial accomplishment of the goal can effect a major enhancement of the group's ability to do its work well—and that, after all, is what organizational development is all about.

Not infrequently, the organization's climate will appear to be inappropriate to its current or anticipated needs. This is not so much because organizations tend to ossify and get out of touch with their environments (although that does happen) as because most organizational-development programs are undertaken when management sees the need for one. The problem then is how to induce change or, more precisely, how to begin a process through which selected changes, and only those changes, will be likely to occur at an acceptable cost in money, time, and human satisfaction. To induce such changes is still an art, not a science. As a rule, the objective is to cause new habits to be learned and thereby to change the pattern of communication flow, rather than simply to change the cast of characters who comprise the group. Organization development is focused on enhancing the effectiveness of existing groups, not on merely altering their composition. This does not rule out personnel changes, but it does relegate that tactic to the status of a radical treatment which is not to be resorted to lightly.

The art of inducing changes in organization climate has developed a few strategies. One of these is to "make a maverick" by deliberately introducing a new management style to a group that is more susceptible to change than others in the organization. Susceptibility may come from mere newness, rapid growth, internal conflicts, or recent management changes. The function of the maverick group is to provide a model of effectiveness on which the other groups can then pattern themselves. However, susceptibility to change need not be merely awaited; it can be created deliberately. Since creating it may entail considerable cost, it is obviously not a strategy to be used without considerable forethought. Susceptibility can be induced through enlargement or reduction of the group's size, reorganization, relocation, merger or spinoff, or indeed any major change in the basic dimensions of the organization. In fact, changes of this kind nearly always induce changes in organizational climate anyway. The difference between those changes and the kind that are induced by successful organizational development is essentially the difference between what is haphazard and what is planned. This is why the consequences to organizational climate of any move of this kind should always be considered in advance and should, where possible, be guided instead of merely being allowed to happen.

Although the training aspect of organization development has had by far the most publicity and the most time and money spent upon it, it is clear that the objectives of organization development can be accomplished, at least to some extent, by administrative means as well. Indeed, unless the company's administrative apparatus is attuned to the needs of organization development and in sympathy with them, it is questionable whether any form of training can have a lasting impact. After all, any attempt to alter adult behavior must cope with an enormous inertia. A man spends decades learning his characteristic ways of listening, expressing himself, and thinking about himself and others. Changing those ways permanently by means of a few weeks of training is impossible *unless* the environment in which he works supports and reinforces those changes. This is why most organizational-development programs are deliberately begun with the top levels of management and then worked down into the organization, instead of starting at the bottom and working up. (It is also the source of the chief weakness of training, about which more later.)

Administration and training are, in fact, indispensable to each other if the purposes of organization development are to be served effectively. Administration can be attuned to making an organization adapt itself to changes in its environment, instead of insulating itself against them. Among the tactics that can help to accomplish this are assignment of people to temporary task forces that deal with specific missions, instead of to permanent departments with general (therefore endless) missions; building feedback mechanisms such as attitude surveys into the routine audit cycle of the organization; and basing compensation in part on the effectiveness of the manager's response to that feedback, rather than on the nature of the feedback itself.

In commenting thus far about training for organizational effectiveness (which we will refer to here simply as "training"), some reservations have been indicated about its effectiveness. There can be no serious quarrel with the *need* for some kind of supplementary education; and while there is some danger that current forms of training could be psychologically damaging to a few individuals, that problem is manageable. The central question with regard to training is not whether it is necessary or whether it is hazardous, but whether it works. The evidence on this point is still rather sketchy, notwithstanding the enthusiasm for and popularity of various training approaches. The answer to this central question must, for the present at least, be clearly marked as tentative. On balance, however, the most *practical* position to take with regard to the effectiveness of training is probably this: For all its deficiencies and the questions that remain unanswered about it, training is our best available instrument, and also our most promising current instrument, for accomplishing the goals of organizational development.

Let us review those goals. The weight of research evidence indicates that organizations that function most effectively are characterized by high levels of mutual trust and confidence between individuals and between groups. The needs of individuals and of groups in such organizations are reconciled through open negotiation, not by fiat. Goals are set so as to optimize the demands which the organization makes upon individuals and groups. Dialogues in one form or another are more or less continually in progress, or are started spontaneously on an ad hoc basis, when the need arises, to insure that communication blocks are anticipated and cleared away. The effective organization is characterized, then, by a high degree of awareness on the part of every component of the needs of all other components with which it interfaces. The effective organization is awake to its own information needs and is committed to satisfying them.

The role of training is to create awareness of those needs and to teach the habits that can satisfy them. But since the "students" are themselves elements of the organization—parts of the mosaic, so to speak—learning can proceed only if their own roles in the mosaic are clarified. What is needed, in other words, is an opportunity for people to confront their own ideas and their own behavior convincingly and yet safely. To effectively control their impact upon others, they must learn to distinguish between their overt conduct and their "favorite fictions" about themselves. Everyone has favorite fictions; one of their functions is evidently to protect the individual from threats. When someone seems to challenge anyone's pet ideas about himself, the natural reaction is for those ideas to close in around the individual, reassuring him that he is what he would like to be and that the challenge must be invalid. Thus favorite fictions will submit to examination, and perhaps to modification, only when the individual feels secure from criticism or loss. The objective of training and the key to its methods is to provide the unique requirements for effective learning: an opportunity to be as candid as one wishes with as much security as one wishes.

Organizational training is that aspect of organizational development which involves a formal attempt to teach concepts and habits that enhance group effectiveness. Much of this is academic and involves readings, lectures, seminars, and so on. There are, to oversimplify a bit, two main training approaches that attempt to reorient ideas and habits more or less directly. One is known as sensitivity training, and the other is known as "Managerial Grid" training. Both are sufficiently complex to require descriptive books in their own right,[18] and only a sketch of each will be attempted here.

Sensitivity training is primarily associated with the National Training Laboratories, an affiliate of the National Education Association. It is built around the skills of highly trained professionals who assist training groups (T-groups) to examine the behavior and feelings of participants as these occur during the training sessions themselves. In this way, the immediate personal experience of group members provides a basis for studying the ways in which groups actually function and the impact of individuals and groups upon one another. Sensitivity training is inherently unscripted; there is no prearranged agenda or curriculum, since events within the group provide the raw material for instruction. Similarly, there is no particular set of right and wrong answers that the participants are supposed to learn. What they are supposed to learn, or at least to get some useful practice in, is the habit of examining their own behavior and its antecedent assumptions.

Much of the controversy over the value of sensitivity training stems from a misunderstanding of its objectives. It is not designed to produce dramatic changes in overt behavior, and it does not produce them. A man who has been to a T-group is not a new man; he is the same old man who has had an experience on which he may, or may not, be able to capitalize. The real purpose of sensitivity training is much more subtle than a behavior change: it is to acquaint people with the process of self-discovery and make that process attractive enough to initiate the practice and repetition that can turn it into a habit. As Douglas McGregor put it:

This training is not a cure for anything. It is designed to help normal, competent managers (who are already effective in their relationships with other members of their organizations) gain greater insight and understanding with respect to the complexities of organized human effort and to acquire some of the knowledge that the behavioral sciences can contribute to this field. Moreover, the lasting value of their learning from this training will depend heavily on the degree to which members of the "system" to which they return (and other aspects of the environment) permit and encourage the learning to continue. The man who has gotten all there is from such a program is launched on a long-term educational venture; he is not "educated" in the complex field of organized human effort by a week or two of training.[19]

The *Managerial Grid* training program was developed by Robert R. Blake and Jane S. Mouton and is administered by their firm, Scientific Methods, Inc. of Austin, Texas. In contrast to sensitivity training, it is quite formalized, consisting of six well-defined phases which are designed to take place over a period of years. Beginning with a series of exercises designed to acquaint the individual with the way in which his managerial style is perceived by others and with a series of seminars in which behavioral science concepts are stressed, the Grid program moves to a consideration of the relationships between groups and eventually to an attempt to diagnose the managerial style requirements of larger organizational units. Grid training usually begins at a high managerial level and works its way down, eventually involving a sizable proportion of organization members.

The Managerial Grid program differs from sensitivity training in that it is a prescribed set of procedures. These take place in a sequence of meetings distributed over time, rather than in a single dose. Frequently these meetings are conducted by organization members who have already been through that phase of the program, rather than by specialists. Both the purpose and the methods of Grid training differ from those of sensitivity training. Instead of focusing upon the individual's influence on the group and its influence on him, grid training deals primarily (although not exclusively) with the relationships between groups. However, there are also similarities between the two approaches—chiefly in their emphasis upon feedback (presenting the individual with reports on the way in which his actions are interpreted by others) and in their emphasis upon teaching the concepts of group dynamics.

Both programs are now in large-scale use. The question of their *effectiveness* is quite difficult to address. From an organizational standpoint, the basic question is whether a demonstrable change in organizational effectiveness can be clearly attributed to the use of training programs of this kind. Any attempt to answer this question through behavioral-research techniques must deal with a formidable obstacle, although by no means an insurmountable one. This is the fact that organizations, like individuals, are exquisitely sensitive; they are susceptible to a great many influences. For this reason it is quite difficult to say with any certainty that a given change was a direct and simple result of training. Even if a change is detected, it may reflect the combined influences of training and other factors or be entirely the result of factors other than training. Partly for this reason, relatively little evaluative research on organizational training has been attempted. However, despite the lack of solid underpinnings there has been a certain premature enthusiasm to get on with the "practical" job of training without bothering with such "theoretical" questions as whether training produces any useful results or whether such results are worth the resources that have to be invested in training.

As of this writing, published research on the subject is quite inconclusive. Some studies lack a before-and-after set of measurements and rely entirely on attempts by trainees to recall, after the training had been completed, what their organizations were like prior to the training. Where before-and-after measurements have been used, several steps have been taken in addition to training in hopes of producing an organizational improvement; and it is impossible to say whether the resulting changes are due entirely, partially, or not at all to training. A great deal of research remains to be done, and the fact that it has not been done is largely a reflection of the priorities that have been assigned to it by managers and behavioral scientists alike. The plain truth is that existing forms of organizational training have been regarded in too many quarters as finished products that are ready for liberal use, rather than as partially understood processes in need of considerable testing, research, and development.

In the absence of convincing evidence as to the effectiveness of training, we have two other sources of evaluation, one of which inspires confidence while the other raises doubts. There are plenty of testimonials in the literature in which men who have experienced one form of training or another declare their enthusiasm for it. More often than not, these statements are prepared by executives who have introduced the programs to their companies on the strength of their personal acquaintance with them. Testimonials in themselves prove little, however. By the same token, the mere fact of being a testimonial does not invalidate the writer's experience as a possible clue to what could be an effective program for others. The other source of evaluation consists largely of theoretical and common-sense considerations, which, while not conclusive by any means, do raise serious doubts about the potentialities of training and the claims of training enthusiasts.

All that we know about the nature of human learning suggests that adult habits of long standing are unlikely to be altered *permanently* unless a rather exceptional set of circumstances can be created. First, the training must be repeated fairly frequently and continued for quite some time. Monthly or at most quarterly refresher training, extended over a period of years, would give the new habits and concepts a reasonable chance of replacing the old ones and resisting the natural tendency of the old habits to reassert themselves. While Grid training offers a step in the right direction by distributing its sessions over a period of months, it seems doubtful that the kind of intensive reinforcement of training that we have described would be economically feasible for most organizations.

Second, a permanent change in adult habits would be abetted by an environment that rewarded the new habits and either punished or at least failed to reward the old ones. In other words, the organization must change along with—and possibly even before—the individual. The chicken-and-the-egg problem enters here, because it is a *system of relationships* rather than individuals per se that needs to be changed, even though individuals are the principal components of that system. Trying to alter the environment to which trainees return is not unlike Br'er Rabbit's wrestle with the tarbaby: It can be done, if at all, only by a massive injection of trained people into the environment and by supporting the new habits strongly enough to change the environment permanently. What we know about learning theory suggests that the conditions that would permit lasting changes as a result of organizational training are particularly difficult to create. It is with those conditions, and not with the techniques of training themselves, that managers and behavioral scientists alike should concern themselves.

After considering the three kinds of evidence available to us—research, testimonials, and learning theory—it is difficult to take a stronger stance toward organizational training than one of hopeful skepticism. However, let the emphasis be on hopefulness, and for good reason. Organizational training in its present forms fulfills many of the theoretical preconditions for effecting lasting improvements in group effectiveness: clarifying of roles, distinguishing between overt conduct and favorite fictions, and providing opportunities to experiment with candor in safety. Whether the theoretical objections that can be raised against them are fatal or merely difficult remains to be seen. An enormous amount of time, talent, and money is being invested in these programs, and investments in research, development, and innovation will surely be made as well. Viewed in its larger context, organizational training is a phase—a particularly fruitful, vigorous phase—of the historical process through which man has been learning to manage a comparatively new historical phenomenon: the modern organization. That process still has a long way to go.

Chapter 14

Where We
Are Heading

WHEN WE CONSIDER THE IMPLICATIONS OF MOTIVATION
theory and behavioral research as a whole, rather than focusing narrowly upon any given aspect of them, some rather startling ideas
emerge.

First, to use only a little bit of poetic license, it appears that *the
nature of human nature is changing*. Man's ideas have probably always been shaped by his environment, but in our era the aspects of
the environment that are capable of introducing new values and new
behavior patterns are themselves changing rapidly. Science and technology are radically reshaping our views of the world and of ourselves, and mass higher education is bringing these new ideas to a
much larger proportion of the population than they might have
reached in an earlier era. Mass communications media and jet trans-
portation bring a world of information to people who were previously influenced chiefly by events that occurred within a day's walk
or a day's drive of home.

In brief, people are subject to a much more varied and much less
stable set of influences than ever before. Local traditions and conventional wisdom are no longer the chief determinants of most people's
ideas. Although man's *basic* nature has not changed, the information
available to him for shaping his ideas about himself and his world has

increased explosively. As his ideas (or, if you will, his assumptions) have become less predictable, so has his behavior. This trend will probably accelerate. There will be no return to the good old days; instead it is going to be incumbent upon us to make the unpredictable new days as good as we can.

The people who will be available to do the work in tomorrow's world will be only superficially similar to the ones who sweated through the Industrial Revolution and brought us to the brink of the technological age. For all practical purposes, organizations will be run by and with a new kind of human. It will be management's job to understand that new kind of person as thoroughly and dispassionately as it can. This means, above all else, that management must abandon conventional wisdom as the basis for its actions and rely instead on the most sensitive and reliable instruments it can find. In brief, tomorrow's manager is going to have to learn to be a bit of a behavioral scientist himself—enough, at any rate, to know how to use the contributions of the behavioral scientist in a sensible, discriminating way.

This is not the only burden being placed upon the manager of tomorrow by the pundits of today. Elsewhere the manager will read that he will also have to become a bit of a systems analyst, a bit of a mathematician, a bit of an economist, and a bit of a lot of other things. To all of which most contemporary managers may shake their heads ruefully and say that there just isn't enough time to learn all those esoteric things and still get their jobs done. This leads to the next implication that emerges from a global view of the behavioral sciences.

To capitalize fully upon our existing insights into the nature of motivation and its effect upon human performance, *the manager's job must be changed radically*. The basic motivational deficiency in most organizations today is the lack of sufficient decision-making authority and responsibility in jobs held by people who could respond to such powers with vastly increased energy and commitment. There is no actual shortage of decision-making power; it is simply and unnecessarily monopolized by management, and especially by the higher organizational levels. This in turn is due to the time-honored concept that relatively few people are capable of making effective decisions or willing to accept responsibility—a condition which compelled management to define its principal tasks as deciding what should be done by other people and then making sure that they do it. That definition is already antiquated and will become increasingly out of tune with reality in the future.

If decision making should be more widely distributed, this will impact management jobs in general and higher-level management jobs in particular. What will they then become? What we know today about motivation suggests there is a vital role for management to fill under those circumstances, but one for which it is typically not well prepared today. This role is not too dissimilar from that of a football coach: a man whose principal preoccupation is with the training and condition of his team and with the strategy that his field lieutenants use, but who does not call the plays and leaves the tactics on the field to the discretion of his quarterback. The manager would become more of a teacher and less of a rule enforcer, more of a planner and less of a plan fulfiller, than he is today. At the same time, the jobs of the people beneath him would acquire, in varying degrees, some of the breadth, headaches, and excitement that are as a rule found chiefly in management jobs today.

We have also cited the demotivating effect of insufficient challenge. Basically, challenge is largely a matter of the degree to which an individual recognizes that his job demands skills or wisdom he does not possess; therefore, if he is to succeed at all, he must somehow learn as much as he can from his experience on the job itself. To some extent, challenge can be built into a job by extending the range of responsibility forward or backward into the chain of events in which the job is embedded. (This is one form of job enrichment.) However, this only buys time—although the value of the purchase is hardly to be minimized! Eventually, either people will learn their jobs well enough to eliminate the anxiety of not being able to do it well (thereby also eliminating challenge); or—what is less desirable—they will convince themselves they have learned it well enough when in fact they have not. Either way the motivational impact of a demanding-yet-still-possible job is gradually diluted.

The implication is clear, if not particularly welcome. Most career planning should be based on the assumption that major changes of assignment will have to occur fairly often—perhaps eight or ten times in the full course of a career. To some extent, technological change, organizational growth, and normal promotions will absorb this volume of changes, but when these do not suffice as a source of new assignments management may actually have to move people about for the sake of moving them about. The cost in administrative inconvenience and in recycling the learning curve is likely to be far less, in the long run, than the cost of carrying people on the payroll who have become so accustomed to a lack of challenge in their work that for all practical purposes they become unmotivatable.

However, the function of this book has been to describe the tools available to organizations through the behavioral sciences, and not to prophesy the future. Whether the implications we have read into current research and theory and the conclusions we have drawn from them will be proved correct matters little. What does matter is that the behavioral sciences, while still in a stage of rapid and somewhat uneven development, have generated a body of knowledge and a set of techniques which make the process of motivation considerably less mysterious, and considerably more subject to effective administration, than it has ever been in the past. To that extent, management by motivation is more than a catch phrase. It is a perfectly feasible strategy for any organization that is willing to take the time and trouble to acquaint itself with what the behavioral sciences have learned.

Whether the scientists will ever learn enough about man in general or men in particular to reduce the practical problems of management to a simple system that can be applied without a great deal of judgment, forethought, and luck is problematical. I doubt that they will. But that really does not matter. We already know enough to improve substantially both the individual's contributions to the organization and his satisfaction in belonging to it. We will probably know even more about both in the future. Meanwhile, there is plenty of work to do *now* in putting all this research and theory to work for the benefit of everyone who works in, or depends upon, an organization.

Notes to the Text

1. Some of the more comprehensive recent summaries are Frederick Herzberg, *et al., Job Attitudes: Review of Research and Opinion,* Psychological Service of Pittsburgh, Pittsburgh, 1957; Rensis Likert, *The Human Organization,* McGraw-Hill Book Co., Inc., New York, 1967; Saul W. Gellerman, *Motivation and Productivity,* American Management Association, Inc., New York, 1963; Robert A. Sutermeister, *People and Productivity,* McGraw-Hill Book Co., Inc., New York, 1963; Victor H. Vroom, *Work and Motivation,* John Wiley & Sons, Inc., New York, 1964.
2. R. W. Revans, *Standards for Morale: Cause and Effect in Hospitals,* Oxford University Press, London, 1964 (published for the Nuffield Provincial Hospitals Trust).
3. Harry Levinson, Charlton R. Price, Kenneth J. Munden, Harold J. Mandl, and Charles M. Solley, *Men, Management and Mental Health,* Harvard University Press, Cambridge, 1962.
4. A. T. M. Wilson, "Some Sociological Aspects of Systematic Management Development," *The Journal of Management Studies,* Vol. 3, No. 1, February 1966.
5. Douglas W. Bray and Donald L. Grant, "The Assessment Center in the Measurement of Potential for Business Management," *Psychological Monographs,* Whole No. 625, Vol. 80, No. 17, 1966.
6. Marvin D. Dunnette, *Managerial Effectiveness,* McGraw-Hill Book Co., Inc., New York (in press).
7. Walter J. McNamara, "Retraining of Industrial Personnel," *Personnel Psychology,* Vol. 16, No. 3, Autumn 1963.

273

8. Ernest F. Bairdain, *Employment Stabilization Through Retraining and Job Restructuring,* IBM Data Systems Division, 1962.

9. J. Stacy Adams, "The Effects of Perceived Inequity," unpublished paper read at Conference on Managers and Money Motivation, Tarrytown, New York (sponsored by McKinsey Foundation for Management Research), May 1967.

10. Elliot Jaques, *Equitable Payment,* John Wiley & Sons, Inc., New York, 1961.

11. Edward E. Lawler III, "Managerial Perceptions of Compensation," unpublished paper read at Midwestern Psychological Association Convention, Chicago, April 1965.

12. For a more thorough discussion of McGregor's ideas, see Chapter 7 in *Motivation and Productivity,* or better still, see Douglas McGregor, *The Human Side of Enterprise,* McGraw-Hill Book Co., Inc., New York, 1960; or his *The Professional Manager* (edited by Warren G. Bennis and Caroline McGregor), McGraw-Hill Book Co., Inc., New York, 1967.

13. *The Professional Manager,* p. 125.

14. G. H. Hofstede, *The Game of Budget Control,* Koninklijke Van Gorcum & Comp. N.V., Assen, Netherlands, 1967.

15. Chris Argyris, *Some Causes of Organizational Ineffectiveness Within the Department of State,* Occasional Papers, No. 2, Center for International Systems Research, Department of State, Washington, D.C., 1967.

16. Rensis Likert, *The Human Organization: Its Management and Value,* McGraw-Hill Book Co., Inc., New York, 1967.

17. Chris Argyris, "On the Future of Laboratory Education," *Journal of Applied Behavioral Science,* Vol. 3, No. 2, 1967.

18. See Edgar H. Schein and Warren G. Bennis, *Personal and Organizational Change Through Group Methods: The Laboratory Approach,* John Wiley & Sons, Inc., New York, 1965; and Robert R. Blake and Jane S. Mouton, *The Managerial Grid,* Gulf Publishing Company, Houston, Texas, 1964.

19. Douglas McGregor, *The Professional Manager, op. cit.*

Index

A

Absenteeism, 247
Achievement, stretching of, 107
Adams, J. Stacy, 178-179, 207
Adaptation, learning and, 154-155
Administration, organizational change and, 261
    training and, 261
Age, competence and, 148
    learning ability and, 150
Aggressiveness, in management development, 108
Agricultural approach, to management training, 106-107
American Telephone and Telegraph Company, 119, 125, 127, 132
    Management Progress Study, 120-121, 124-127
Analysis, manager's use of, 17
Analyst, motivational, role of, 25-26
Anger, as teaching tool, 255-256
Anxiety, challenge and, 271
    about income, 192-193
Appraisal. *See* Career counseling; Performance; Performance measurement
Appropriateness, in managerial style, 232-233, 254
Argyris, Chris, 200, 238, 239, 240, 243
Assessment centers, 125-127
Assignment changes, in career planning, 271-272
    competence and, 154-155

Assumptions, challenge to, 224-227
    and changing human nature, 270
    about commitment to organization, 230-232
    about motivation, 227-228
    about organization, 222-227
    about rewards and punishment, 228
    in organizational climate, 253
    tactics related to, 236-237
Attitude, communication of, 46-47
Attitude change, organizational climate and, 244
Attitude surveys, 261
Authority, distribution in organization, 220-221
    of production-centered supervisor, 37
    surrender to, 221
Autonomy, individual's need of, 234
Average, as semantic problem, 72

B

Bairdain, Ernest F., 150, 151
Behavior, job security and, 18-19
Behavioral research, blue collar workers and, 29-30
    definitions of, 27
    idol-smashing in, 28
    implications of, 269
    job satisfaction and, 30-32
    management and, 16-17

Behavioral research (*continued*)
  management style changes and, 243-244
  viewpoint in, 17-18
Behavioral science, organization in light of, 229-232
Behavioral scientists, attitude of, 228
Bell Telephone System, 120-121, 124-127
Bethlehem Steel Company, 151
Bias, of disadvantaged groups, 35
  self-discipline and, 38
  in supervisor, 34-35
Biographical inventories, 96
Blake, Robert R., 264
Blue collar workers, motivational studies among, 29-30
  See also Employee; Factory worker
Boredom, in routine job, 84
Boss, production-centered, 37
British Civil Service, 125
British War Office Selection Boards, 125
Budget, challenge of, 236
  motivation from, 233-237
  organizational climate and, 233-234
Business games, 123

C

Capital gains tax, 215
Career counseling, frankness in, 111-112
  as insurance against risk, 110
  management development and, 110-113
  motivation in, 113
  overoptimism and overpessimism in, 111
  personality and, 110
Career management, 116-118
  performance measurement and, 119
Career planning, assignment changes and, 271-272
  motivation and, 84
Carrot-and-stick philosophy, 28-31
Challenge, demotivating effect of, 271
  vs. job security, 32-33
Chance, in selection system, 87-88
Change, adaptability to, 16
  education and, 14-15
Choice, in personnel selection, 66
Civil service, pay rates for, 184-185

Climate, organizational, 219-249
Coaching, by immediate supervisor, 115
  in management development, 113-115
Coercion, control by, 244
College graduates, increased number of, 148
  inducements for, 21-22
Commitment, behavioral science view of, 230
  degree of, 227
Communication, of attitudes, 46-47
  credibility in, 48-49
  as dialogue, 45
  employee needs in, 47
  feedback in, 45-47
  learning and, 44
  in managerial development, 103
  Manchester group studies in, 42-44
  negotiation in, 46
  organizational climate and, 248
  quality of, 44
  receptive atmosphere in, 48-49
  research in, 40-49
  Revans studies in, 42-44
  sender's attitude in, 46
  supervisor efficiency in, 47-48
  unspoken, 44
Company image, bad news involving, 91
  and company representatives, 90
  improvement of company in relation to, 92
  management of, 91-92
  public relations and, 89-92
  selection process and, 88-89
Company representatives, company image and, 90
Competence, assumptions about, 227
  changeability of, 146
  defined, 146
  education and, 148-149
  enlargement of, 101-118
  laziness and, 167
  learning transfer and, 153
  levels of, 166
  longevity of, 158
  motivation and, 158-159
  preserving of, 167
  responsibility and, 198
  self-concept in, 168
Competence loss, 145-168
  abnormal, 158
  age groups and, 147-148

O

Obsolescence, learning ability and, 154
Occupational groups, pay rates for, 182
Occupational interests, tests of, 96
Occupational role, as self-concept, 54
Office of Strategic Services, 125-126
Orchestration, of organization, 251-252
Organization, assumptions about, 222-227
    authority in, 220-221
    behavioral science approach to, 229-231
    climate of, 219-249. *See also* Organizational climate
    coercion in, 244-245
    commitment to, 227, 230-231
    control in, 228-229, 247
    defined, 219
    demands of on employee, 51
    development of. *See* Organizational development
    emotional interactions and, 49
    employees' likes and dislikes concerning, 245-246
    feedback in, 252
    as group of people, 219
    homogenization of, 241
    individual and, 220
    information-dependent, 253
    as living system, 239
    managerial styles and, 222-223
    membership in, 172-173
    motivational dependency in, 270
    "orchestration" of, 251
    performance and, 212-213
    proper function of, 251-267
    psychological contract with employees, 51-55
    readiness for development, 257
    "selecting out" system in, 241
    structural change in, 25
    tactics and assumptions in, 236-237
Organizational change, decision making and, 25
    problems of, 115-116
Organizational climate, assumptions in, 253
    attitude in, 255
    communication and, 248
    deference in, 241
    in Dutch manufacturing plants, 233-234
    group efficiency and, 251-252

    inducing changes in, 260
    managerial style and, 243-244
    mutual trust in, 262
    rewards and punishments in, 242
Organizational development, 251-267
    administration and training in, 261
    assignment changes and, 271-272
    feedback in, 239, 252, 261
    information processing in, 256
    intellectual basis of, 257-258
    learning in, 256
Organizational goal, commitment to, 230
Organizational homogenization, 226
Organizational training, 262-263
    effectiveness of, 265
    learning and, 266
    See also Training
Output, restriction of by production workers, 30-31, 204
Overestimation, of job requirements and skills, 150-151
Overoptimism, in career counseling, 111
Overpay, job classification and, 195
"Oversolving," tendency toward, 19-20

P

Pay differentials, reconciling of, 177-178
Pay increment. *See* Income increment
Pay programs, merit basis of, 176-177
Pay satisfaction, employee, 172-177
    secrecy and, 183-186
Pay scales, compression of, 185, 196
    disarray in, 184
    equitability in, 176-183
    merit increase and, 194
    occupational groups and, 182
    range of, 177
    relative increment and, 188-191
    secrecy about, 183-186
    union demands and, 199-200
    upgrading of, 182
Perceptions, change in, 35-36
Performance, achieved results in, 139
    appraisal, 108-110, 135-138, 141-144
    biographical survey and, 131
    components of, 211
    "crown-prince" problem and, 133-134
    current vs. future, 134-136

About the Author

Dr. Saul W. Gellerman is president of Saul W. Gellerman and Company, management consultants. He was with International Business Machines Corporation for more than eight years as personnel research associate, manager of personnel research for IBM World Trade Corporation, and most recently executive research consultant.

Dr. Gellerman has appeared in the Bureau of National Affairs film series on "Motivation and Productivity," and he is author of *People, Problems and Profits* (McGraw-Hill), *The Management of Human Relations* (Holt, Rinehart & Winston), and *Motivation and Productivity* (American Management Association), which won the McKinsey Foundation Award for Excellence in Management Literature in 1963.